## THE PRINCIPALS:

MR. DELLINGER: There has to be some way of speaking the truth. We have to speak the truth some way. If you won't allow it to come in other ways, we have to stand up and tell it because it is true.

\* \* \*

MR. A. HOFFMAN: It . . . said . . . that Yippies hate America. It is that they feel the American dream has been betrayed . . . I was there when Paul Revere rode right up on his motorcycle and said, "The pigs are coming, the pigs are coming." . . .

\* \* \*

MR. HAYDEN: We would hardly be notorious characters if they had left us alone in the streets of Chicago last year . . . We were invented. We were chosen by the Government to serve as scapegoats for all that they wanted to prevent happening in the 1970's . . . If you didn't want to make us martyrs, why did you do it?

\* \* \*

THE COURT: I would tell you sir, that the United States District Judge who practiced law in the courts of the United States and sat on state and federal benches for 50 years has to sit here, sir, and have a defendant call him a pig? Listen to him now.

MR. KUNSTLER: Your Honor, we cannot hear him because of the binding and gag on him.

**THE OBSERVER:**

THE HON. JOHN V. LINDSAY,

"The blunt, hard fact is that we in this nation appear headed for a new period of repression—more dangerous than at any time in years. The frenzy, the bitterness, the tumult of the last few years have led many people—including many in positions of power—to expect peace and order to come by whittling away at the Bill of Rights of our Constitution. . . .

". . . We all know the danger of using courtrooms as political forums. And it is important to oppose political extremists who make illegitimate use of our courts.

"But that is exactly why we must speak out when officials and when governments do the same thing.

"All of us, I think, see the recent Chicago trial as a defeat for the integrity of the judicial process. All of us, I think, see in that trial a tawdry parody of our judicial system.

"But it is important to understand the roots of

this disaster. When you try political activists under a conspiracy charge—long considered to be the most dubious kind of criminal charge—difficult to define or to limit—and when a trial becomes fundamentally an examination of political acts and beliefs—then guilt or innocence becomes almost irrelevant. The process becomes a matter of political opinion instead of legal judgment, and the sense of a courtroom as an independent, open and judicious tribunal becomes lost.

"And we lost something else, too. Whatever the ultimate verdicts, who has really won in this case? Think of yourself as a young man or woman, emerging into political concern. If you had witnessed what happened in Chicago, which of you would believe that our system was open, fairminded, and humane? Which of you would come away from this trial with a renewed faith in our judicial system?"

A brilliant mosaic of revealing moments from the transcript of the Chicago Conspiracy trial—the most significant *kulturkampf* of our time.

—Dwight Macdonald

# THE
# TALES
# OF
# HOFFMAN

Edited from the official transcript by

## MARK L. LEVINE
## GEORGE C. MCNAMEE
## DANIEL GREENBERG

Introduction by Dwight Macdonald

Including 32 pages of on-the-scene sketches

· BANTAM BOOKS ·
TORONTO   ®   LONDON
NEW YORK
A NATIONAL GENERAL COMPANY

THE TALES OF HOFFMAN
*A Bantam Book / published March 1970*

*Bantam Books are published by Bantam Books, Inc., a National
General company. Its trade-mark, consisting of the words "Bantam
Books" and the portrayal of a bantam, is registered in the United
States Patent Office and in other countries. Marca Registrada.
Bantam Books, Inc., 666 Fifth Avenue, New York, N.Y. 10019.*

PRINTED IN THE UNITED STATES OF AMERICA

# ACKNOWLEDGMENTS

Joan Hochman, Jane Dickerman, Andrew Horn, Lynn Moloshok and Paul Shemin rendered constant and invaluable advice and assistance to the editors in this project and deserve our sincere thanks.

We are also grateful to those who, at various times and in various ways, assisted us in this endeavor:

John Books Beinecke, Howard Cady, Nancy Davis, Sophie Engelhard, Justine Fischer, Mary Jane Frye, Judy Halberstadt, Elliott Hefler, Debbie Hirsch, Wendy Hutton, Harvey Ishofsky, Kenneth Kahn, Esther R. Levine, Walter Lord, Lauree McMahon, Julie Osler;

Laura Banfield, Ellen Carlstein, Sarah Chasis, Andy Dolan, Shura Gardner, Andrea Gilbert, Peter and Betty Hutcheon, Joanne Jablow, David Langston, Peter Millock, Annie Parson, Debbie Peretz, Amanda Porterfield, Tod and Gail Roberts, Joan Ross, Brian and Bonnie Toohey, Ray Vickers.

In addition, we extend our gratitude for long-time support and encouragement to: Irving and Beatrice Greenberg, Shep Greenberg, Sophie Greenblatt Levine, the late Saul Levine, Daniel and Barbara McNamee, Roger and Giles McNamee, Ashna Pincus.

THE EDITORS

# CONTENTS

# INTRODUCTION

by Dwight Macdonald

*United States of America, Plaintiff, vs. David T. Dellinger et al., Defendants, No. 69 Crim. 180* began in the Federal District Courthouse in Chicago on September 26, 1969, before the Hon. Julius J. Hoffman (and a jury) and ended five months later after some 200 witnesses had been heard—more or less, depending on the Judge's iron whim; Mayor Daley didn't get much beyond giving his name, not to his displeasure—and 22,000 pages of transcript had been accumulated. *The Tales of Hoffman,* a title that understates the fantastic atmosphere of the trial, is a mosaic of the more significant moments.

It is hardly news by now, at least here in the effete East, that if the defendants were out to show up American bourgeois justice, as they were, Judge Hoffman aided and abetted them beyond their fondest, most alienated dreams of revolutionary glory. Even editors of *The New York Times* have perceived this, even Max Lerner. Let me pass over, for the moment, the Judge's courtroom manner, arrogant without dignity, wisecracking without wit, a combination of Torquemada and a Borscht-circuit *tummeler.* I'm also willing to stipulate, as we say in court, that his sustaining all the prosecution's objections and overruling all the defense's—to be fair, the ratio was maybe only 98 to 2—that these rulings were called as he saw them, honestly and without bias or prejudice. (Gotta watch your step with Julie, fastest draw in the Midwest with a contempt citation.) But there is something peculiar, assuming the Judge was not in cahoots with the defendants to undermine our legal system, already reeling from the assaults of our Attorney General—as I do assume, holster that citation, Judge—about the consistency with which he perpetrated injudicial outrages from beginning to end of the trial. He rushed through jury selection in half a day, solo, refusing to question the panel on most of the points the defense asked him to, including previous exposure to the case from press and television. He tried to arrest for contempt four lawyers who didn't show up on the first day because they had been engaged by the defense only for pre-trial work, a position he backed down from under horrified pressure from the legal establishment. He refused to postpone the trial until Bobby Seale's lawyer, Charles Garry, recovered from an operation, refusing to let Seale defend himself and thus goading him into constant interruptions—always sensible and rarely obscene, by the way, if you read the complete transcript and not just the press reports—which the Judge solved catastrophically by having Seale gagged and bound, finally severing him from the case with a four-year contempt sentence to give him a head start on his separate trial later. He excluded basic defense documents (as on the Convention and the police riots) and witnesses such as Ramsey Clark, who as Attorney General at the time had had the responsibility of insuring a peaceful Convention and who had tried to negotiate with Mayor Daley to that end. Judge Hoffman wound it all up in an orgy of sabotage of due process, justice and mere decency, sentencing all of the defendants and both their lawyers to prison for contempt of court before the verdict. When the jury, after being hung up for four days (unexpectedly, and a tribute to them but not to Judge Hoffman) acquitted two defendants on both charges (conspiring to incite a riot, and actually doing so) and the other five on the conspiracy charge, the odd—and to a hopeful believer (like me) in the jury system, the intolerable—outcome was they were all sentenced anyway for contempt, from six months to two years. What price justice when Hoffman is telling the tale?

Their lawyers got the works: 4 years, 13 days for William Kunstler; 1 year, 8 months, 5 days for Leonard Weinglass. These neat calculations show an unexpected rationality, in a way, as does the Judge's novel salami tactics with the contempt sentence. Hitherto the accepted maximum sentence for refractory lawyers had been six months; by slicing up Kunstler's crime into twenty-four separate offenses, the Judge was able to give him a lenient two months on each and still come out with four years. A pity to see a brain like that wasted on the right side of the law. Finally, despite the jury's long hesitation and eventual compromise, the Judge gave the five defendants still within his reach the maximum five years, adding a Hoffmaniac turn of the screw with $5,000 fines apiece plus "the costs of prosecution," whatever that means. It's a novel concept to me, no doubt a tidy sum once the Judge's slide rule gets into action, say $58,612.57 apiece, give or take a few cents.

In short, Judge Hoffman made the kind of legal history Tom Hayden, David Dellinger, Rennie Davis, Abbie Hoffman and Jerry Rubin wanted him to make. It looks fishy—a federal judge playing into the hands of the revolutionaries he appeared to be persecuting. And who, or what, is behind him? That's the interesting question. How can we account for the present situation unless we believe that men high in the Government are concerting to deliver us to disaster? This must be the product of a great conspiracy, a conspiracy so immense as to dwarf any previous such venture in the history of man. What can be made of this unbroken series of decisions and acts contributing to the strategy of defeat? They cannot be attributed to incompetence. If Hoffman were merely stupid, the laws of probability would dictate that part of his decisions would serve his country's interest.

The last five sentences above are, of course, not mine—one hopes the reader sensed the style had become rather gamey—but, except for substituting "Hoffman" for "Marshall," they are quoted from the once-famous 60,000-word speech the late Senator McCarthy delivered in the Senate on June 14, 1951, exposing the then Secretary of State, George Marshall, as a traitor working for the Kremlin. I didn't believe then that General Marshall, granted his incompetence, was an agent of Stalin, nor do I now believe that Judge Hoffman, granted his, is an agent of the New Left. But a clever prosecutor—not Mr. Foran or Mr. Schultz—could make as good a case for this paranoiac hypothesis as they did for their own in the trial.

Chicago has become our new Dallas: first the "police riot" against demonstrators (and others, anybody within club reach) at the 1968 Democratic Convention, and a year later, a judicial riot when the leading demonstrators went on trial for having tactlessly provoked the police riot by insisting on exercising their rights as guaranteed by the First Amendment to the

Constitution: "the freedom of speech . . . the right of the people peaceably to assemble, and to petition the government for a redress of grievances." It is true that the Chicago Eight weren't respectful to their Judge and prosecutors any more than they had been to Mayor Daley's cops, but in both cases the repressive reaction was out of all proportion to the provocation, and their disrespect fed and grew on the professional incompetence of the forces of law and order—policemen are supposed to control themselves, judges are supposed to "have ice water in their veins," as former Justice Abe Fortas put it. Whatever was in Judge Hoffman's veins, it wasn't ice water; aquavit maybe. He was spoiling for a fight, a confrontation, from the first day, and as the months wore on, it becomes obvious from the evidence in the present book that he was enjoying it. And not just sadistically, though that too, but also in a sly, masochistic way—he was asking for it, begging for it, and often he seems to deliberately provoke the disrespect he instantly complains about. One understands why Kunstler at the end says he feels "nothing but compassion" for Hoffman, also why the other Hoffman, Abbie, was given a relatively light contempt sentence although he, of all the defendants, was the most personally, and effectively, insulting to his namesake. A complex neurotic, Julie. (I apologize for the familiarity, Judge; it's not my style, but I feel I really know you after reading this book—you're so freely self-expressive on the bench. *Hoffman's Complaint.*)

The defense lawyers have been criticized for not sitting down when told to and for not repressing their charges (though, as Weinglass says to the Judge at one point, "Do you really think we could?" or words to that effect) and for talking back and other nonprofessional practices, such as making an issue about when and where their clients may go to the bathroom and, on a higher level, asking for relaxation of procedure on various irrelevant, and political, occasions. As to the low-comedy scenes about going to the bathroom, not much to my taste, the Court takes part with gusto. Likewise with Kunstler's requests for unlegal favors such as a recess on October 15 to allow the defendants to participate in Moratorium Day activities, permission to have his clients present in court a cake to Bobby Seale on his thirty-third birthday, a "moment of silence for Dr. King" on January 15, etcetera. The Judge rejects them all, I think properly, but with unjudicial side remarks that are here pleasant enough—"I won't even let anybody bring me a birthday cake. . . . This is a courthouse and we conduct trials here. I am sorry."—but that become nasty and provocative when the same uncorseted style is applied to serious matters. (One of the Judge's few witty remarks—as against his usual *tummeler* cross talk—came after he had granted a five minute recess so that the defendants could consult Dr. Spock, who had dropped in to see the show. "We would like to introduce him to your Honor," suggested Kunstler, ever alert with the innocent needle. "My children are grown, Mr. Kunstler," replied his Honor.)

His constant ridicule of the two defense lawyers would alone be grounds for a mistrial, I should think. In one session we get first:

Mr. Weinglass: That is permissible procedure?

The Court: I said it was. You don't have to ask me after I said it.

Mr. Weinglass: I am sorry. I object to it.

The Court: Sometime I am going to take an oath before I talk to you, you ask me so many questions.

Then:

Mr. Kunstler: Your Honor, there is an old maxim in law that if the police are brutal to one group, there is an inference they may be brutal to other groups, and that is a—

The Court: That is a maxim of the law I never heard of, and I sustain the objection.

Mr. Kunstler: You heard the maxim that "False in one thing, false in all." That is what I am saying:

"Falsus in uno, falsus in omnibus." That is the maxim.

The Court: You ought to put on your striped trousers and be a professor.

Mr. Kunstler: Your Honor, I am afraid I don't have striped trousers.

The Court: I didn't ask you for a lecture. . . . I don't know all of those fancy phrases that you used.

This simple-guy put-down of the Eastern city slicker was one of the Judge's favorite ploys, sometimes affectation ("I think your Honor does [know what the 'fancy phrase' means]," Kunstler replied—I hope he's right), but more often the kind of genuine provincial resentment our Vice President is making a career, of sort, by expressing (in five-dollar words and ten-dollar syntax—that'll show 'em!). As:

The Court: He [Seale] is being treated in accordance with the law.

Mr. Kunstler: Not the Constitution of the United States, your Honor, which is the supreme law. He has a right to defend himself.

The Court: I don't need someone to come here from New York or wherever you come from to tell me that there is a Constitution in the United States.

And:

The Court: You speak of the Constitution as though it were a document printed yesterday. [A very good way to speak of it—D.M.] We know about the Constitution way out here in the Middlewest, too, Mr. Kunstler.

Mr. Kunstler: Oh, your Honor, this is a little unfair, isn't it?

The Court: We really do. You would be amazed at our knowledge of constitutional law.

Mr. Kunstler: Isn't that a little unfair, your Honor? We are not here from different parts of the country—

The Court: I am getting a little weary of these thrusts by counsel and I don't want any more of them. [The Judge should move to New York and find what thrusts can be—D.M.] I had occasion to admonish you before.

Mr. Kunstler: I know, but you said I could argue as long as I wanted.

The Court: As long as you are respectful, sir.

Mr. Kunstler: I am respectful.

The Court: No, you haven't been.

Mr. Kunstler: You implied, I thought, Chicago people didn't understand the Constitution, only Easterners understand it. That isn't true.

The Court: Bring in the jury.

The trouble with the editors' excerpts is you can't stop quoting them, like eating peanuts. There's always something interesting. Here my point was made in the first two exchanges but I added the rest because it illustrates the dominant impression I got from the whole book, how sensible and courteous the defense lawyers were (their clients were also sensible but not so polite) and how unsensible and rude the Judge. I skip over his Honor's personal remarks (as when he asked Kunstler if he used Chanel No. 5) and his frequent questioning of the defense lawyers' competence, in front of the jury, item no. 78 on the mistrial docket ("a defense, if you can call it that"; when they asked for explanations of his bizarre rulings, advising them to consult a lawyer), and I will conclude, your Honor, with item no. 79, The Weinglass Mystery, or The Case of the Amnesiac Judge. For some antic, Torquemada-*tummeler* reason, Hoffman throughout the trial affected to forget the junior counsel's name, calling him Weinstein, Feinstein, Fineglass, Weinberg, Weinramer, forever being corrected and forever apologizing. This doubtless accompanied by one of those rubberlipped smirks I'm told he indulged in—unlike the defendants' laughter that bothered him so much, they don't appear in the record. Nor do his intonations, which are reported to have been so expressive in merely reading the indictment at the beginning of the trial that a lady juror felt she couldn't give a fair verdict and got herself excused. Toward the end, the resourceful defense table produced a large placard inscribed "WEINGLASS" which they hoisted up on occasion to refresh the Judge's memory. But he still got it wrong. At the very end, after he had modulated to "Weinrob," his victim wearily observed: "I was hopeful when I came here that after twenty weeks the Court would know my name . . ." To which, The Court: "Well, I am going to tell you about that. . . . I have got a very close friend named Weinruss and I know nobody by the name of Weinrob—[something wrong here with the transcript, or the Judge—D.M.] and somehow or other the name of Weinruss stuck in my mind and it is your first appearance here. You have seen lawyers pass before this bar all during your four to five months here whom I know intimately and I scarcely ever forget a lawyer's name even when he hasn't been in for twenty years." The garrulity makes no sense as an explanation, since "Weinruss" was not even the most common of the pseudonyms by which he addressed Mr.—it *is* "Weinglass," isn't it? And, as an apology, it is also defective, the last sentence adding the clinching insult. Not the most consecutive mind, his Honor's. But still, why? What method in his madness? I think the clue is his remark, overheard by a reporter in an elevator: "Now we are going to hear this wild man Weinglass." (See Transcript page 397.) For once, he got the name right. It reminds me of another injudicious remark made in a public place, the bar of a country club as I recall, by another unjudicial judge, the Hon. Webster Thayer of the Massachusetts bench, apropos a trial he was about to conduct with all due legal decorum, including that great black maxi-robe: "I'm going to get those anarchist bastards!" The Hon. Thayer did get Sacco and Vanzetti but I don't think the Hon. Hoffman will do well in the appellate courts. If he does, I'll have to agree that Tom Hayden for once is right about something.

What Judge Hoffman and his two more sober but equally obtuse allies at the Government table, Mr. Foran and Mr. Schultz, didn't realize—a fatal error that played into the receptive hands of the defense and made a shambles of the trial—was that dissidents have developed in the last year or so a new kind of courtroom behavior which makes unheard-of demands on the judge. In old-style political trials, from the pre-revolutionary trial in which Peter Zenger was successfully defended against His Majesty's prosecutors on a charge of publishing seditious matter, to the recent trial of Dr. Spock et al., in Boston, both sides, in dress and behavior, accepted the conventions of the ruling establishment. The lawyers sat down when the judge told them to and didn't ask for permission to bring birthday cakes into court, the defendants wore business suits and neckties (or stocks and tie-wigs) and not purple pants, Indian headbands, or—as Abbie and Jerry did at one point—judicial robes, nor did they laugh or make abusive or witty remarks —and the spectators didn't shout "Right on!" or "Oink!" or, indeed, anything at all. Repression reigned. The defense behaved as if they shared the values and life style of the Court, even when they didn't, as in the big IWW trial in 1918 under the Espionage Act. There were over a hundred defendants, the entire leadership plus of the Wobblies, the only American anarchists who ever got through to the people. Their trial lasted five months—there were 17,000 separate offenses, a salami-slicing record beside which Judge Hoffman's is amateurish—the jury took sixty-five mintues to find 100 of the defendants guilty, and Judge Kenesaw Mountain Landis, later the "Czar" of baseball after the "Black Sox" scandal, also made Judge Hoffman look like a piker, handing out sentences ranging from ten days to twenty years, plus a cool $2,300,000 in fines, plus costs. That was the end of the Wobblies in our history. But although the defendants were anarchists to a man, as bold and ingenious in anti-establishment disruption outside the courtroom as their lineal descendants, Tom Hayden's SDS and Abbie Hoffman's Yippies, they behaved themselves inside it. Judge Landis, as mean a patriot as Judge Hoffman, and fully as tough a jurist, didn't feel obliged to hand out any contempt sentences. They respected those sacred precincts, not from any civic illusions—they were as cynically anti-bourgeois as the next Yippie—but because, like most radicals before the present generation, their public style was separate from their personal style. Today's radicals have merged the two and have created a functioning community which, unlike the nineteenth-century Fourierist and Owenite experiments, is not set apart geographically, but lives in and takes part in everyday life, swimming against the current but in the common river. As Chairman Mao well puts it, "The people are to the revolutionary as the water is to the fish." In the case of our New Left, read "mass media" for "people."

The Spock trial, which took place only a year and a half ago, how time flies, was perhaps the last in the old mode we shall see. Dr. Spock, after getting a load of the Chicago jurodrama, had second thoughts: "We sat like good little boys called into the principal's office. I'm afraid we didn't prove very much," he said recently. He meant that, as Jessica Mitford's excellent book, *The Trial of Doctor Spock,* showed, the moral and political issues the defendants hoped to promote by their defiant acts and by the trial were never brought out. Judge Ford was as bigoted and legalistic as Judge Hoffman. And so, given an old-style defense by old-style lawyers (for such they were, even Louis Boudin, the most sophisticated in left-wing defense cases) who shut up when they were overruled and were, like true professionals, psychologically distant from their clients' cause—given this, the Boston judge was in control and could repress the meaning of the trial in a way the Chicago judge, confronted by new-style defendants and lawyers, could not. Toward the end, one of the prosecutors complained that Kunstler and Weinglass were part of the same radical ambiance as their clients. (It was one of his few perceptive remarks.) The closeness revolted him, as a professional gladiator might be outraged if his opponent hacked away at him in the name of some abstract doctrine like Christianity.

In the new-style radical courtroom tactics, either the lawyers share the alienation and often the hair style of their clients, or there are no lawyers. Also, as in the Living Theatre and other avant-garde dramatic presentations, the audience gets into the act; the spectators raise their voices, or, worse, their laughter, at crucial moments despite all those beefy marshals. And the defendants, hitherto passive except when they had their meagre moment on the witness stand—"Please answer the question, yes or no" —feel free to make critical comments on the drama when the spirit moves them. The Chicago trial is the richest specimen of the new free-form trial to date, owing to the ingenious tactics of the defense (and the Judge's collaboration), but there are two other examples that compare, and contrast, interestingly with it: the current trial of Black Panthers in New York before a city magistrate, Judge Murtagh, on charges of conspiracy to blow up various business and police premises; and the trial a year ago of the "Milwaukee Fourteen" before Judge Larson, of the state judiciary, on charges of having incinerated ten thousand draft cards with homemade napalm.

The Black Panther trial hasn't begun yet, technically—in its first three weeks only two of sixteen pre-trial motions have been disposed of—and it promises to last even longer than the Chicago one did. But already a quite different pattern has emerged. The defendants are as indignant as the Chicago Eight were at what is being done to them in the name of legality, and with even more reason. They have been imprisoned for almost a year under $100,000 bail apiece, which means no bail. The Chicago Eight were free on bail. The Panthers aren't charged with any actual bombings, only with a conspiracy to intend to bomb, while the bail for four white radicals recently indicted in New York on charges of complicity in some real bombings was set at a reasonable $20,000 each; a year's imprisonment, and possibly two if the trial drags on at its present pace, seems excessive for innocent people, as the Panthers are until they are proven guilty in court. So there has been flak from the defendants—what have they to lose, they're in jail already—and outbursts from the spectators. Judge Murtagh's response has been tough but cool. He has ignored static from the defendants when he could—"Let's get on with it"—and when he couldn't, engaged in chilly dialogue like a hostess with a drunk on her hands. He has established some control over the spectators by making it clear he would jail them for contempt if they persisted in shouting "Right on!" to the defendants' morning greeting, "Power to the People!" and has sentenced two on the spot, after summary court-martials, to thirty days. At this writing, he seems to have established a precarious control over the courtroom. It may blow up any day, but it is at least a possible approach to the problem from the old-style viewpoint: play it by ear, modulating between fatherly admonitions and drumhead executions, and above all, don't get involved the way Julie did.

Judge Larson's approach was different from either Murtagh's or Hoffman's: he did get involved, but in a sympathetic way, like a psychiatrist. His problem was easier than theirs, it is true: the fourteen defendants were mostly Catholic priests, scholars and laymen; the crime they were accused of was destroying records that might send American youths to die in what many Americans think an unjust war; they admitted their guilt, indeed insisted on it as an act of conscience; and they defended themselves, no lawyers, old or new style, around to recall the judge to his professional role. This last was perhaps the decisive factor in making the Milwaukee trial a benign and sensible expression of our court system as against the Boston blank, the New York minuet and the Chicage circus. At any rate, Judge Larson allowed the defendants considerable leeway in expressing the ideals and ideas that had led them to their illegal action, whether from sympathy with them as moralists or as babes in the legal woods, or both. And when he sentenced them—leniently—he was regretful and, when it came to Father Mullaney, a Benedictine monk with a PhD in clinical psychology who had been especially eloquent and moving in his courtroom discourse, he cried.*

The legal basis for the Chicago trial was as rickety as its conduct under the Master of the Revels, also called the Lord of Misrule in the old days, Julius J. Hoffman—namely, the 1968 "Anti-Riot Act," fathered by Strom Thurmond. The anti-riot act was a congressional reflex to the ghetto riots following the murder of Martin Luther King and to such forgotten black bogeymen as H. Rap Brown and Stokely Carmichael. It is worthy of its sire. It makes it a federal offense (5 years, $10,000) to cross state lines with the *intention* of inciting, promoting, encouraging or participating in a riot, which is defined as any assemblage of three or more persons in which one or more persons injure another person (or more) or *damage property,* or *threaten to do so* (my emphasis). It seems obvious that such a "law" would convict anybody—and, in the case of the Chicago Five, did so—who travels any distance with the aim of exercising his First Amendment rights to talk out and peaceably assemble to ask the governing powers for redress of grievances, since if the demonstration is a success, somebody is bound to get knocked around by the cops, and a window or two may be broken in the heat of the moment. So who's to say what his intentions were? That's for a psychiatrist not a judge or jury. It seems likely the higher courts will throw out this Thurmondity as unconstitutional, but Judge Hoffman botched up the Chicago trial so thoroughly that they will be able to avoid the issue, with some relief, one imagines, by limiting themselves to correcting his errors.

From the legal viewpoint, the trial was—disap-

---

* For a detailed account of this remarkable trial, see Francine Gray's article in the *New York Review of Books* for Sept. 25, 1969 —as imaginative reportage as I've read in a long time. The *Review* has also printed, in its Dec. 4, 1969, and Feb. 12, 1970, issues, the complete transcripts of the parts of the Chicago trial record concerning Bobby Seale and Allen Ginsberg, with excellent introductions by Jason Epstein, which give a sense of context and continuity that is of necessity lacking in the present volume. It is reassuring that the mosaic excerpts here give about the same general picture as the *Review*'s complete-text episodes do.

pointing. But it was of unique significance in a way the defendants understood from the start and the prosecution and judge never caught on to: as a head-on collision, a public confrontation between the extremes of American politics and life styles, the radicalized, alienated youth versus the bourgeois Establishment. A *kulturkampf* which the young won hands down, on points. (Not that they were *really* young, the Chicago Five—Dellinger was a senile fifty-three, and the others were close to the age barrier of thirty; even revolutionaries grow old, if not up.) This is not a vaudeville theater, the Judge complained, asking the marshals to ask the defendants to stop giggling. And another time he asked the marshals to exclude from the courtroom anyone who applauded. The Court, he said, isn't a theater. But Jerry Rubin was right when he said, explaining he had been unavoidably detained and hadn't meant to walk out on the trial: "I like being here. It is interesting. . . . It is good theater, your Honor."

A long procession of singers, writers and intellectuals took the witness stand during the five months, and the contrast between their minds and feelings and those of the Court was dramatic. The testimony of Allen Ginsberg (who was allowed three O-o-m-m-m's and no more) and Norman Mailer (who replied to Prosecutor Schultz's request to stick to the facts—"Facts are nothing without their nuance, sir") was especially educational. It was all wasted on the Judge, however. When Mr. Schultz complained Mailer was not being "responsive" to his questions—i.e., was trying to tell the complicated truth—the Judge said: "You are too high-priced a writer to give us all that gratis, Mr. Mailer. Just answer the question." And to Tom Hayden's "So, your Honor, before your eyes you see the most vital ingredient of your system collapsing because the system does not hold together," the Judge replied: "Oh, don't be so pessimistic. Our system isn't collapsing. Fellows as smart as you could do awfully well under this system. I am not trying to convert you, mind you."

But the tone of the whole affair was set by Abbie Hoffman; it was his show, a chance to act out in largest publicity his ideas about radical politics as theater, about "putting on" the squares and goosing the media. His testimony is the crux of the trial, the

xxiii

most extensive and intensive expression of the new-radical style. It's also extremely amusing and penetrating; Abbie combines wit, imagination and shrewdness in a way not so common, and he has mastered his peculiar style so thoroughly that he can play around in and with it like a frisky dolphin. They can't even get him to give his name and address. When the Judge asks him for the former, he replies "Just Abbie. I don't have a last name, Judge. I lost it." (He told the press he was going to legally change his name after getting a load of his Honor.) Later: "My name is Abbie. I am an orphan of America." "Where do you reside?" "I live in Woodstock Nation." "Will you tell the Court and jury where it is?" "Yes. It is a nation of alienated young people. We carry it around with us as a state of mind in the same way the Sioux Indians carried the Sioux nation around with them. It is a nation dedicated to cooperation versus competition . . ." "Just where is it, that is all." "It is in my mind and in the minds of my brothers and sisters." Even his age provokes a poetic cadenza:

Q. Can you tell the Court and jury your present age?

A. My age is 33. I am a child of the 60's.

Q. When were you born?

A. Psychologically, 1960.

. . .

Q. Can you tell the Court and jury what is your present occupation?

A. I am a cultural revolutionary. Well, I am really a defendant—

Q. What do you mean?

A. —full time.

It is a wonder the trial ever got finished at all. And that the Judge, Government lawyers and federal marshals were physically able to stay in the same room with such defendants. Some of them may have been educated by the experience. I have been, and I've enjoyed it.

# Editors' Foreword

What you will read in the ensuing pages are the exact words of the participants, as officially recorded by the court stenographer, in the case of *United States v. Dellinger et al.*, more popularly known as the "Chicago Conspiracy" trial.

None of the words have been changed. The 22,000 pages of transcript have been edited to capture the emotional drama of this controversial trial and the substance of the opposing positions. We have attempted to do this with a just eye, despite our personal biases, in an effort to adequately and fairly portray what occurred.

We have excerpted those portions which not only highlighted the trial, but typified it. The factual descriptions are there, but so is the outrage, the philosophy and the humor.

The transcript of a trial is one long continuous recording of the words of the participants, broken only by recesses for lunch and adjournments at days' ends. Natural breaks in conversations and colloquies are not given, nor are the dramatic pauses which arise from the situations themselves or the participants' language. It is these natural pauses that we attempted to supply by dividing the transcript into segments, each segment presenting as nearly as possible the moment in time as it took place in the courtroom, with all the emotions and nuances that normally occur in such repartee.

Because this is a book for the nonlawyer, all legalistic colloquies unnecessary to the main action have been deleted. And because we want the trial to speak for itself, we have kept editorial comments to a minimum. Thus comment appears within each chapter in order to place the printed segments in context by summarizing prior background, or by informing the reader when a new subject is about to be discussed or a new witness to take the stand.

Three asterisks divide the segments and indicate that unnecessary dialogue has been deleted at that point. Occasionally, two asterisks divide the segments, indicating a pause in the dialogue but no omission of material. Deletions of irrelevant dialogue have been indicated by ellipses between paragraphs. The editors have taken special care to ensure that nothing has been removed from its context, most omissions being made merely to maintain the continuity of the action.

The book, like the trial, is divided into seven major parts. Beneath each part title, we have indicated the page numbers of the official court transcript from which the dialogue in that part is taken. Because the trial lasted four and a half months and spanned 22,000 pages, we often found it necessary to delete testimony of witnesses, in whole or in part, where we felt that it was not essential to following or understanding the proceedings.

We again remind the reader that the dialogue that follows is the verbatim language of the participants in the trial.

MARK L. LEVINE
GEORGE C. McNAMEE
DANIEL GREENBERG

February 1970

# THE TALES OF HOFFMAN

*Excerpts from the Verbatim Transcript*

---

UNITED STATES OF AMERICA
          *Plaintiff*
     vs.

DAVID T. DELLINGER, RENNARD   No. 69 Crim. 180
C. DAVIS, THOMAS E. HAYDEN,
ABBOTT H. HOFFMAN, JERRY C.
RUBIN, LEE WEINER, JOHN R.
FROINES and BOBBY G. SEALE,
               *Defendants*

---

TRANSCRIPT OF PROCEEDINGS had at the trial of the above—entitled cause before the HON. JULIUS J. HOFFMAN AND A JURY, commencing on the 26th day of September, A.D. 1969, at the hour of 10:00 o'clock a.m.

   *PRESENT:*
       HON. THOMAS A. FORAN,
             United States Attorney
       MR. RICHARD G. SCHULTZ,
             Asst. United States Attorney, and
       MR. ROGER CUBBAGE,
             Attorney, Department of Justice,
             appeared on behalf of the Government;
       MR. WILLIAM KUNSTLER and
       MR. LEONARD I. WEINGLASS,
             appeared on behalf of the defendants.

# I

# Opening Statements

Transcript pages 1-81

**September 26, 1969**
Officer of the Court:

> THEREUPON a panel of twelve venire-
> men and four alternates were called to the
> jury box and duly sworn for examination
> upon their voir dire, and examined until
> twelve jurors and four alternate jurors were
> accepted by the Counsel for the Plaintiff
> and Counsel for the Defendants.

> AND THEREFORE, the panel of twelve
> jurors and four alternates was duly sworn
> to try the issues.

       \*     \*     \*

[Prior to the introduction of evidence and testimony of witnesses, the attorneys for the opposing parties are granted the
opportunity to explain to the jurors the issues they intend to
prove—ed.]

*Opening statement on behalf of the Government by Mr.
Schultz*

Mr. Schultz: . . . The Government, ladies and gentlemen
of the jury, will prove in this case, the case which you will
witness as jurors, an overall plan of the eight defendants in
this case which was to encourage numerous people to come
to the city of Chicago, people who planned legitimate protest
during the Democratic National Convention which was held
in Chicago in August of 1968, from August 26 through August
29, 1968. They planned to bring these people into Chicago
to protest, legitimately protest, as I said, creat[ing] a situation

3

in this city where these people would come to Chicago, would riot . . . [T]he defendants, in perpetrating this offense, they, the defendants, crossed state lines themselves, at least six of them, with intent to incite this riot.

\* \* \*

[*Without the presence of the jury*]

The Court: This will be but a minute, Mr. Marshal. Who is the last defendant you named?

Mr. Schultz: Mr. Hayden.

The Court: Hayden. Who was the one before?

Mr. Schultz: Davis, and prior to that was Dellinger.

The Court: The one that shook his fist in the direction of the jury?

Mr. Hayden: That is my customary greeting, your Honor.

The Court: It may be your customary greeting but we do not allow shaking of fists in this courtroom. I made that clear.

Mr. Hayden: It implied no disrespect for the jury; it is my customary greeting.

The Court: Regardless of what it implies, sir, there will be no fist shaking and I caution you not to repeat it.

\* \* \*

[Mr. Schultz continuing with his opening statement—ed.]

Mr. Schultz: . . . The Defendants Dellinger, Davis and Hayden joined with five other defendants who are charged in this case in their venture to succeed in their plans to create the riots in Chicago during the time the Democratic National Convention was convened here.

Two of these defendants, the Defendant Abbie Hoffman who sits—who is just standing for you, ladies and gentlemen—

The Court: The jury is directed to disregard the kiss thrown by the Defendant Hoffman and the defendant is directed not to do that sort of thing again.

\* \* \*

Mr. Schultz: . . . Ladies and gentlemen of the jury, the Government will prove that each of these eight men assumed specific roles in it and they united and that the eight conspired together to encourage people to riot during the Convention. We will prove that the plans to incite the riot were basically in three steps. The first step was to use the unpopularity of the war in Vietnam as a method to urge people to come to Chicago during that Convention for purposes of protest. The first was to bring the people here.

The second step was to incite these people who came to

Chicago, to incite these people against the Police Department, the city officials, the National Guard and the military, and against the Convention itself, so that these people would physically resist and defy the orders of the police and the military.

So the second step, we will prove, was to incite, and the third step was to create a situation where the demonstrators who had come to Chicago and who were conditioned to physically resist the police would meet and would confront the police in the streets of Chicago so that at this confrontation a riot would occur. . . .

\* \*

First they demanded, when these people arrived in Chicago, to sleep in Lincoln Park. At one point they were talking in terms of up to or exceeding 500,000 people who were coming to Chicago to sleep in Lincoln Park and they demanded free portable sanitation facilities, they demanded free kitchens and free medical facilities.

The second demand, non-negotiable demand which was made by those defendants I just mentioned, was for a march to the International Amphitheatre where the Democratic National Convention was taking place. They said they were going to have a march of up to or exceeding 200,000 people. Although they were told that the United States Secret Service which was charged with the protection of the President of the United States, the Vice President of the United States and the candidates for nomination—although they were told that the Secret Service said that a permit could not be authorized because of the danger to the security of these individuals, the President and the Vice President and the candidates, the defendants demanded a permit for a march. . . .

So, ladies and gentlemen, of the jury, the Government will prove with regard to the permits that I have just mentioned that the defendants incited the crowd to demand sleeping in Lincoln Park and to demand that march to the Amphitheatre so that when the police ordered the crowd out of Lincoln Park at curfew and when the police stopped the march, the crowd, having been incited, would fight the police and there would be a riot.

\* \*

. . . The Government will not prove that all eight defendants met together at one time, but the Government will prove that on some occasions two or three of the defendants would meet together; on other occasions four would meet; on some occasions five of them would meet together to discuss these

5

actions, and on several occasions six of the defendants met together to discuss their plans. . . .

In sum, then, ladies and gentlemen, the Government will prove that the eight defendants charged here conspired together to use interstate commerce and the facilities of interstate commerce to incite and to further a riot in Chicago; that they conspired to use incendiary devices to further that riot, and they conspired to have people interfere with law enforcement officers, policemen, military men, Secret Service men engaged in their duties; and that the defendants committed what are called overt acts in furtherance of the conspiracy—that is, they took steps, they did things to accomplish this plan, this conspiracy. . . .

\*    \*    \*

The Court: Is it the desire of any lawyer of a defendant to make an opening statement?

Mr. Kunstler: It is, your Honor.

The Court: All right. You may proceed, sir.

Mr. Kunstler: Your Honor, it is 12:30.

The Court: I know, I am watching the clock. You leave the— What does that man say—you leave the time-watching to me—on the radio or TV—leave the driving to me. Mr. Kunstler, I will watch the clock for you.

Mr. Kunstler: Your Honor, will you permit us to complete the opening statements?

The Court: I will determine the time when we recess, sir. I don't need your help on that. There are some things I might need your help on; not that.

\*    \*    \*

*Opening statement on behalf of certain defendants by Mr. Kunstler*

Now the Government has given you its table of contents. I will present to you in general what the defense hopes to show is the true book. We hope to prove before you that the evidence submitted by the defendants will show that this prosecution which you are hearing is the result of two motives on the part of the Government—

Mr. Schultz: Objection as to any motives of the prosecution, if the Court please.

Mr. Kunstler: Your Honor, it is a proper defense to show motive.

The Court: I sustain the objection. You may speak to the

6

guilt or innocence of your clients, not to the motive of the Government.

Mr. Kunstler:  Your Honor, I always thought that—

Mr. Schultz:  Objection to any colloquies, and arguments, your Honor.

The Court:  I sustain the objection, regardless of what you have always thought, Mr. Kunstler.

\* \* \*

Mr. Kunstler:  The evidence will show as far as the defendants are concerned that they, like many other citizens of the United States, numbering in the many thousands, came to Chicago in the summer of 1968 to protest in the finest American tradition outside and in the vicinity of the Convention, the National Convention of the party in power. They came to protest the continuation of a war in South Vietnam which was then and had been for many years past within the jurisdiction of the party in power which happened to be the Democratic Party at that time. . . .

There was, as you will recall, and the evidence will so indicate, a turmoil within the Democratic Party itself as to whether it would enact a peace plan, as part of its platform. This, too, would be influenced by demonstrators. The possibility of this plank was what motivated many of the demonstrators to come to Chicago. The possibility of influencing delegates to that National Convention to take an affirmative strong stand against a continuation of this bloody and unjustified war, as they considered it to be along with millions of persons was one of the prime purposes of their coming to Chicago. . . .

At the same time as they were making plans to stage this demonstration and seeking every legal means in which to do so, the seeking of permits would be significant, permits in the seeking of facilities to put their plans into operation in a meaningful and peaceful way.

\* \*

At the same time as all of this was going on, the evidence will show that there were forces in this city and in the national Government who were absolutely determined to prevent this type of protest, who had reached a conclusion that such a protest had to be stopped by the—the same phrase used by Mr. Schultz—by all means necessary, including the physical violence perpetrated on demonstrators. These plans were gathering in Washington and they were gathering here in this city, and long before a single demonstrator had set foot in the city

7

of Chicago in the summer of 1968, the determination had been made that these demonstrations would be diffused, they would be dissipated, they would essentially be destroyed as effective demonstrations against primarily the continuation of the war in South Vietnam. . . .

We will demonstrate that free speech died here in the streets under those clubs and that the bodies of these demonstrators were the sacrifices to its death. . . .

\* \*

. . . [T]he defense will show that the real conspiracy in this case is the conspiracy to which I have alluded, the conspiracy to curtail and prevent the demonstrations against the war in Vietnam and related issues that these defendants and other people, thousands, who came here were determined to present to the delegates of a political party and the party in power meeting in Chicago; that the real conspiracy was against these defendants. But we are going to show that the real conspiracy is not against these defendants as individuals because they are unimportant as individuals; the real attempt was—the real attack was on the rights of everybody, all of us American citizens, all, to protest under the First Amendment to the Constitution, to protest against a war that was brutalizing us all, and to protest in a meaningful fashion, and that the determination was made that that protest would be dissolved in the blood of the protesters; that that protest would die in the streets of Chicago, and that that protest would be dissipated and nullified by police officers under the guise of protecting property or protecting law and order or protecting other people. . . .

Dissent died here for a moment during that Democratic National Convention. What happens in this case may determine whether it is moribund.

\* \* \*

*[At this point in the trial the Court summarily held in contempt of court two Defense Lawyers, Michael J. Kennedy and Dennis J. Roberts, who attempted to withdraw from the case. Mr. Sullivan is their counsel]*

The Court: I don't think there is any doubt that those two lawyers are in contempt. I will sign the order. I said substantially these things orally already.

Mr. Sullivan: May I be heard on this, your Honor?

The Court: Yes.

Mr. Sullivan: I object on behalf of Messrs. Kennedy and

8

Roberts to the entry of this order. I would like an opportunity to respond.

The Court: No, I will sign the order, Mr. Sullivan.

\* \* \*

The Court: Is there any other defense lawyer who wishes to make an opening statement to the jury?

I take it that your standing there means yes, you do, Mr. Weinglass.

\* \* \*

Mr. Weinglass: . . . I leave the judgment of what is a non-negotiable demand to you, but you are going to hear some interesting evidence in the course of this case on that issue, because the city, the people who were in charge of granting to these young people the right which they have as citizens to congregate, and meet, and we contend even sleep in our public parks which are publicly-owned property held in trust for the public by the public officials, were reasonable demands which the city could have met if the persons responsible for that decision would not have been persons who were so fearful and so misunderstood the young in this country that they could not meet and talk to them in a reasonable, rational way. . . .

\* \* \*

The Court: I have repeatedly cautioned you. I caution you again, Mr. Weinglass. I think you understand me. You persist in arguing and telling the jury what you propose to do in respect to objections.

Mr. Weinglass: Yes, I thought that was the purpose of an opening statement.

The Court: That is not the function of an opening statement. I have cautioned you time and time again. I caution you once more.

Mr. Weinglass: I thought that was the purpose of an opening statement. Thank you, your Honor.

The Court: Don't thank me. I didn't do it as a favor to you. I am cautioning you not to persist in it. . . .

The Court: Mr. Weinglass, I have repeatedly admonished you not to argue to the jury, not to tell the jury anything other than what in your opinion the evidence will reveal.

I think your persistency in disregarding the direction of the Court and the law in the face of repeated admonitions is contumacious conduct, and I so find it on the record.

\* \* \*

9

The Court:  Does any other defense lawyer wish to make an opening statement?

Just a minute, sir. Who is your lawyer?

Mr. Seale:  Charles R. Garry.

Mr. Foran:  Your Honor, may we have the jury excused?

The Court:  Ladies and gentlemen, I am sorry, I will have to excuse you again.

[*Without the presence of the jury*]

The Court:  Mr. Kunstler, do you represent Mr. Seale?

\* \* \*

Mr. Kunstler:  No, your Honor, as far as Mr. Seale has indicated to me, that because of the absence of Charles R. Garry—

The Court:  Have you filed his appearance?

Mr. Kunstler:  Filed whose appearance?

The Court:  The appearance for Mr. Seale.

Mr. Kunstler:  I have filed an appearance for Mr. Seale.

The Court:  All right. I will permit you to make another opening statement in behalf of Mr. Seale if you like. I will not permit a party to a case to—

Mr. Kunstler:  Your Honor, I cannot compromise Mr. Seale's position—

The Court:  I don't ask you to compromise it, sir, but I will not permit him to address the jury with his very competent lawyer seated there.

# II

# Case for the Government

Transcript pages 82-9763

Officer of the Court:

> THEREUPON the government, to maintain the issues in its behalf, presented the following evidence, to-wit:

[With these words the case for the government officially begins. In the ensuing pages you will read the highlights of that presentation.

We remind the reader that the dialogue which follows is the verbatim language of the participants in the trial—ed.]

Mr. Weinglass: To avoid unnecessary repetition, may I have a standing objection?

The Court: I don't deal in standing objections on anything.

Mr. Weinglass: I will state my objection once again.

The Court: Every time you have an objection, you make it, and every time you make one, I will rule on it. I might sustain it, too.

[A standing objection is a single objection which if granted, would obviate the need for individually objecting to a future series of similar questions—ed.]

* * *

The Court: . . . I think Mr. Schultz' suggestion that subpoenas be stayed—I think you said or one of the lawyers said that a man named Johnson, Lyndon B. Johnson, was subpoenaed also, is that right?

Mr. Kunstler: We don't know if he has been served yet but the subpoena is out.

The Court: It wouldn't be nice to take him from the comforts of his ranch in Dallas or wherever it is, Johnson City, if we couldn't reach him on Monday . . .

* * *

[*Discussion concerning request of four defense lawyers to withdraw from the case*]

The Court: . . . Now, Mr. Sullivan, have you resolved your differences?

Mr. Sullivan: I think so, but at least I would like to give it a college try. . . .

It is my understanding that these defendants are willing that Messrs. Tigar, Lefcourt, Kennedy and Roberts not be present during the trial of this case and not participate in the trial as defense counsel, and they are willing to agree to their withdrawal as trial counsel. They are, as I understand it, satisfied to be represented in the trial of this case by Messrs. Garry, Kunstler and Weinglass, and that they do not waive any claim of prejudice arising from the absence of Mr. Garry.

That is my understanding, your Honor, and in light of that understanding, if that is the case, then I ask your Honor to take such action as you may deem appropriate, and I would suggest—

The Court: I don't care to participate in negotiations. I don't want to bargain here before the Court. I don't want to participate in a bargaining session. As you know, I am not a bargainer. . . .

\* \* \*

The Court: First of all, before I consider that motion there will be a finding that the respondents Michael E. Tigar and Gerald B. Lefcourt are in contempt of this Court. I direct the United States Attorney to prepare the same kind of order that was submitted in connection with Michael J. Kennedy and Dennis J. Roberts.

Mr. Sullivan: May I be heard?

The Court: I deny the motion, the other motion, in its entirety, the motion submitted here.

Mr. Sullivan, I am not going to have lawyers flaunt the authority of this Court and not have the other lawyers be fair with the Court and try to intimate or suggest that while they filed appearances, they don't really represent them. . . .

. . .

The Court: I commit them without bail. I deny the motion for bail.

Mr. Sullivan: If the Court please—

The Court: I don't bail a lawyer contemner.

Mr. Sullivan: Your Honor, are they to remain in custody for—

The Court: Yes.

Mr. Sullivan: —for the rest of their lives?

The Court: For when?

Mr. Sullivan: For the rest of their lives? Is there no term?

The Court: I will determine on the disposition of this case Monday morning at ten o'clock.

Mr. Sullivan: Your Honor—

The Court: That will be the disposition. They are now held in contempt. I didn't say—don't put words in my mouth, Mr. Sullivan. I didn't intend and you know you were talking foolishly when you said the rest of their lives. . . .

## September 29, 1969

The Court: . . . I have always followed the practice, and it is the law, to require lawyers in criminal cases to present a motion for leave to withdraw, not to send a telegram and say they are withdrawing, but to present a motion for leave to withdraw, giving evidence that they have served such notice of the motion not only on the Government but on their own clients. That was not done in this case.

It appears now that in the opinion of the Court all defendants are adequately and responsibly represented and as far as this Court is concerned, I have no desire to damage the professional careers of young lawyers; but even young lawyers who have corresponding lawyers here must comply with the law.

Agreeable with the motion and suggestion of the Government, the contempt proceedings against the two lawyers who were here and the other two lawyers who were not here—you have their names, Mr. Clerk?

The Clerk: Yes, your Honor.

The Court: —will be vacated, set aside, and leave will be given to them to withdraw . . .

* * *

The Clerk: There is a motion, your Honor, on behalf of amicus curiae, one hundred lawyers, to declare a mistrial and drop contempt proceedings.

The Court: I deny that motion not only as moot, partially moot, but I deny the motion because you have no standing, sir.

Mr. Meyers: Certainly the mistrial application is not moot.

The Court: I said in part it is moot. Is your hearing good?

Mr. Meyers: Yes, but I am here on behalf of a hundred lawyers.

The Court: In respect to amicus curiae, one hundred lawyers, I deny that because they do not have standing at the trial under this indictment and the pleas of not guilty entered pursuant thereto.

Mr. Meyers: May I have the privilege of stating my—

The Court: No, no.

13

Mr. Foran:   Your Honor—

The Court:   No. This is not a public forum. It is a branch of the United States District Court.

\*    \*    \*

*[Argument on defense motion for mistrial. Such a motion, if granted by the Court, would immediately terminate the present proceedings without a finding of innocence or guilt]*

Mr. Kunstler:   Your Honor, without repeating any of the long history of the controversy with reference to the lawyers which was disposed of this morning, I am moving on behalf of all defendants for a mistrial in this case or, in the alternative, again for the disqualification of this Court. Your Honor, we have set forth some seven or eight grounds of this motion.

Our first ground is that your Honor illegally, unlawfully and unconstitutionally ordered and directed the arrest of some of the pretrial lawyers in the case; that equally illegally you effectuated the imprisonment and appearance in court while in custody of these attorneys; that you refused, again we claim unconstitutionally, to set bond for these attorneys, and again, number four, equally unconstitutionally, you attempted to coerce the defendants by these arrests and imprisonment and denial of bail to waive their Sixth Amendment rights to counsel of their choice; and that you have during the course of the trial degraded, harassed and maligned in diverse ways and fashions these and other of defendants' attorneys, and because of this you have so prejudiced this case that there can no longer be a fair and impartial trial—all we claim in violation of the Constitution and laws of the United States. . . .

In addition we claim that you have consistently and systematically harassed, humiliated, maligned and degraded all of these attorneys by the following—and I have set forth starting on page 4 some of the following—that you have refused to permit them to complete oral argument and that you have frequently interrupted their presentation; that you have threatened them with contempt and that you have adjudicated two of them in contempt.

I might add, your Honor, I believe you also have adjudicated Mr. Weinglass in contempt from the language on the record of last Friday. That you have stressed in a highly derogative fashion the fact that lead trial counsel are from other states; that you have insisted on the daily presence of local counsel whom you knew were never intended to participate in the actual trial, and that you have converted routine courtroom language by these attorneys into criticism of both Chicago and the prospective jurors, and that you have granted only one

14

trial motion by the attorneys and that was to adjourn four minutes earlier than usual with the observation in words or substance that the defense have finally won one. And I believe the words "finally won one" is a quote. . . .

* * *

The Court: Mr. Clerk, the motion styled "Emergency Motion" filed by the defendants over the signature of William N. Kunstler and a signature of Leonard Weinglass signed as represented by William N. Kunstler for a mistrial or, in the alternative, for the disqualification of the Court, will be denied. The Court directs the Clerk of the Court to impound this document for such consideration as the Court may give to it at some future time during or after this trial.

Mr. Marshal—

Mr. Kunstler: Your Honor, I object to that last statement. There is another intimidation being practiced here upon the attorneys that we now have to worry about what happens to us for filing the paper, and I would like the record to so indicate.

The Court: You always have to worry in this courtroom, Mr. Kunstler, when you make remarks or make allegations in a document such as you made over your signature. That will be all.

Mr. Kunstler: We made—

The Court: That will be all, sir.

* * *

The Court: Mr. Weinglass, will you continue, please, with your cross-examination of this witness.

Mr. Weinglass: May we have the presence of the jury, your Honor?

The Court: Oh, I thought they were ordered out. That is not a bad idea.

*(Whereupon, the following further proceedings were had herein, in open court, within the presence and hearing of the jury)*

The Court: You must expect to do pretty well for the remainder of your cross-examination. . . .

*Cross-examination of Government Witness Raymond Simon, Corporation Counsel for the city of Chicago, by Defense Attorney Kunstler*

A. Yes, Mr. Kunstler, and there I was trying to point out the reason how that comes about to Mr. Feinglass, and that is because—

Q. I think his name is Weinglass instead of Feinglass.

A. I beg your pardon, Mr. Weinglass.

15

Q. Just so we will have no problems in the future.
A. Your name is Mr. Kunstler?
Q. Yes.
A. I apologize, Mr. Weinglass, for saying Feinglass. . . .

\* \* \*

Q. Just one last question. Now that it is all over, don't you think that the city made the wrong decision—
A. No, sir.
Q. —to force those people out of Lincoln Park?

. . .

A. I don't know what would have happened if that wasn't done. That is kind of speculation. I represent the city of Chicago, Mr. Kunstler. I know what they were doing at that time. They were striving as hard as they could and in as deep earnestness as they could to have it be orderly in the city. They didn't want another Robert Kennedy assassination here. They didn't want Senator McCarthy or McCarthy workers, or all the rumors that were bouncing in in the intelligence reports, they didn't want that to happen in an assembly in the middle of the night in Lincoln Park, and have a young girl supporter of Senator McCarthy killed. We didn't want that to happen, and it didn't happen. I think we made the right decision by not letting them take over the park. They were honest judgments.

## September 30, 1969

The Court: . . . You say, as I read from the motion slip, "Motion of Stanley A. Bass, local counsel, to be excused from required attendance for the duration of this trial." That to me means you want to get out.

Now if you want to get out and there is no objection either by your client, any of your clients, and they will so state for the record themselves, and there is no objection by the Government, I am disposed to allow your motion to withdraw.

. . .

The Court: . . . You may call them in the order their names appear in the indictment.

Mr. Dellinger: I only require Mr. Kunstler and Mr. Weinglass and Mr. Garry.

The Court: Ask him his name, first, for the record.

. . .

Mr. Davis: Your Honor, my name, on the record, is Rennard C. Davis. My friends call me Rennie. It was never my intention that Mr. Bass represent me in this trial. It has only been my intention from the beginning that we have a trial

16

team of three, so I am going into this trial with not full representation since Mr. Charles Garry is not here, but I do again, for I don't know how many times, release Mr. Bass from obligations to the trial.

. . .

Mr. Bass: Mr. Hayden, please.

Mr. Hayden: I consent to the withdrawal also.

Mr. Bass: Mr. Hoffman.

Mr. Hoffman: I consent to the withdrawal.

Mr. Bass: Mr. Rubin.

Mr. Rubin: I consent with the understanding that the trial is illegitimate because Charles Garry is not here, our head counsel.

Mr. Bass: Mr. Weiner.

Mr. Weiner: I consent.

Mr. Bass: Mr. Froines.

Mr. Froines: I consent.

Mr. Bass: Mr. Seale.

Mr. Seale: I fired all of these lawyers a long time ago. Charles Garry ain't here, and I want my legal counsel here.

[Mr. Bass's motion to be excused was subsequently granted —ed.]

\*     \*     \*

Mr. Kunstler: . . . We have filed a renewed emergency motion to disqualify your Honor in this case, and I would just briefly summarize it.

The Court: I have read it carefully.

Mr. Kunstler: I understand, sir.

The Court: I have read every line of it.

Mr. Kunstler: But I think it is important at least to indicate generally what is in it.

The Court: May I suggest to you that was the reason for my delay in coming to the bench, for which I ask your pardon most humbly.

Mr. Kunstler: You notice my inquiry was directed at the prosecution, not at your Honor.

The Court: I am sorry, but you did send this motion in, and I look at the papers here, and the bar of this Court knows that I am not considered a loafer.

Mr. Kunstler: Your Honor, you are misinterpreting.

The Court: You were complaining at my late arrival.

\*     \*     \*

[*In reference to a motion that Judge Hoffman disqualify himself, Mr. Kunstler made the following statement*]

Mr. Kunstler: . . . Now apparently, according to one newspaper reporter who is under subpoena and is waiting outside to testify if your Honor would have a hearing on this matter, you were overheard to say in the elevator, as I understand it, and we have included Mr. Von Hoffman's article in the Washington Post as Exhibit A, you were overheard to say, "Now we are going to hear this wild man Weinglass."

Now Mr. Von Hoffman is prepared to take the stand and swear that that is what he heard in the elevator from your Honor's lips.

If that statement is true and correct, and Mr. Von Hoffman so testifies, and your Honor finds it to be true and correct, then I think that there is absolutely a valid just cause for your Honor to disqualify himself in this matter, and when you add this with all the other objections which the defendants have had up to this time, the cumulative effect is, I think, so overwhelming that in all justice, your Honor should disqualify himself.

. . .

The Court: Mr. Clerk, the motion of the defendants styled "Renewed Emergency Motion to Disqualify the Honorable Julius J. Hoffman as Judge in This Matter" will be denied, because the papers filed in support thereof do not state grounds for the relief sought. . . .

\* \* \*

[Colloquies concerning possible disqualification of two jurors. Out of the presence of the jury]

Mr. Foran: Judge, the reason we were late this morning and then the reason for the request for the interruption was I was informed just about the time we were to come to court by the FBI that they had been informed that one of the jurors had received a letter or her family had received a letter that certainly could be of a threatening nature. . . . I have a copy of it here, your Honor, marked as Government's Exhibit A. It is addressed to the King family, 81 South Caroline, Crystal Lake, Illinois 60014. It is written in script, "You are being watched. The Black Panthers. . . ."

. . .

The Court: Now my own marshal, gentlemen, was handed this morning this communication addressed to the Peterson family. . . .

. . .

The Court: . . . [I]t is not unlike Government's Exhibit A for identification . . .

. . .

Mr. Weinglass: I think this does raise the flag of caution that more than one has received a similar document. Perhaps we ought to ask all of the jurors.

18

Mr. Kunstler: I think the record should also indicate that the newspapers in Chicago did publish the addresses of each one of the jurors. I saw it in at least two newspapers.

Mr. Foran: Yes, they did.

The Court: There is a suggestion by Mr. Feinglass—

Mr. Kunstler: Mr. Weinglass is going to be Mr. Feinglass before this trial is over. I may put in a change of name application for him.

The Court: It is Feinglass—oh, it is Weinglass? Did I say Feinglass?

Mr. Kunstler: You were, I think, overinfluenced by Mr. Simon yesterday.

The Court: It is Weinglass.

. . .

Mr. Kunstler: . . . [W]e are at the point, your Honor, where the defendants have seriously made a statement that they believe that the two letters in question were sent in some way by some agent of the Government in order to prejudice them further in this trial. That is their position. I think they have publicly stated it, and that is the position which they take.

The Court: I will let you try to prove that right now. That is a very grave charge against an officer of the Government.

Mr. Kunstler: Well, we obviously can't prove it, your Honor.

The Court: Then don't say it.

Mr. Kunstler: This is the clients' position. That is my statement.

. . .

The Court: To make a statement like that is irresponsible.

\* \* \*

[*The following passages are from the proceedings of October 6, 1969*]

Mr. Kunstler: . . . We would hope that your Honor would set this down for a hearing so that what your Honor has termed and we agree with your Honor is a very serious allegation can at least begin to unravel in this courtroom.

. . .

Mr. Foran: Your Honor, the Government objects to the totally frivolous, idiotic proposal that you have hearings to determine inferences of possibilities of circumstantial evidence of a totally unjustified, totally ridiculous charge. I wish really—well, your Honor, the Government objects to it. It is so—I wish the showboat tactics would stop.

\* \* \*

[*Returning to the proceedings of September 30, 1969*]

The Court: . . . Mr. Marshal, will you please go to the jury room and request Juror Kristi A. King and Juror Ruth L. Peterson to accompany you to the courtroom, one at a time. . . .

. . .

The Court: Miss King, will you please look at Government's Exhibit A for identification—

Mr. Marshal, will you show it to the juror.

—and let me know whether you have seen the original of that document at any time.

Miss King: No, sir, I haven't.

The Court: You have never seen it?

Miss King: No, sir.

The Court: Do you know whether any member of your family brought it to your attention or not?

Miss King: It wasn't brought to my attention, no, sir.

The Court: All right.

Read it, Miss King. Read it, please.

Miss King: It says, "You are being watched. The Black Panthers." It's addressed to the King Family.

\* \*

The Court: Having now seen it—and assuming that anyone in your family has seen it—will you please tell me whether, having seen and read that document, you can continue to be a fair and impartial juror in this case, treating the United States of America and all rights of the defendants fairly and impartially, and render a verdict or verdicts according to the evidence and the law which will be given to you in this case? Do you still think you can do that?

Miss King: No, sir.

The Court: What did you say?

Miss King: No, sir.

The Court: You do not think so.

Miss King: No.

Mr. Kunstler: Your Honor, I must make an objection for the record.

This juror had never seen this letter before your Honor showed it to her. The most minimal investigation by the Federal Bureau of Investigation would have revealed from her father and from her mother that she had not so seen it.

. . .

Mr. Kunstler: . . . [A]t that point in your Honor's interrogation this morning when Miss King said she had not seen that letter, I think it was your Honor's duty then to discontinue questioning in this case, because now the Court has revealed the letter. The Court has made the contact with the juror, rather than anyone else at this moment, and revealed the letter to the juror.

[Thereupon, the Court excused Miss King as a juror and appointed an alternate in her stead—ed.]

\* \* \*

The Court: I know of no judge anywhere who goes as far in a voir dire [here, an oral examination of potential jurors to determine their acceptability—ed.] in that area as I do.

Mr. Kunstler: Your Honor has not been around very much.

\* \* \*

[*Ruth Peterson was the second juror alleged to have received a threatening note*]

The Court: The Marshal is handing you Government's Exhibit B-2 for identification. Have you ever seen it before?

Juror Peterson: Yes.

. . .

The Court: Having seen that letter or that document entitled or, rather, identified as Government's Exhibit 2 for identification, B-2, do you still feel that you can fulfill your assurances given to the Court on a prior occasion when you were being examined by the Court, you remember, upstairs in the larger courtroom, that you can be a fair and impartial juror, continue to be here?

Juror Peterson: Yes.

The Court: And that you can give these eight defendants who sit at that table as well as the United States of America—

Juror Peterson: Yes, I do.

The Court: —a fair and impartial trial?

Juror Peterson: Yes.

The Court: You do?

Juror Peterson: Yes, I think it is my duty to.

. . .

The Court: . . . Do you have any knowledge as to who sent this letter to your home?

Juror Peterson: No, I don't. I don't think anybody did. I think they are just trying to play a hoax.

\* \* \*

*Direct examination of Government Witness David E. Stahl, Chicago Deputy Mayor, by Mr. Foran*

The Court: Ladies and gentlemen of the jury, the testimony which this witness is about to give is offered by the Government only with respect to the Defendant Derringer and to no other defendant at this time.

Mr. Kunstler: I think your Honor meant Dellinger.

21

The Court:   Dellinger, that's right.

*By Mr. Foran:*

Q. Will you give the conversation, Mr. Stahl.

A. Mr. Dellinger said that we must issue a permit—

The Court:   I am going to get back at you, Mr. Witness. I mispronounced the defendant's name. You said Dillinger. It's Derringer. We were both wrong. You mean Mr. Derringer, do you not?

Mr. Foran:   Dellinger.

\* \* \*

*Cross-examination of Mr. Stahl by Mr. Weinglass*

Q. Now if my understanding is correct, all of the meetings with Abbie and Jerry occurred in City Hall, the three meetings?

Mr. Foran:   Your Honor, I object to the constant reference to these two little—to Abbie and Jerry. Let's call the defendants by their proper names.

The Court:   I agree.

Mr. Foran:   It is an attempt to give a diminutive attitude to men who are over 30.

The Court:   They should not be referred to in the United States District Court by their—I nearly said Christian names; I don't know whether that would be accurate or not, but not by their first names. . . .

\* \* \*

Q. Now in your August 10 meeting with the National Mobilization where you testified on direct that Rennie and Mark were present as well as three other people—

Mr. Foran:   Your Honor, here we go again. Now another 29-year-old being "Rennie Baby." I object to the diminutive familiar child terms for mentally grown men.

Mr. Kunstler:   Your Honor, I did not hear "Rennie Baby."

Mr. Weinglass:   Rennie Baby?

Mr. Foran:   Rennie and Mark and Helen Runningwater —I mean, that is foolishness.

Mr. Kunstler:   I object to that, your Honor.

The Court:   I sustain the objection to the question.

Mr. Kunstler:   Would your Honor order the jury to disregard the "Rennie Baby" remark as unfounded?

The Court:   If the United States Attorney said that, I certainly do.

Crowd the "Baby" out of your minds. We are not dealing with babies here.

\* \* \*

Mr. Foran:   . . . [Mr. Kunstler] is in this argumentative fashion trying to once again play Perry Mason.

Mr. Kunstler: He does pretty well, your Honor. If I can do half as well as Perry Mason—

Mr. Foran: As a television actor, you do, Mr. Kunstler.

* * *

The Court: I know what you are trying to do but I am talking about documents not in evidence.

Mr. Kunstler: I offer it in evidence, your Honor.

The Court: I don't receive defendant's exhibits during the Government's case.

Mr. Foran: Your Honor, look at that now. Your Honor, is this a man of his experience trying to pretend that he doesn't know that is grossly improper?

. . .

Mr. Foran: Your Honor, will you let the man try to remember he has got a law degree?

Mr. Kunstler: Your Honor, every time there comes this despairing anguished cry from Mr. Foran about the defense counsel for which I use the term dying quail, I believe, to describe it, and it occurs every time.

The Court: I have never heard that. That is a new one.

. . .

* * *

The Court: You know Mr. Mies van der Rohe designed that lectern for the use of counsel and I wish you would stay behind it, sir.

Mr. Kunstler: Your Honor, sometimes for a free spirit, it is quite confining, so I move a little, and I am sorry.

* * *

Q. But you think that was a rather important thing that was said to you about tearing up the town?

Mr. Foran: Oh, your Honor, here we go again.

Mr. Kunstler: Your Honor, if the remark "here we go again" is an objection, I never heard it.

Mr. Foran: I really am going to refer you to Wigmore's [a legal treatise on the rules of evidence—ed.] tonight, Mr. Counsel. Instead of watching yourself on TV, you can study evidence.

. . .

Mr. Kunstler: . . . The proper way to object is to say "I object," not "Channel 7" or "Channel 5."

* * *

Mr. Foran: . . . And by the way, your Honor, I would like to have your Honor tell counsel's group in the courtroom that they are not to respond by laughter and comments.

23

The Court: I have already admonished the Marshal to see to it that order is maintained.

Mr. Kunstler: Your Honor, a bit of laughter is not disorder, and I think sometimes—

The Court: It is in this courtroom. This is either a serious case or it isn't. I don't waste my time.

Mr. Kunstler: I know, but when your Honor makes a quip and makes people laugh, there is no such statement by the U.S. Attorney.

The Court: It is not intended to provoke laughter.

Mr. Kunstler: But it does, your Honor, and we all know that it does.

The Court: I am not a humorist.

## October 2, 1969

*Continued cross-examination of Mr. Stahl by Mr. Kunstler*

The Court: I can only use the voice the Lord gave me. This is the first time in about twenty-two years serving on state and federal benches that anybody has complained about my voice. They have complained about other things but nobody has complained about my voice. And it is amusing—you know, I am not forbidden to read the newspapers, I haven't forbidden myself, but I did see even some press friends of mine refer to my voice as being rasping. Then, on the other hand, I heard it referred to by your associate—what is the name of that actor—

Mr. Kunstler: Orson Welles, your Honor.

The Court: —as Orson Welles, who has a magnificently resonant voice.

Now take your choice. It is either rasping or it is as resonant as Orson Welles.

Mr. Weinglass: Well, I don't want to characterize the voice of the Court. However—

The Court: I do my best to use the vocal facilities the Lord has endowed me with.

\* \* \*

Mr. Kunstler: But I want the record to quite clearly indicate that I do not direct Mr. Seale in any way. He is a free independent black man who does his own direction.

The Court: Black or white, sir—and what an extraordinary statement, "an independent black man." He is a defendant in this case. He will be calling you a racist before you are through, Mr. Kunstler.

Mr. Kunstler: Your Honor, I think to call him a free independent black man will not incite his anger.

24

*By Mr. Kunstler:*

Q. Now, in all of your discussions with either Jerry Rubin, Abbie Hoffman, Dave Dellinger, Rennie Davis, or any of the people with them at any of the meetings to which you testified, did anyone ever say to you, "If we don't get the permits, we're going to do violent acts in this city"?

A. Not in precisely that language, no.

Q. Well, did they do it in any language?

A. Yes. Mr. Dellinger said on Monday that permits for the use of the parks should be issued in order to minimize destruction.

Q. To minimize destruction. And did he indicate to you from whence the destruction would come?

A. It certainly wasn't coming from the Chicago Police Department.

\* \* \*

*[Redirect by Mr. Foran]*

Q. At the August 7 meeting with Rubin and Hoffman, was there any discussion of any violence?

A. Yes. Mr. Hoffman indicated that he was prepared to tear up the town and the Convention.

\* \* \*

*[Recross by Mr. Weinglass]*

Q. On the August 7 meeting with Abbie Hoffman and Jerry Rubin, did Mr. Hoffman and Mr. Rubin indicate to you that if the yippies would be permitted to stay in the park, that everything would be OK and not violent?

A. I don't recall words exactly to that effect being—or statements exactly to that effect being made at that meeting.

Q. Was that the general tenor of their remarks, Mr. Stahl?

A. They opened the meeting by saying they wanted to avoid violence. They also followed that statement subsequently with statements about their willingness or about Mr. Hoffman's willingness to tear up the town and the Convention and to die in Lincoln Park.

Q. But in between that first statement you made and the second did they not indicate to you that if the city would permit them to stay in the parks, that there would be no violence and everything will be all right?

A. I would suspect they made a statement something along those lines in the course of the meeting.

Mr. Weinglass: Thank you.

\* \* \*

Q. Would you relate what you heard, please.

A. I heard Mr. Rubin saying that the pigs started the violence, and he says, "Tonight we're not going to give up the park. We have to meet violence with violence." He says, "The pigs are armed with guns and clubs and MACE, so we have to arm ourselves with"—with any kind of weapon they could get.

Q. Did he say anything more that you can recall? Do you recall any further statements by him at this time?

A. I don't recall what else he said, but he ended it with saying, "And don't forget our gigantic love-in on the beaches tomorrow."

\* \* \*

Q. When the police car came, the marked police car came behind the barricade, did any of the people turn and face the police car?

A. Yes, they did.

Q. Then what occurred, please?

A. Well, they began to throw rocks at it, boards, 2 x 4's that were cut in half, hitting the car with it, breaking the windows. One took a piece of board that looked like an axe handle and started swinging at the blue light on the roof. The car went into the barricade and hit the barricade and then backed out and they were yelling, "Kill the pigs. Get them. Get those pigs in the car." . . .

Q. After this squad car left the area of the barricade, Mr. Murray, what occurred?

A. Shortly after, eight to ten patrolmen approached and they were spread out—

. . .

Q. And what occurred, please?

A. Objects came from the crowd, from behind the barricade again, bricks and stones, mostly, bottles and cans, and one policeman turned, started running back, fell down, and they cheered, and the policemen retreated.

\* \* \*

Mr. Kunstler: Your Honor, may we excuse the jury?

The Court: What did you say?

Mr. Kunstler: May we excuse the jury?

Mr. Schultz: Yes we have no objection to that, your Honor.

The Court: You want the jury excused?

Mr. Kunstler: Yes, your Honor.

26

The Court: You mean "should I excuse the jury." You say, "we." You don't do that.

Mr. Kunstler: No. We are not partner in that, your Honor.

The Court: You are suggesting that the Court excuse the jury.

Mr. Kunstler: I thought that is what I said.

The Court: No, you didn't. I thought I made clear our respective—what our respective functions were.

Mr. Kunstler: To which I have wholeheartedly agreed, your Honor.

## October 3, 1969

[*Colloquy between the Court and Defense Counsel*]

Mr. Kunstler: Just in closing, I would like to object to the constant reference that your Honor has made to contempt cases of other lawyers, to statements you are going to deal with us at an appropriate time. I think that has an intimidating effect on counsel.

The Court: The law requires me to do it, Mr. Kunstler. The law of the circuit requires me to do it.

Mr. Kunstler: I am just making my observations, your Honor, because we both know that—

The Court: Don't always say what we know. Don't say what I know because I don't know what you know.

Mr. Kunstler: That "we" did not include your Honor. That is Mr. Weinglass and myself both know that these remarks are made often and we both think that they have a very intimidating effect on a lawyer defending his client.

\* \* \*

*Cross-examination of Government Witness Murray by Mr. Kunstler*

A. . . . [A]s soon as the park got dark—as soon as it got dark each night, the crowd, the people in the park would change, you know. During the daylight hours and the evening, they were sleeping, some of them, making love, some of them, sitting around talking, listening to music, little talks, and as the night, you know, as it got dark and more people would enter the park—and not only Hippies or Yippies, it was people that were anti-police. I saw people from the North Side coming into the park.

Q. How do you know an anti-police person when you see him?

A. I can't tell when I see him but when they open their mouth and yell, "Kill the pigs," I assume he is anti-police.

\* \* \*

Mr. Schultz: I have a very short series of questions. It might take me just a couple of minutes.

27

The Court:   A lawyer's short series or really a short series?
Mr. Schultz:   Really a short series, your Honor.

\*     \*     \*

Mr. Kunstler:   It is a very simple matter, your Honor. It has to do with the fact that some of the defendants have asked me to ask your Honor whether from time to time, if the occasion arises and they do have to go to the men's room, they might leave without interrupting the trial and come right back.

The Court:   Well, if it be understood that they waive their constitutional right to be present here.

Mr. Kunstler:   I think under those circumstances, your Honor, they would certainly waive their constitutional rights.

\*     \*     \*

*On redirect examination by Mr. Schultz*

Q. What if anything, did Rubin say during the preceding ten minutes before the policemen were assaulted and during the time the policemen were assaulted which would encourage the crowd to assault the policemen?

. . .

A. He said "Let's get the m-f-en pigs out of here." He said, "Take off your guns and we'll fight you," and "you're shitheads," and "You're m-f-s" and "Your kids are f-n pigs."

*On recross examination by Mr. Weinglass*

Q. Did you see Mr. Rubin on the street Wednesday night?
A. No, sir.
Mr. Schultz:   Objection, if the Court please.
*By Mr. Weinglass:*
Q. Did you see Mr. Turner—
The Court:   I have sustained the objection. You are getting beyond the redirect examination.

Mr. Weinglass:   Well, your Honor, the prosecutor, if I recall, on redirect was permitted to go extensively into Mr. Turner's activities over my objection and I objected because it wasn't related to the Defendant Rubin, and now I am trying to elicit from the witness the fact that it was not, in fact, in any way related to the Defendant Rubin. I am being obstructed in that effort.

Mr. Schultz:   Mr. Weinglass—
The Court:   Be careful of your language.
Mr. Schultz:   Mr. Weinglass isn't being obstructed.
The Court:   I don't obstruct anybody.
Mr. Weinglass:   I meant obstructed by the objection.
The Court:   I make legal rulings, sir. I am not an obstructionist. I am here to conduct this trial fairly and impartially,

28

sir. Do not characterize me as an obstructionist. Don't do it again.

Mr. Weinglass: I don't believe I did, your Honor, but—

The Court: You said you were being obstructed.

Mr. Weinglass: I did not say by the Court.

The Court: You are not being obstructed at all. A lawyer has a right to make an objection. The Court is obligated to rule. You have made objections. You have a right to make them in behalf of your client. You are not an obstructionist when you make an objection. . . .

\* \* \*

*Direct examination of government witness Mary Ellen Dahl, a Chicago policewoman, by Mr. Schultz*

Q. Do you know a person named Abbott Hoffman?

A. Yes, sir.

Q. Do you see that person in the courtroom at this time?

A. Yes, sir.

Q. Would you point him out, please.

A. Yes, sir. He's hiding behind the gentleman in the maroon shirt. Him, right behind you.
    *(Indicating)*

Mr. Kunstler: Your Honor, I think the word "hiding" is a little strong. He happens to be sitting, I thought, behind Mr. Davis.

The Court: Well, in any event, the record may indicate that the witness has identified the Defendant Hoffman in open court.

. . .

*By Mr. Schultz*

Q. . . . Now will you relate, please, to the Court and to the jury what you heard the Defendant Hoffman say.

A. Yes, sir. He said, "Tomorrow we're going to meet in Grant Park, and we're going to storm the Hilton. We got to get there singly because if we go in groups the blank pigs are going to stop us."

Q. You say "blank pigs." Did he say "blank pigs"?

A. No, sir.

Q. Did he use another word other than "blank"?

A. Yes, sir.

Q. Was it a four-letter word?

A. Yes, sir.

Q. What was the first letter of that four-letter word, please?

A. "F."

\* \*

Q. All right. Please go on.

A. And he said that "We're going to storm the Hilton. We

29

can't make it without weapons. We are going to need a lot of weapons, so we should bring rocks, bottles, sticks, and another good weapon is a brick. But we have to break the bricks in half so that it will be easier to conceal and it will be easier to conceal and it will be easier to throw and the girls can throw them too," and then he asked if anybody had any suggestions or ideas on other weapons, and someone behind me in the group said, "Yes. We should take the bottles and break them in half because if we throw broken bottles, they are going to do more damage broken than whole," and he said, "Yeah, that's a good idea." And he said, "Another good idea is golf balls with—"

Q. Who said, "Another good idea is golf balls"?

A. Hoffman said, "Another good idea is golf balls, with nails pounded through them at all different angles, so that when you throw them, they will stick," and he said, "But don't forget the vaseline for your faces to protect against the MACE, because there's going to be a lot of MACE flying, and don't forget your helmets, because you're going to need them to protect against the pigs. If you haven't got helmets, try to get them somewhere." And then someone asked about holding the park that night, and he said, "Yeah, we should hold the park at all costs. It's our park, and the blank pigs have no right to push us out. It's our park. We're going to fight," and at this point my partner and I left.

\* \* \*

[*Colloquy between Court and counsel*]

The Court: Are you saying that all evidence received in a criminal case as a result of a surveillance is inadmissible? If you are right, there are a lot of people languishing in the penitentiary who don't belong there.

Mr. Weinglass: I probably will have to agree with that.

The Court: If you can get a list of those people, maybe you can get some valuable clients.

Mr. Weinglass: I hope there aren't more added to that list, but—

The Court: Don't be a pessimist.

**October 7, 1969**

*The Government having completed its direct examination of a witness*

The Court: You may proceed with the cross-examination of this witness.

Mr. Kunstler: I suggest that the jury hear it.

30

The Court: Oh, that is a good idea. I have an abundance of marshals here but sometimes they forget to bring in the jury.

Certainly you know now that I never look at a jury.

Mr. Kunstler: I thought you were going to say that you were fallible.

\* \* \*

*Colloquy regarding examination of a witness*

The Court: I sustain the objection, and I admonish counsel not to repeat the question. It has been previously asked.

Mr. Weinglass: I am finished.

The Court: You won't do it now since you are finished. My admonition went for naught.

Do you want to ask this witness some questions?

Mr. Kunstler: I might take a fling at it.

The Court: Oh, don't fling. Oh, no. We don't allow flings, but we will let you cross-examine the witness.

\* \* \*

The Court: The motion of the defendants to strike—I will wait until the laughter ceases. I didn't intend to be funny this time.

Do you approve of your client laughing out loud while the Court is making a decision on a motion made by them, sir?

Mr. Kunstler: I didn't hear it. I was talking to Mr. Davis.

The Court: You seemed to be enjoying their laughter because you smiled yourself.

Mr. Kunstler: Your Honor, a smile is not forbidden in the Federal Court, I don't think.

\* \* \*

Mr. Kunstler: I think I ought to put it on the record. Mr. Davis complimented Mr. Foran on making a good point with that observation and I smiled.

The Court: As long as you are putting things on the record, I think I will put on the record the posture of one of your clients. This is the United States District Court. Have a look at him lying down there like he is on the ground. I won't discipline him at this time but I call attention to it on the record, as you put it.

Mr. Kunstler: It may reflect his attitude, your Honor, toward what is going on in the courtroom.

The Court: Oh, I think it does. I think it does reflect his attitude.

Mr. Kunstler: Then it is free speech.

The Court: And that attitude will be appropriately dealt with . . .

31

**October 8, 1969**

*Direct examination of Government Witness Robert Pierson, an undercover investigator for the Cook County State Attorney's office, by Government Attorney Schultz*

Q. Did you in any way alter your physical appearance to conduct your assignment as undercover agent?

A. Yes, I did.

Q. Would you describe to the Court and jury, please, what you did to alter your appearance for the assignment.

A. I allowed my hair to grow long. I allowed myself to go without a shave for approximately four to six weeks. I purchased the attire of a motorcycle gang member, which is motorcycle boots, a black T-shirt, black levis and a black leather vest and a motorcycle helmet.

. . .

Mr. Weinglass: . . . I could not possibly know what the prosecution was going to present by way of circumstances surrounding the speech even though the speech is alleged in the indictment, so this is the first opportunity we have had to raise the motion.

The Court: You might have asked your clients about it.

Mr. Weinglass: Beg pardon?

The Court: You might have asked your clients about it.

Mr. Weinglass: Well, it is our experience [that] our clients' understanding of reality and what is being produced in this courtroom are two different things, and I would have to wait until I heard what the government is going to put into evidence before I would know what the circumstances are surrounding the speech. . . .

**October 9, 1969**

Mr. Weinglass: I am sure the Court will hear from Mr. Foran as to whether the United States Government will take the risk of jury participation. I only represent the defendants, and I represent to this Court that the defendants feel that the benefits to be gained by jury participation far outweigh the possible disadvantages of a prejudicial question. We are willing to take that risk.

The Court: I again—have you finished your presentation?

Mr. Weinglass: Yes, I have.

The Court: Mr. Weinglass . . .

\* \* \*

Mr. Foran: Your Honor, may I address the Court? Now that comment, your Honor, is consistent. Mr. Kunstler is intentionally generating objections from the prosecution and with his claque back in the courtroom giggling and groaning and that claque over there giggling and groaning, your Honor, the impression is attempted to be given to this jury that the prosecution is attempting to hide the truth in this case. And that is intentional, your Honor.

On behalf of the Government, I protest that kind of conduct.

Mr. Kunstler:   Your Honor, if we are going to have tactics like this in front of the jury, this is old line prosecutorial tactics, we are familiar with them, to get up in front of the jury and make an impassioned speech which he has just done. I think, myself, he ought to be admonished for that kind of conduct in front of the jury, and referring to claques back there in the court here. These are defendants fighting for their rights.

Mr. Foran:   People have no right in a courtroom to react by groans and giggles and discussions on what occurs in the courtroom, and that has been happening since the beginning of the trial.

\*     \*     \*

*Appearance of Mr. Daniel Feldman, attorney*

Mr. Feldman:   My name is Daniel Feldman, Isham, Lincoln and Beale.

I am here on behalf of Mr. Arthur Petacque, who is an employee of the Chicago Sun-Times.

At 10:30 Mr. Petacque was served with a subpoena asking for his presence before your Honor at 10:00 a.m. this morning.

The Court:   By whom?

Mr. Feldman:   By the defendants.

. . .

Mr. Feldman:   . . . I suggested to Mr. Petacque that he ought not risk a contempt citation by not appearing at all, and, therefore, I would ask your Honor for instructions in the matter in the circumstances.

I have no idea, nor does Mr. Petacque as to why he has been subpoenaed.

The Court:   He has employed a high-priced lawyer, and you want me to instruct him, Mr. Feldman?

. . .

Mr. Weinglass:   The subpoena will be withdrawn.

Mr. Feldman:   Thank you.

The Court:   You have won a bloodless victory, Mr. Feldman. Here is your subpoena. Let your client keep it among his souvenirs. . . .

33

**October 10, 1969**

  *Continued cross-examination of undercover investigator Pierson by Mr. Weinglass*

Mr. Weinglass: Your Honor, that is improper impeachment. I cite Goldstein on Jury Trials [a legal treatise—ed.].

The Court: I would like to preside over a class in evidence, but I haven't the time today.

* * *

*[Mr. Weinglass questioning Mr. Pierson]*

Q. Do you also have a definition for Black Panther talk?
A. No, sir.
Q. Do you have any definition of what barbecuing the pork might mean?

[The Government's objection to the question was sustained —ed.]

. . .

Mr. Weinglass: If your Honor please, I spent a good deal of time with this witness—

The Court: I have spent a good deal of time listening to you also. What do you want me to do? Do you want a gold star for the time you spent?

Mr. Kunstler: Your Honor, I object to that, those insulting remarks to co-counsel.

The Court: I don't insult lawyers.

Mr. Kunstler: Sir, you just have, your Honor.

The Court: I suggest to you don't make a suggestion like that again, sir.

I don't know that a lawyer has to say he spent a great deal of time with the witness. We are all spending time.

Mr. Weinglass: You didn't let me finish.

Mr. Kunstler: You didn't let him finish.

Mr. Weinglass: If you will let me finish.

The Court: If you will sit down, Mr. —

Mr. Kunstler: Kunstler is the name, K-u-n-s-t-l-e-r.

* * *

Mr. Weinglass: No, your Honor, I did not want to make any request on that basis alone, but I am afraid, again, that you interrupted me in the middle of my request. I was going to ask the Court if the witness could have the time, and I would also like to request the time myself. As your Honor knows, I have a medical problem.

. . .

The Court: If you feel you have to do something to your tooth, of course I will give you a recess. You didn't say that to me.

34

Mr. Weinglass:   I was cut off in the middle as I was about to proceed.

The Court:   I do not cut lawyers off, sir, and especially you. . . .

\* \* \*

[*Description of events of Wednesday, August 28.*] *By Mr. Weinglass*

Q. As things quieted down, as you have just indicated, did you see the police form a line?

A. The line that I recall seeing had already formed and it was partially into the crowd where the speakers on the microphone systems were telling the crowd to sit down and then as the crowd sat down, then the police retreated also.

Q. So you saw the police come into the crowd at one point?

A. Yes, sir, I did.

Q. Can you tell the jury in what manner the police came into the crowd? Was there a formation?

A. Yes, sir, there was.

Q. Describe the formation of the police.

A. It was a wedge-type formation.

Q. How would you describe a wedge formation specifically?

A. A "V" shape.

. . .

Q. Were these policemen armed?

A. Well, all uniformed police officers are armed.

Q. What where they armed with?

A. From what I could see, they had their standard equipment.

Q. Will you describe what they had in their hands as they went into that crowd.

A. They had batons.

Q. How were they holding their batons. Could you indicate that to the jury?

A. (*indicating*) When the wedge first started coming into the crowd, they were holding their batons, I believe, with both hands.

Q. And did they then begin to use their batons?

A. Yes, sir, I believe they did.

Q. With one hand?

A. Yes, sir.

Q. In a swinging fashion?

A. Yes, sir.

Q. Striking people in front of them?

A. Yes, sir.

Q. Did you see a number of people go down under the force and impact of the batons?

35

A. Of the wedge coming in, yes, the people were falling down and running back.

Q. Did you see anyone get hit in the head with a baton?

A. I don't recall seeing someone go down as a result of being struck with a baton.

Q. Did you see anyone get hit in the head with a baton?

A. No, I couldn't say that.

Q. Did you see anyone get hit on the head with a baton?

A. I saw clubs swung at people's heads, yes.

Q. By policemen?

A. Yes.

Q. They were swinging their clubs over their heads and down on the demonstrators?

A. Yes, sir.


**October 13, 1969**

*[Direct examination of Detective Frank Riggio of the Chicago Police Department by Mr. Foran]*

Q. Calling your attention to August of 1968 during the Convention, were you given any specific assignment?

A. Yes, I was.

Q. What was that?

A. I was to keep Rennie Davis under surveillance.

Q. What was your tour of duty at the time?

A. I started at two in the afternoon and finished at two in the morning.

. . .

Mr. Weinglass: At this point, this witness having identified himself now as a surveillance agent, on behalf of the Defendant Rennie Davis I make the objection that a 24-hour surveillance constitutes a constitutional invasion of a citizen's privacy contrary to the Fourteenth Amendment and I object to this witness being permitted to give any testimony in a court of law on the ground that his conduct constituted a violation of the United States Constitution.

The Court: I will overrule the objection.


**October 14, 1969**

*[On a motion by Defense Attorney Kunstler that Court recess on Wednesday, October 15, 1969, to allow the defendants to participate in Moratorium Day activities]*

Mr. Kunstler: . . . In closing, Your Honor, I would just like to stress that the defendants feel very strongly that because of the refusal of institutions of government to recognize the depth and breadth of the protest of the war in Vietnam, a lot of trouble which besets this country has arisen. It is felt

36

very strongly by them, and I might say very personally, by myself and Mr. Weinglass, that this refusal is why we are here in court today, the refusal to give permits to marches of protest is probably one of the main reasons why we are all before you this moment, and we are asking for much the same thing as they asked in Chicago a year ago. We are asking your Honor for a permit for people to go and express themselves in support of an opposition that has grown to such proportions that tomorrow you will have what is virtually a national holiday in the United States—not declared by the President but declared by the supreme holder of all power in this country, the people, and I would say in this case that the people are as strong as the President and in my own humble opinion much stronger. That is where the Constitution says all power rests anyway, and the people have declared a national holiday and this I think your Honor ought to respect and permit these defendants to join in it.

. . .

Mr. Foran: . . . Your Honor, these men have been charged by a federal grand jury, and there has been some evidence presented in this case that these men partook in a cynical plan to use two of the tragic issues of American society, the war and the tragic flaw of American character, racism, to generate for themselves the right to tear down the legal and formal structure of the Government of the United States.

That these men should now with such cynicism ask to join what may well be a totally sincere effort by a great many people, American citizens, to protest a war—and I might add that many of us feel the tragedy of war, especially some of us who have fought in one—your Honor, it is a situation where there were photographs in the newspapers last week of some of these defendants participating in activities with the Weatherman group of the SDS . . .

\*　　\*　　\*

Mr. Kunstler: . . . The flags in New York are flying at half-mast not because these defendants are the ones that are doing it but because the Mayor of that city has ordered that they be flown at half-mast which was the same order President Nixon gave with reference to General Eisenhower.

And I think it is as important, your Honor, to protest more than some thirty thousand American deaths and Lord knows how many Vietnamese deaths that have occurred in that country as it is to mourn one man in the United States, and if courts can close for the death of one man who lived a full life, they ought to close for the deaths of thousands and millions of innocent people whose lives have been corrupted and rotted

37

and perverted by this utter horror that goes on in your name
and my name—

The Court: Not in my name.

Mr. Kunstler: It is in your name, too, in the name of the
people of the United States.

The Court: You just include yourself. Don't join me with
you. Goodness. Don't you and I—

Mr. Kunstler: You are me, your Honor, because every
citizen—you are a citizen the way I am a citizen.

The Court: Only because you are a member of the bar of
this court and I am obligated to hear you respectfully as I have
done.

Mr. Kunstler: No, your Honor, you are more than that.
You are a citizen of the United States.

The Court: Yes, I am.

Mr. Kunstler: And I am a citizen of the United States, and
it is done in our name, in Judge Hoffman's name and William
Kunstler's name.

The Court: That will be all, sir. I shall hear you no
further.

\* \* \*

[*In response to a statement by Mr. Weinglass to Judge
Hoffman concerning Defendant Seale*]

Mr. Seale: Hey, you don't speak for me. I would like to
speak on behalf of my own self and have my counsel handle
my case in behalf of myself.

How come I can't speak in behalf of myself? I am my own
legal counsel. I don't want these lawyers to represent me.

The Court: You have a lawyer of record and he has been
of record here since the 24th.

Mr. Seale: I have been arguing that before the jury heard
one shred of evidence. I don't want these lawyers because I
can take up my own legal defense and my lawyer is Charles
Garry.

The Court: I direct you, sir, to remain quiet.

Mr. Seale: And just be railroaded?

The Court: Will you remain quiet?

Mr. Seale: I want to defend myself, do you mind, please?

The Court: Let the record show that the Defendant Seale
continued to speak after the Court courteously requested him
to remain quiet.

Bring in the jury, Mr. Marshal.

\* \* \*

[*In response to a statement by Mr. Kunstler on the previous dialogue concerning Seale*]

38

The Court: I will let you speak as long as you want to on that question because your appearance is still of record.

Mr. Kunstler: That is right, your Honor, but when a man stands up and says he wants to defend himself—

The Court: That is not the law in the middle of a trial.

Mr. Kunstler: That is the law. The constitution says any man that wishes to defend himself may do so.

The Court: You speak of the Constitution as though it were a document printed yesterday. We know about the Constitution way out here in the Middle West, too. Mr. Kunstler.

Mr. Kunstler: Oh, your Honor, this is a little unfair, isn't it?

The Court: We really do. You would be amazed at our knowledge of constitutional law.

Mr. Kunstler: Isn't that a little unfair, your Honor? We are not here from different parts of the country—

The Court: I am getting a little weary of these thrusts by counsel and I don't want any more of them. I had occasion to admonish you before.

Mr. Kunstler: I know, but you said I could argue as long as I wanted.

The Court: As long as you are respectful, sir.

Mr. Kunstler: I am respectful.

The Court: No, you haven't been.

Mr. Kunstler: You implied, I thought, Chicago people didn't understand the Constitution, only Easterners understand it. That isn't true.

The Court: Bring in the jury.

Mr. Kunstler: You are not letting me argue as long as I want to.

The Court: No. You haven't anything to say that is important right now.

* * *

[*Cross-examination of Detective Frank Riggio by Mr. Kunstler*]

Mr. Foran: Your Honor, I object. It has been asked and answered. He said he didn't see him. We will be here until spring—

The Court: I sustain the objection.

Mr. Kunstler: Your Honor, I think we can avoid the references to "We can be here until spring." We don't want to be here at all.

The Court: I didn't hear that.

Mr. Kunstler: The prosecutor says we will be here until spring because I am asking the questions.

39

Mr. Foran:   Your Honor, I made some side comment and I withdraw it.

The Court:   I didn't hear that.

Mr. Foran:   I will withdraw my comment.

The Court:   You mean it might not be? We can be assured that it might not be until spring? Is that what you mean Mr. Kunstler?

All right, I will let you withdraw it. I direct the jury to disregard the reference to spring.

Mr. Kunstler:   Without any implication we have anything against spring, your Honor.

\* \* \*

[*Colloquy concerning the correct date for the issuance of a Government subpoena*]

Mr. Schultz:   I didn't mean to suggest we were having a difference, your Honor. He did not object to it, to the issuance of the subpoena.

Mr. Kunstler:   Just made an agonized groan, your Honor.

The Court:   Agonized groan?

Mr. Kunstler: Agonized groan when he said October 31.

The Court:   Will you settle for that?

Mr. Kunstler:   For an agonized groan?

The Court:   Yes.

Mr. Kunstler:   I have already settled for that.

**October 15, 1969**

[*The following happened as the defendants attempted to observe Moratorium Day*]

Mr. Dellinger:   Mr. Hoffman, we are observing the moratorium.

The Court:   I am Judge Hoffman, sir.

Mr. Dellinger:   I believe in equality, sir, so I prefer to call people Mr. Or by their first name.

The Court:   Sit down. The clerk is about to call my cases.

Mr. Dellinger:   I wanted to explain to you we are reading the names of the war dead.

The Marshal:   Sit down.

Mr. Dellinger:   We were just reading the names of the dead from both sides.

\* \* \*

Mr. Foran:   Your Honor, that is outrageous. This man [Kunstler—ed.] is a mouthpiece. Look at him, wearing a[n] [arm] band like his clients, your Honor. Any lawyer who comes into a courtroom and has no respect for the Court and acts in conjunction with that kind of a conduct before the Court, your Honor, the Government protests his attitude and would like to

40

cite—to move the Court to make note of his conduct before this Court.

The Court: Note has been duly made on the record.

Mr. Kunstler: Your Honor, I think that the temper and the tone of voice and the expression on Mr. Foran's face speaks more than any picture could tell.

The Court: Mr. Kunstler—

Mr. Foran: Of my contempt for Mr. Kunstler, your Honor.

Mr. Kunstler: To call me a mouthpiece, and your Honor, not to open his mouth and say that that is not to be done in your court, I think violates the sanctity of this Court. That is a word that your Honor knows is contemptuous and contumacious.

The Court: Don't tell me what I know.

Mr. Kunstler: Well, then, you tell me, your Honor, if you have ever heard that word used in your court before.

The Court: I know that he is here in this courtroom, Mr. Kunstler—

Mr. Kunstler: I am wearing an arm band in memoriam to the dead, your Honor, which is no disgrace in this country.

I want him admonished, your Honor. I request that you do that. The word "mouthpiece" is a contemptuous term.

The Court: Did you say you want to admonish me?

Mr. Kunstler: No, I want you to admonish him.

The Court: Let the record show I do not admonish the United States Attorney because he was properly representing his client, the United States of America.

\*   \*   \*

The Court: In the circumstances of this case, this situation, sir, you a lawyer in the United States District Court permitting your client to stand up in the presence of the jury and disrupt these proceedings. I don't know how to characterize it.

Mr. Kunstler: Your Honor, we do not permit or not permit our clients. They are free independent human beings who have been brought by the Government to this courtroom.

. . .

The Court: To place the flag of an enemy country—

Mr. Kunstler: No, your Honor, there is no declared war.

Defendant Hayden: Are you at war with Vietnam?

The Court: Any country—I say it with your approval.

Let that appear on the record also.

Bring in the jury. I don't want—

Mr. Kunstler: Are you turning down my request after this disgraceful episode? You are not going to say anything?

The Court: I not only turn it down, I ignore it.

41

Mr. Kunstler: That speaks louder than words, too, your Honor.

The Court: And let that appear of record, the last words of Mr. Kunstler, and, Miss Reporter, be very careful to have them on the record.

\* \* \*

[*Recross-examination of Detective Frank Riggio by Mr. Kunstler*]

The Court: Mr. Kunstler, if you want your question answered, you will wait, please, for the witness to complete his answer. Otherwise I will forbid you to continue in this manner.

Mr. Kunstler: Your Honor, I already—

The Court: You can't finish—

Mr. Kunstler: I acknowledge my error, your Honor. I don't need a lecture. I acknowledged it.

The Court: I accept your apology.

Mr. Kunstler: I apologize.

\* \* \*

*Direct examination of Government Witness Oklepek, an undercover newspaper reporter, by Mr. Foran*

Q. Would you state the conversation, Mr. Oklepek?

A. Mr. Hayden told the group that this formation was the same type of formation that Japanese students had used to precipitate riots in Japan in 1960, which prevented then President Eisenhower from visiting that country. He said that "Getting people together in this kind of formation, getting the[m] moving and chanting and yelling, aroused their emotions, sustained their spirits, got them very excited."

He said that "This formation was very good for breaking through police lines and that in the event of an arrest situation, this formation would be used during the Convention Week to break police lines and to try to escape from Lincoln Park, for instance." . . .

**October 16, 1969**
*Cross-examination of Mr. Oklepek by Mr. Kunstler*

Q. Did you ever see any person in Mobilization wearing a gun?

A. Not that I could see, no.

Q. You say not that you could see. Are you saying that you saw the outlines under their coats?

A. I saw bulges under their coats.

Q. Oh, you saw bulges. Did you say to yourself at that time, "Those are guns"?

A. I said to myself at that time, "Those are bulges."

Mr. Foran: I object to this, your Honor.

The Court: I sustain the objection if you are reading from that document. It is not in evidence.

Mr. Kunstler: Your Honor, I still say this is classic impeachment, form of impeachment, and I don't know any way that any of the authorities say to do it except the way I have done it.

.   .

The Court: . . . I don't know what you mean by "classic impeachment." To me impeachment is impeachment. We are not dealing with the classics, and that is not the way we do it, and since there is no objection, you may ask the question.

\* \* \*

Mr. Foran: I object to the form of that question. There is a simple way to—

The Court: That is reason enough. I sustain the objection. You are not going about this in the right way, I am sorry, Mr. Kunstler. I don't want to assume a professional attitude, but you should know that your questions have been bad [as] a matter of form.

Mr. Kunstler: I will try to redo them, your Honor.

The Court: Borrowing your word, they are classically bad.

Mr. Kunstler: In the Roman or Greek sense, your Honor, or in the modern sense?

The Court: Just plain English.

\* \* \*

The Court: I never have tried a case where I did not have at least one marshal in the courtroom.

Mr. Kunstler: No, your Honor, I understand that, your Honor, but four standing—

The Court: If you understand it, don't comment. And, moreover, I must refer you to the Supreme Court again. The Supreme Court has said that the judge is the governor of the trial and you will leave the governing of the trial to me. You just represent your client.

Mr. Kunstler: No, your Honor, we have to do it because the Supreme Court has also said when the courtroom has the appearance of an armed camp, that reversible error might have occurred, and I think we have a duty to our clients to put that on the record.

The Court: I see no evidence of an armed camp. I think you are grossly unfair to make this statement.

Mr. Kunstler: Your Honor, I would like to record to show one, two, three, four, five, six, seven marshals—one just left, which was eight marshals in the courtroom at one time, and then outside there are other people who are searched coming

43

in. I think that this is the basis for a possible attack on the trial as being an armed camp and I think I owe it to my clients to put that on the record which I have done.

The Court: It is on the record that you said it was an armed camp. I am presiding over a trial in the United States District Court. That is all I know.

\* \* \*

The Court: . . . [A]ll I get from your clients constantly is a laugh. Just this last second they sit there and laugh at a judge of the highest trial court in the United States. That is what I have been getting. Perhaps you think that is proper as a lawyer admitted to practice here by the courtesy of this court. . . .

Mr. Kunstler: I just want to say, your Honor, for the record, I don't think that a laugh is always out of place in a Federal Court. I am not sure that your Honor is always interpreting these laughs as being directed at you. I think that that is your Honor's subjective reasoning.

The Court: I am perfectly competent to know how they are laughing. You leave that to me.

\* \* \*

Q. And did you see any instance in which a woman was being clubbed by a policeman?
A. Yes.
. . .
Q. What did you see happen to her while she was being clubbed or afterwards? Did she fall down?
A. Afterwards she was dragged to a police car.
Q. Dragged to a police car across the pavement?
A. About 25 feet.
Q. Across pavement? Is that correct?
A. Yes.
Q. That is macadam pavement?
A. I am not familiar with pavement as to the different types.
Q. It is not grass, is it?
A. No, sir, certainly not.

**October 17, 1969**

The Court: Ladies and gentlemen of the jury, good morning.

Mr. Feinglass, will you please continue with the cross-examination of this witness?

Mr. Kunstler: Your Honor, so the record may be clear, I don't think Mr. Weinglass noticed the Feinglass. It is Mr. Weinglass.

The Court: Oh, I did misspeak myself. I said Feinglass.

44

I correct myself. I meant Weinglass. I am sorry I worked an F in there instead of the W that you deserve, Mr. Weinglass.

* * *

Q. Can you tell the jury what you recall of that conversation now?

A. At that time in several of the Chicago papers there were stories about rumors that were being passed on by the Yippies, two of which I recall. One was to put LSD in the city water supply—three, excuse me. One was to put LSD in the water supply. The second was to scatter sharp objects on all of the expressways leading into the city so that incoming vehicles would have all of their tires flattened. And the third was to release simultaneously all over the city at various points 20 different pigs which were the Yippie symbol for—well, it was the pig they were running for President.

Mr. Hoffman was joking about all of these things to the people who were present in the office at that time. . . .

* * *

Q. . . . [D]o you recall stating to the FBI the following:

"My own reaction and feelings at this point as a result of having heard various discussions by NMC leaders concerning its plans, was that the desires and efforts of NMC leaders to have a peaceful demonstration were sincere." . . .

. . .

A. This statement was made on September 30, about a reaction and feeling on August 21. If you will look at the top of the page. The phrase at this point referring to August 21, 1968 before the Convention Week had commenced, and before everything that happened during Convention Week had happened. My own reactions and feeling at this point, August 21, 1968, that is what this statement is in reference to and yes, I did make it, and that is the way I felt on August 21, 1968 [i.e., the week preceding the Democratic Convention—ed.].

* * *

[*On redirect, concerning Wednesday evening's events*]

Q. Did you see police and demonstrators in hand-to-hand wrestling and fighting?

A. Yes, I did.

Q. How big a crowd was there?

A. I would say 5,000 people.

. . .

Q. What was the crowd chanting?

A. They were chanting, "Hell no, we won't go. Dump the

Hump. Daley must go. NLF is going to win. Ho, Ho, Ho Chi Minh." Things like that.

* * *

[*Recross by Mr. Kunstler*]

Q. Mr. Oklepek, did you tell the grand jury anything about guns emanating from Mr. Hayden's mouth?

The Court: That question will look awfully bad on paper, Mr. Kunstler. Nobody objected to it, but I just want you to have a good record.

Mr. Kunstler: I bow to your grammatical comments, and I withdraw the question and will ask you another.

The Court: I just wanted you to know too I was listening to you.

Mr. Kunstler: I understand, your Honor. I have never doubted for a moment that you were listening.

* * *

Mr. Kunstler: Unless my ears fail me—I will object. I am hearing the same question and I expect the same answer that I heard on redirect.

The Court: I will let him answer over objection, even if your ears don't fail you.

* * *

*Direct examination of Government Witness Carl Gilman, a California news cameraman, by Government Attorney Schultz*

Q. Will you relate to the Court and jury the last part, the very last part of the speech which Dr. Dellinger gave?

Mr. Weinglass: If your Honor please, I object to this question. I object to this witness relating any speech given by a person before an open public rally at a college campus as being a violation of the First Amendment of the United States and I would like to argue this outside of the presence of the jury.

. . .

A. "Burn your draft cards. Resist the draft. Violate the laws. Go to jail. Disrupt the United States Government in any way you can to stop this insane war."

* * *

*Cross-examination of Mr. Gilman by Mr. Kunstler*

Mr. Kunstler: Your Honor, is someone being removed from the courtroom? Again another black person, I see.

Mr. Schultz: Say—this repeated comment about "another black person"—

A Spectator: You hate black people or something?

Mr. Schultz: This constant repetition is not warranted,

this attempt to make it appear that there is racism in this courtroom. And that response, your Honor, is so outrageous —it is so wrong and it is so deliberate by these men, it must stop. It is they who are engendering and who are looking for racism. . . .

. . .

Mr. Kunstler: Your Honor, it's only been black people ejected that I have seen. I have never seen a white person removed from this courtroom when I have turned around, and this makes about the eleventh black person that's been—

The Court: I don't know how from your position you can see what person has been ejected. I'm facing the door. I've never seen anybody ejected. I've seen people go out. I can't say that they were ejected, and I don't think that it is proper for a lawyer to refer to a person's race.

. . .

The Court: And I direct you now, I order you now, not to refer to the ejection of a black person again.

Mr. Kunstler: I will not, your Honor, if black people are not constantly ejected from this Court.

The Court: I order you not to, sir. That is my order.

Mr. Kunstler: I think that violates the constitutional rights, your Honor, of these clients.

The Court: I think I am as familiar with the Constitution as you are, sir, and you will now proceed with your cross-examination of this witness.

\* \* \*

Q. . . . Mr. Gilman, what is your employment when you are not working for the FBI?

A. I work for Channel 8 Television, Midwest—

Q. Can you speak up? I can't hear you.

A. I work for KFMB Television in San Diego, California.

Q. How long have you worked for KFMB?

A. Five years and a few months.

Q. And what is your job at KFMB?

A. A reporter and a newsreel cameraman.

. . .

O. And do you have a press card which indicates that you are a member of the journalism fraternity?

A. Yes, sir.

Q. Now, there came a time, did there not, when you began to inform for the FBI, is that correct?

A. Yes.

. . .

Q. When was that?

47

A. Around March of 1968.

Q. And can you indicate to me whether you approached them or they approached you?

A. I approached them.

. . .

Q. And what did you tell Mr. Evans [FBI agent—ed.]?

A. That I was concerned about things that I was reporting on, information I had received I considered to be a threat to the security of the United States, and I felt that the FBI should be aware of the information that I had.

Q. How many times after the first meeting did you call the FBI to bring something to their attention?

A. Since now?

Q. Since you started.

A. Hundreds of times.

[*Mr. Kunstler questioning Mr. Gilman about a speech by Defendant Dellinger*]

Q. What did he say about the draft?

A. I cannot remember.

Q. You can't remember any other words about the draft except—

A. Except that he was opposed to the draft.

Q. I would imagine so.

Mr. Schultz: Objection, if the Court please. I move to strike it.

The Court: "I would imagine so." Those words may go out, spoken by Mr. Kunstler, and I direct the jury to disregard them.

Please don't make any observations about your imagination.

Mr. Kunstler: It was an involuntary thing, your Honor.

Mr. Schultz: I don't think Mr. Kunstler does anything involuntary.

Mr. Kunstler: He ought to talk to my wife.

The Court: You carry on and I won't be able to take you seriously, Mr. Kunstler.

You are not inviting me to consult your wife about whether what you say is involuntary?

Mr. Kunstler: I was going to remark, your Honor, she would say the same thing to me.

* * *

Q. Just one last question: Do you not remember that in discussing problems in Chicago that Mr. Dellinger made reference to a statement that went something like "Shoot to kill, shoot to maim"?

A. I do not remember that.

48

**October 20, 1969**

*Direct examination of Government Witness Robert Casper, an FBI special agent, by Mr. Foran*

Q. Could you explain to the jury what the interest of the FBI is in an outdoor demonstration, public rally?

A. Well, as I said, we obtained a leaflet a couple of weeks before this from the organization that was sponsoring the rally. It called for the rally, as a matter of fact, and because of this and this leaflet—the organization which was called the Coalition for an Anti-Imperialist Movement was the sponsor of this rally, and from this leaflet—this is why we were there. It was a militant type of leaflet, sir.

Q. A militant type of leaflet?

A. Yes, sir.

Q. Did it call for any legal action?

A. Not that I can recall, sir.

Q. Was there any possibility of this rally violating federal laws?

A. There has been at some rallies, sir, violations of federal law. Yes, there was a possibility.

Q. Can you explain to the jury what violations of federal law are involved in a rally?

A. Well, at some rallies desecration of the flag for instance, burning of the flag, tearing it apart is one.

Q. You were there to make sure there wasn't any violation of federal law like burning a flag?

A. Well, in part; yes, sir.

\* \* \*

*Direct examination of Government Witness James Tobin, a Chicago police officer, by Mr. Schultz. Commenting on the demonstration]*

Q. Would you relate the conversation that occurred.

A. The first person to speak was the marshal, and he said, "I don't think we can hold them down. The tension is too high. They want to go." And at that, Rennie Davis, the defendant, said, "OK, but I want you to do this—" and at that, he pointed to the base of the grass and said, "You see down there, replace those people with marshals."

Q. Where was he pointing, please?

. . .

A. He was pointing [down toward the sidewalk, and then—ed.] to directly in front of the Conrad Hilton Hotel by the door where there was a TV camera elevated approximately 20 feet up in the air . . . and he said, "You see

49

those cameras, those are live cameras. Now what I want you to do, I want you to instruct your marshals to sit on that front line and I want you to instruct your marshals to kick the police in the shins and kick them in the legs and when they do, the police will react and they will react by clubbing the demonstrators and the TV cameras will pick this up and when they pick this up—"

\* \* \*

Q. Did you hear Rubin say anything other than the things you have already related?

A. Yes. As the march proceeded north, I heard Rubin use numerous obscenities. I heard obscenities in the crowd.

Q. All right. Would you relate the obscenities, please. Yes, you may relate the obscenities.

A. I may? Rubin would yell to "Fu - - the pigs," "Off the pig."

Q. "Off the pig"?

A. Yes.

Q. What is "Off the pig"? Have you ever heard that terminology before?

A. Yes, I have. It's a street terminology for "Kill the pigs."

Q. Go ahead.

A. He would yell—he was putting his finger up in the air and yelling, "Off the pig, off the pig," and he would use these obscenities back and forth to the people on the sidewalk, to the people in the cars, any police car that went by in the vicinity he would yell to them and he was jumping up and down, he was waving his arms, he was telling everybody, "Cheer it up, chant it up, chant it up."

\* \* \*

*[Colloquy on Defendant Seale's motion to act as his own counsel]*

The Clerk: There is a motion here of Defendant Bobby Seale pro se to be permitted to defend himself.

The Court: I will hear you, Mr. Seale.

Mr. Seale: I want to present this motion in behalf of myself and I want to place some statements concerning past— well, it is what has been described as in one manner and another interrupting the Court, but I am not and have not been— I am not a lawyer, but I do know that I as one of the defendants have a right to defend myself and I feel and know that it should be looked into by the Judge of this Court, Judge Hoffman, and I feel that it has not been looked into. . . .

Also I think my reasons should be clear that prior to the

50

beginning of this trial my understanding of my legal representation here was so that this motion can have some validity and understanding to it. I understood quite a while back after arraignment, immediately after arraignment, in fact, the same day that I was arraigned on these charges, that Charles R. Garry would be the only one who would defend me here, that all other lawyers who would appear in court would appear in court only for pretrial motions and pretrial proceedings. There is where I stood and this has been my contention all along. . . .

I, Bobby Seale, demand and move the Court as follows: Because I am denied this lawyer of my choice, Charles R. Garry, I cannot represent myself as my attorney would be doing, but because I am forced to be my own counsel and to defend myself, I require my release from custody, from the bail presently in force, so that I can interview witnesses, do the necessary investigating, do necessary factual research and all other things that being in custody makes impossible.

2. The right to cross-examine witnesses and examine witnesses of my choice.

3. The right to make all necessary motions that I as a layman can think of to help my defense and prove my innocence and to argue those motions. . . .

\*   \*   \*

Mr. Seale: . . . I know I have gotten some attacks from the Government saying we were playing games over here. I am not playing no game with my life, being stuck on the line, and I want to put that into the record to explain my situation.

The Court:   Mr. Schultz.

Mr. Schultz:   May we briefly reply, your Honor?

Your Honor, this is a ploy. It's just a simple obvious ploy.

\*   \*

'. . . [O]n the first day of trial, September 24 . . . Mr. Kunstler filed an appearance in court—and so told the Court and told us and asked for leave to file instanter, and they did file, an appearance to represent the defendant, Bobby Seale, and then we proceeded to pick a jury and we were going to trial.

Then on the Friday—that's about the 26th, that Friday— Mr. Seale stood up and said, "I fire all my lawyers." It's true it's true that an individual has the right if he wants, to defend himself. We are not arguing that, and I think that's well established. If one wants to represent himself, he can. But he can't under the circumstances in this case, and that is, having a total . . . of five lawyers, and then fire four of them and

51

say, "I want the one or I won't go ahead," and saying that after the trial has begun.

Under those circumstances, when a lawyer files an appearance and goes into court representing a client, he has no right, without the Court's approval, to stop representing that individual, and you have not granted that right, because one of the reasons why we went ahead is because there were other lawyers representing Mr. Seale. And the ploy is so obvious.

\* \*

. . . The defendants are trying to make a record, they are trying to create error in a record.

Now, they know perfectly well that if Mr. Seale were to cross-examine witnesses here and argue to the jury, we would have a mistrial in this case in two minutes. He would destroy the other defendants' rights to a fair trial. There is absolutely no doubt about that. Other defendants are subject here. Other defendants are affected by what witnesses say on cross-examination or on direct examination in front of a jury, and they know that, and they know perfectly well, him not being a lawyer, him not being versed in the law, that there would be reversible error and there would be nothing that we could do about it.

. . . They are doing everything possible, making all the waves they can, not only to create error in the record, which I am certain—I am absolutely certain—they haven't done. That's irrelevant practically to them. It's what publicity value they can get out of it. It's a mockery, they say. That's what they are looking for. It's a mockery because he doesn't have the lawyer of his choice and he can't represent himself. It looks very good in those words, but that's not the fact at all. It's a game they are playing with this Court. . . .

\* \* \*

Mr. Seale: . . . I stated that it was my understanding and my agreement that only Mr. Charles R. Garry would represent me right after arraignment. I saw all these other lawyers the defendants brought in, and it was my understanding and agreement that they would only represent me while I was in California, pretrial motions and proceedings, and that Charles R. Garry would represent me here. . . .

The Court: . . . Mr. Seale has moved to be allowed to act as his own counsel and for relief on bail and ordered to perform certain functions he deems necessary to his defense. . . .

In exercising its discretion, the Court should deny a motion to defendant pro se when such procedure would be disruptive of the proceedings and when denial would not be prejudicial to the defendant. . . .

I find now that to allow the Defendant Seale to act as his own attorney would produce the same disruptive effect. Moreover, the denial of the defendant's motion to appear pro se would not be prejudicial to his case. On the contrary, the complexity of the case makes self-representation inappropriate and the defendant would be more prejudiced were he allowed to conduct his own defense than if his motion were to be denied. . . .

\* \* \*

*[As the defense is about to cross-examine Government Witness Robert Allen Tobin]*

Mr. Seale: I would like to say, Judge, that you denied my motion to defend myself and you know this jury is prejudiced against me.

The Court: I will ask you to sit down.

. . .

Mr. Seale: They have been made prejudiced against me, I know. I should be allowed to defend myself. I should be allowed to speak so I can defend myself.

The Marshal: Be quiet.

Mr. Seale: Don't tell me to shut up. I got a right to speak. I need to speak to defend myself.

The Court: Mr. Seale, I must admonish you that any outburst such as you have just indulged in will be appropriately dealt with at the right time during this trial and I must order you not to do it again.

Mr. Seale: In other words, Judge—

The Court: If you do, you do it at your own risk, sir.

Mr. Seale: In other words, you are saying you are going to put me in contempt of court for speaking on behalf of myself?

The Court: I will not argue with you.

Mr. Marshal—

\* \* \*

Mr. Seale: . . . Now you are saying you are going to put me in jail, you are going to put me in jail, that's one thing. You are going to put me in contempt of court because I am speaking in behalf of myself.

. . .

The jury is prejudiced against me all right and you know it because of those threatening letters. You know it, those so-called jive threatening letters, and you know it's a lie. Now how can that jury give me a fair trial?

53

The Court: Mr. Marshal will you go to that man and ask him to be quiet?

* *

Mr. Seale: . . . You know, the black man tries to get a fair trial in this country. The United States Government, huh. Nixon and the rest of them.

Go ahead and continue. I'll watch and get railroaded.
. . .

The Court: Gentlemen, I want to say just one word and my remarks are addressed particularly to Mr. Seale.

Several times during this trial he has disobeyed the injunction of the Court not to stand and talk out. I feel that in fairness to him I should admonish him and his lawyers as well, to the extent that they have any influence over him, that there is competent authority for dealing with a defendant who persists in talking out against the order of the Court and I want Mr. Seale to know that. I am sure the lawyers know it. I do this only in the interest of the other defendants. . . .

**October 21, 1969**

[*Cross-examination of Government Witness Carcerano by Mr. Weinglass*]

Mr. Foran: And I object to that style of questioning, of misstating direct examination.

The Court: I sustain the objection.

Mr. Kunstler: Your Honor, I just want to object. I think objections can be made without editorial speeches for the jury's benefit.

Mr. Foran: They can when they are made by error and not intentionally. I object—excuse me, your Honor.

Mr. Kunstler: He has a double lick in now.

The Court: They make an editor out of you, Mr. Foran. Don't be an editor.

Mr. Foran: All right, your Honor. I am sorry.

**October 22, 1969**

Mr. Kunstler: . . . Mr. Seale informed me again on or about October 16th of this year that he was going to move before your Honor for permission to represent himself, and reiterated to me that he had discharged me and all other attorneys except Mr. Garry representing him, and that I should take no further action with reference to him and that I should withdraw formally. Accordingly, I am doing so through this motion which I have filed with your Honor yesterday, and a copy has been served upon the United States Attorney. . . .
. . .

The Government:   . . . [I]t is then subject to the sound discretion of the court as to whether or not this prior right prior to the beginning of the trial of a client to defend himself is overcome in the Court's discretion by the strong likelihood that the discharge of a lawyer in the midst of a trial would result in total destruction of court proceedings—total disruption of court proceedings to the prejudice of a fair trial.

On that basis, your Honor, the Government asks the Court to deny the motion.

Mr. Kunstler:   Your Honor—

Mr. Seale:   Can I speak on that and answer his argument?

The Court:   No. This is not your motion, sir. Your motion has been decided.

\* \* \*

[*Following eviction of a spectator from the court room*]

Mr. Seale:   You are a pig for kicking him out.

Spectators:   Right on. Right on.

The Marshal:   This Honorable Court will now resume its session.

The Spectators:   Oink oink.

\* \* \*

Mr. Kunstler:   Your Honor, if I could make one application—the other seven defendants have purchased a birthday cake for Chairman Bobby Seale whose 33rd birthday is today and they have requested me to ask your Honor's permission since the marshals would not let them bring the cake to Mr. Seale . . . to at least bring it to him and present him with the cake before the jury comes in.

The Court:   Mr. Kunstler, I won't even let anybody bring me a birthday cake. I don't have food in my chambers. I don't have any beverages. This is a courthouse and we conduct trials here. I am sorry.

. . .

Mr. Davis:   They arrested your cake, Bobby. They arrested it.

**October 23, 1969**

The Court:   Ladies and gentlemen of the jury, good morning.

Mr. Seale:   Good morning. I hope you don't blame me for anything.

The Court:   Ladies and gentlemen of the jury, it is my obligation to tell you that the parties to a lawsuit have no right to address the jury, and Mr. Seale just made a remark to you that was entirely out of order. I direct you to disregard it . . .

\* \* \*

55

Mr. Schultz:   He held up the newspaper for them [the jury] to see and—

Mr. Hoffman:   It ain't a newspaper. It is the Berkeley Tribe and doesn't tell lies, so it isn't a newspaper.

**October 27, 1969**

Mr. Seale:   What about my constitutional right to defend myself and have my lawyer?

The Court:   Your constitutional rights—

Mr. Seale:   You are denying them. You have been denying them. Every other word you say is denied, denied, denied, denied, and you begin to oink in the faces of the masses of the people of this country. That is what you begin to represent, the corruptness of this rotten government or four hundred years—

The Marshal:   Mr. Seale, will you sit down.

Mr. Seale:   Why don't you knock me in the mouth? Try that.

The Marshal:   Sit down.

The Court:   Ladies and gentlemen of the jury, I regret that I will have to excuse you.

Mr. Seale:   I hope you don't blame me for anything and those false lying notes and letters that were sent that said the Black Panther Party threatened that jury, it's a lie, and you know it's a lie, and the Government did it to taint the jury against me.

*(The following proceedings were had in open court, out of the presence and hearing of the jury)*

Mr. Seale:   You got that? This racist administrative Government with its superman notions and comic book politics. We're hip to the fact that Superman never saved no black people. You got that?

* * *

Mr. Foran:   Mr. Weinglass just asked me—

The Court:   You just let me do my job, and you do yours properly, and we'll get along, Mr. Fein— Weinstein.

Mr. Kunstler:   Your Honor, I think it is Weinglass.

The Court:   Weinglass. I corrected it. I got in ahead of you. I corrected it.

**October 28, 1969**

The Court:   I deny the motion [for a one-day adjournment].

Mr. Kunstler:   Now in the event that your Honor has denied this motion, would your Honor—

The Court:   Not in the event; I have denied it.

Mr. Kunstler:   I was speaking from anticipation, your Honor.

Now that it has been denied, I would ask your Honor to grant permission for one of co-counsel here, Mr. Weinglass or myself, to be absent tomorrow to consult with Mr. Garry.

The Court:   Only on these conditions, Mr. Kunstler; that first each and every defendant in this case stand up at his place at the defense table and agree that either you or Mr. Feinglass look after his interests.

Mr. Kunstler:   Weinglass, your Honor.

\* \* \*

[*Colloquy between the Court and Defendant Dellinger*]

The Court [to Mr. Kunstler]:   You don't expect me to answer a question put to me in that way, do you?

Mr. Dellinger:   Why not?   You expect us to answer a question.

The Court:   Mr. Marshal, will you tell Mr. Derringer to remain quiet?

Mr. Kunstler:   That is Dellinger.

The Court:   Dellinger.

\* \* \*

*Cross-examination of Government Witness William Frapolly, an undercover agent (?), by Defense Attorney Kunstler*

Q. . . . I understand yesterday you testified that you had been or were a student at Northeastern Illinois State College?

A. That is right, sir.

Q. You were expelled, were you not, for throwing the president off the stage physically?

A. No, I wasn't, sir.

Q. What were you expelled for?

A. I was expelled for being with a group of people that threw the president off the stage.

\* \* \*

Q. Do you remember today whether you told the grand jury that someone told you jeeps passed by?   Do you recall?

Mr. Foran:   Your Honor, I object to this.

The Court:   I repeat, that is not the way to do it.   I sustain the objection.

Mr. Kunstler:   Your Honor, I guess the Appellate Court will have to tell me how to do it then.

Mr. Foran:   They will.

The Court:   Oh, I don't threaten very easily, sir.

57

Mr. Kunstler: I am not threatening, your Honor. I just think it is classic impeachment.

The Court: I don't try to second guess an appellate court, and I don't want a cheap remark like that made again by you, sir.

Mr. Kunstler: Your Honor, it is not a cheap remark. It is a heartfelt remark, and we are following the book on this.

The Court: Yes, it is. I will not permit a lawyer to threaten me.

Mr. Kunstler: I am not threatening. I am saying we will take it somewhere else.

The Court: Your client has a right to appeal, sir.

**October 29, 1969**

Mr. Kunstler: . . . Today we were informed by the marshals that there is a new rule in effect which has come from somewhere to search our staff members. The staff members bring with them legal papers, legal documents, results of investigations, and other matters which we don't want to disclose to anybody or have anyone, particularly anyone connected with the Government of the United States, which is in essence, as your Honor has indicated many times the plaintiff in this action, and we think it violates—

The Court: Not many times. Once.

Mr. Kunstler: —rights of counsel.

What was that?

The Court: Not many times. Just once.

Mr. Kunstler: Once? All right, your Honor. I will amend my sentence . . . [W]e think it violates the Sixth Amendment rights of these defendants to have United States marshals look through their material when they come in here. . . .

\* \* \*

The Court: . . . The record in this case thus far compels me to insist that the marshals search everybody but the lawyers; members of the press have never been searched.

Mr. Kunstler: I don't understand that, your Honor. If you would elaborate—

The Court: If you don't—there are a lot of things you don't seem to understand. I tell you it is for the security and that will be all, sir.

. . .

Mr. Kunstler: Your Honor, I haven't seen a violent episode in this courtroom, and I don't think you have, either. If a few chuckles once in a while is need for security, I just don't see it.

The Court: . . . These are precautions that I am taking for the security of people who come into this courtroom, and I intend to see that they are observed.

Mr. Kunstler: Your Honor realizes this is brand new. It didn't happen yesterday with our staff.

The Court: New or old—

Mr. Hayden: This is the same accusation made at the Democratic Convention last year.

\* \* \*

Mr. Hoffman: May I talk to my lawyer?

There are 25 marshals in here now . . .

Mr. Kunstler: Your Honor, we are objecting to this armed camp aspect that is going on since the beginning of this trial.

The Court: It is not an armed camp.

Mr. Kunstler: It is not right, and it's not good, and it's not called for.

Mr. Schultz: If the Court please, before you came into this courtroom, if the Court please, Bobby Seale stood up and addressed this group.

Mr. Seale: That's right, brother.

Mr. Schultz: And Bobby Seale said if he is—

Mr. Schultz: . . .—that if he's attacked, they know what to do.

Mr. Seale: I can speak on behalf of my constitutional rights, too.

Mr. Schultz: He was talking to these people about an attack by them.

Mr. Seale: You're lying. Dirty liar. I told them to defend themselves. You are a rotten racist pig, fascist liar, that's what you are. You're a rotten liar. You're a rotten liar. You are a fascist pig liar.

. . . I hope the record shows that tricky Dick Schultz, working for Richard Nixon and administration all understand that tricky Dick Schultz is a liar, and we have a right to defend ourselves, and if you attack me I will defend myself.

Spectators: Right on.

Mr. Seale: A physical attack by those damned marshals, that's what I said.

\* \* \*

The Court: Let the record show the tone of Mr. Seale's voice was one shrieking and pounding on the table and shouting. That will be dealt with appropriately at some time in the future.

Mr. Kunstler: Your Honor, the record should indicate that Mr. Schultz shouted . . .

The Court: . . . [I]f what he said was the truth, I can't blame him for raising his voice.

\* \* \*

The Court: The last statement was made by the Defendant Abbie Hoffman.

Mr. Hoffman: I don't use that last name any more.

\* \* \*

The Court: If you speak once again while the jury is in the box and I have to send them out, we will take such steps as are indicated in the circumstances.

Bring in the jury, Mr. Marshal.

. . .

Mr. Seale: Good morning, ladies and gentlemen of the jury.

\* \* \*

*Further cross-examination of Government Witness William Frapolly by Mr. Weinglass*

Q. Mr. Frapolly, you testified yesterday and I believe on Friday that you were functioning in an undercover capacity for the Police Department of the city of Chicago on August 17, 1968, when you were at a meeting in Grant Park . . .

. . .

Q. . . . and I believe you testified yesterday and on Friday that it was you who suggested to the meeting the method and the manner and the way in which lavatories, public lavatories could be sabotaged, is that correct?

A. No, sir.

Q. Then correct me on that. What did you tell the group?

A. I related a story.

Q. In relating that story did you tell the group that another group of people placed balsam wood balls in the lavatory and that caused the lavatory not to function?

A. Yes; that was part of the story.

. . .

Q. Was it part of your instruction or part of your police assignment to tell demonstrators in this city funny stories about how they could sabotage public lavatories?

A. I don't recall, sir.

. . .

Q. At that meeting [another, two days earlier—ed.] it was you who suggested that grappling hooks and ropes be

60

used to stop jeeps which had barbed wire on the front of them, is that correct?

A. That is not correct, sir.

Q. Tell us what you suggested to Rennie Davis?

A. I suggested to Rennie Davis and some other people that a grappling hook be thrown into barbed wire as it was being strung out from a truck.

Q. From a truck?

A. Yes, sir.

Q. Is that from a military truck?

A. I don't know, sir.

Q. What kind of truck did you have in mind when you said it?

A. Truck.

Q. Any kind of a truck? A moving van?

A. Do you want my exact description of the truck, sir?

Q. Yes, if you can give us the description of it, if you have it.

A. Something like a two and a half ton military truck with a canopy on the back of it.

. . .

Q. You suggested that a grappling hook be used to somehow interfere with the wire mechanism of that truck? Is that correct?

A. Yes, I did, sir.

. . .

Q. People were asking for suggestions but you were the only one who volunteered that a military vehicle should be sabotaged, isn't that true?

A. I think there were other suggestions, sir.

\* \* \*

Mr. Kunstler: Your Honor, if I could interrupt for just a moment and ask for a five-minute recess.

Dr. Benjamin Spock is in the courtroom, and the defendants would like to consult with him. He has to leave at 11:50.

. . .

The Court: All right. We will take a brief recess so that the defendants can consult with Dr. Benjamin Spock.

Mr. Kunstler: We would like to introduce him to your Honor. He is sitting in the courtroom.

Mr. Foran: Your Honor, I object to that.

The Court: My children are grown, Mr. Kunstler.

Mr. Seale: Before the redirect, I would like to request again—demand—that I be able to cross-examine the witness. My lawyer is not here. I think I have a right to defend myself in this courtroom.

The Court: Take the jury out, and they may go to lunch with the usual order.

Mr. Seale: You have George Washington and Benjamin Franklin sitting in a picture behind you, and they was slave owners. That's what they were. They owned slaves. You are acting in the same manner, denying me my constitutional rights . . .

\* \* \*

Mr. Foran: . . . [N]ever have I been in a courtroom—again, for twenty years and for many years daily in courtrooms all over this state and in many instances all over the United States—have I seen the type of conduct that is not only constantly going on in this courtroom, with noise, with giggling, with laughter, with movement, with refusal to stand when the Court gets on the bench, with comments being made by defendants to a jury, with outbursts in front of the jury, with participation in this conduct not only by the defendants but by many of the spectators.

\* \* \*

The Court: . . . Well, I have been called a racist, a fascist—he has pointed to the picture of George Washington behind me and called him a slave owner and—
Mr. Seale: They were slave owners. Look at history.
The Court: As though I had anything to do with that.
Mr. Seale: They were slave owners. You got them up there.
The Court: He has been known as the father of this country, and I would think that it is a pretty good picture to have in the United States District Court.
Mr. Kunstler: We all share a common guilt, your Honor.
The Court: I didn't think I would ever live to sit on a bench or be in a courtroom where George Washington was assailed by a defendant in a criminal case and a judge was criticized for having his portrait on the wall.

\* \* \*

The Court: I will not hear you now. I am asking you to be silent.
Mr. Seale: I want to know will you—Oh, look—it's a form of racism, racism is what stopped my argument.
. . .
The Court: Mr. Seale, do you want to stop or do you want me to direct the Marshal—
Mr. Seale: I want to argue the point about this so you can get an understanding of the fact I have a right to defend myself.
The Court: We will take a recess.
Take that defendant into the room in there and deal with him as he should be dealt with in this circumstance.

\* \* \*

[*Speaking to defendant Seale*]

The Court: . . . If you will assure the Court that you will be respectful and not cause the disorder and commotion that you have up to now, I am willing that you resume your former place at the table, and in the same physical condition that you were in prior to now.

I ask you, therefore, and you may indicate if you choose, by raising your head up and down or shaking your head . . .

\* \* \*

Mr. Kunstler: I wanted to say the record should indicate that Mr. Seale is seated on a metal chair, each hand is hand-cuffed to the leg of the chair on both the right and left sides so he cannot raise his hands, and a gag is tightly pressed into his mouth and tied at the rear, and that when he attempts to speak, a muffled sound comes out as he has done several times since he has been bound and gagged.

\* \* \*

Mr. Seale: You don't represent me. Sit down, Kunstler.

The Court: Mr. Marshal, I don't think you have accomplished your purpose by that kind of a contrivance. We will have to take another recess.

Let the record show again the defendants have not risen.

### October 30, 1969

[*Pursuant to an order by the Court, Defendant Seale has again been strapped into a chair in an attempt to silence his outbursts*]

Mr. Weinglass: If your Honor please, the buckles on the leather strap holding Mr. Seale's hand is digging into his hand and he appears to be trying to free his hand from that pressure. Could he be assisted?

The Court: If the Marshal has concluded that he needs assistance, of course. . . .

. . .

Mr. Kunstler: Your Honor, are we going to stop this medieval torture that is going on in this courtroom? I think this is a disgrace.

Mr. Rubin: This guy is putting his elbow in Bobby's mouth and it wasn't necessary at all.

Mr. Kunstler: This is no longer a court of order, your Honor, this is a medieval torture chamber. It is a disgrace. They are assaulting the other defendants also.

Mr. Rubin: Don't hit me in my balls, motherfucker.

Mr. Seale: This motherfucker is tight and it is stopping my blood.

Mr. Kunstler: Your Honor, this is an unholy disgrace to

the law that is going on in this courtroom and I as an American lawyer feel a disgrace.

Mr. Foran: Created by Mr. Kunstler.

Mr. Kunstler: Created by nothing other than what you have done to this man.

Mr. Hoffman: You come down here and watch it, Judge.

Mr. Foran: May the record show that the outbursts are the Defendant Rubin.

Mr. Seale: You fascist dogs, you rotten low-life son-of-a-bitch. I am glad I said it about Washington used to have slaves, the first President—

Mr. Dellinger: Somebody go to protect him.

Mr. Foran: Your Honor, may the record show that that is Mr. Dellinger saying someone go to protect him and the other comment is by Mr. Rubin.

Mr. Rubin: And my statement, too.

The Court: Everything you say will be taken down.

\* \*

Mr. Kunstler: Your Honor, we would like the names of the marshals. We are going to ask for a judicial investigation of the entire condition and the entire treatment of Bobby Seale.

The Court: You ask for anything that you want. When you begin to keep your word around here that you gave the Court perhaps things can be done.

\* \* \*

The Court: Don't point at me, sir, in that manner.

Mr. Kunstler: If we are going to talk about words, I'd like to exchange some.

The Court: Don't point at me in that manner.

Mr. Kunstler: I just feel so utterly ashamed to be an American lawyer at this time.

The Court: You should be ashamed of your conduct in this case, sir.

Mr. Kunstler: What conduct, when a client is treated in this manner.

The Court: We will take a brief recess.

Mr. Kunstler: Can we have somebody with Mr. Seale? We don't trust—

The Court: He is not your client, you said.

\* \* \*

The Marshal: The Court will now resume its session.

The Court: Will you continue with your cross-examination?

Mr. Weinglass: If your Honor please, just before that I would like to inform the Court that the reason why the other defendants are not rising I am told is because Mr. Seale is not able to rise due to the fact that he is shackled to his chair and they are sitting in silent protest of that fact. . . .

* * *

Mr. Weinglass: . . . I would be remiss in my duty to my client if I stood in this courtroom with fifteen marshals standing at the door, one man gagged and bound, the marshals striking at him and not asking the Court the simple question or not asking the jury if they could continue to deliberate in this trial. I see nothing improper with that. . . .

If my motion is not well founded in the law Mr. Foran can come to this lectern and cite case law. All he does is launch out on a personal attack and you have permitted it. Not only have you permitted it, you have added to it your own intimidation of me personally that I will be dealt with later.

The Court: That wasn't intimidation, sir, that was—

Mr. Weinglass: I accepted that as intimidation.

The Court: You are mistaken. This Court doesn't intimidate lawyers.

Mr. Weinglass: What does your Honor intend—

The Court: It cautions you not to repeat your conduct.

* * *

The Court: . . . I again caution you you not to say—utter the kind of remark you have made here this morning.

Mr. Weinglass: I would like to know what remark I have made that—

The Court: I shall not answer your question, sir, because when I attempt to answer them you interrupt me.

Mr. Weinglass: I give the Court my assurance that I will not.

The Court: I wouldn't take your assurance because you have violated it on many occasions.

* * *

The Court: I would tell you, sir, that the United States District Judge who practiced law in the courts of the United States and sat on state and federal benches for 50 years has to sit here, sir, and have a defendant call him a pig?

Listen to him now.

Mr. Kunstler: Your Honor, we cannot hear him because of the binding and gag on him.

The Court: You bring that to the Judicial Conference or wherever you want to bring it.

* * *

Mr. Schultz: May we be informed of the number, if the Court please, of the last exhibit?

The Court:   What did you say?

Mr. Schultz:   The number was not disclosed.

. . .

The Court:  . . . What is the number, Mr. Weinstein— Weinwer—Weinberg—

Mr. Weinglass:   Weinglass, your Honor.

\*   \*   \*

*Cross-examination of Government Witness Lieutenant Joseph Healy by Mr. Kunstler.*

Q: Lieutenant Healy, do you know who I am?

A. Yes, I do.

Q. We met before, didn't we?

A. Yes, we did.

Mr. Schultz:   Objection, if the Court please.

Mr. Kunstler:   Objection that we met, your Honor?

The Court:   It is hardly material. If you want to introduce yourself—

Mr. Kunstler:   That is what I am doing.

The Court:   All right. Then tell him who you are.

Mr. Kunstler:   I am trying to find out if he knows.

The Court:   That wastes time. He is Charles Kunstler, the lawyer.

Mr. Kunstler:   Your Honor, William Kunstler.

The Court:   Oh, is it William?

Mr. Kunstler:   Charles is the French author.

**October 31, 1969**

*[Lieutenant Healy, a Government witness, has just re- sumed the stand to start the day's session.]*

Mr. Weinglass:   If your Honor please, Mr. Seale is having difficulty. The Marshal has noticed it. He is in extreme dis- comfort. He has written me a note that the circulation of blood in his head is stopped by the pressure of the bandage on the top of the skull and would it be possible to have those bandages loosened? He is breathing very heavily. I think both marshals can note it.

. . .

Mr. Kunstler:   I would like to reiterate I am calling for an end to this. I think this is absolutely medieval. I don't think you have seen it in your experience nor I have seen it in mine.

I am moving now in behalf of the other seven defendants that this be stopped. Let this man defend himself. You could stop this instantly, stop any disturbance in the courtroom if you let him defend himself.

66

The Court: The record does not indicate that I could stop Mr. Seale.

Mr. Kunstler: You can, your Honor. He asks one thing of you and that is the right to defend himself.

. . .

The Court: . . . You are his lawyer and if you were any kind of a lawyer you would continue to do it.

Mr. Kunstler: If I were any kind of a lawyer I would protest against what is being done in this courtroom and I am so protesting . . .

\* \* \*

The Court: He [Mr. Seale—ed.] is being treated in accordance with the law.

Mr. Kunstler: Not the Constitution of the United States, your Honor, which is the supreme law. He has a right to defend himself.

The Court: I don't need someone to come here from New York or wherever you come from to tell me that there is a Constitution in the United States.

Mr. Kunstler: I feel someone needs to tell someone, your Honor. It is not being observed in this Court, if that is the treatment a man gets for wanting to defend himself.

The Court: Read the books. You will find that the Court has the authority to do what is being done and I will not let this trial be broken up by his conduct.

. . .

The Court: Why should I have to go through a trial and be assailed in an obscene manner.

Mr. Kunstler: But, your Honor, that is a reaction of a black man to not being permitted to defend himself. If you had said to him, "Defend yourself," none of this would have happened.

The Court: I have had black lawyers in this courtroom who tried cases with dignity and with ability. His color has nothing to do with his conduct.

Mr. Kunstler: But, your Honor, he feels—

The Court: Not at all.

Mr. Kunstler: He feels he is being denied a right which the Constitution gives him . . .

The Court: If that is a motion, I deny the motion. . . .

\* \* \*

Mr. Kunstler: Your Honor, before the jury comes in, the defendants would like to move to adjourn for the day until Monday so that we can have an opportunity to send the lawyers to California to consult with Mr. Garry, and we feel that we ought to do this both for humanitarian and for legal reasons . . .

. . . We feel as attorneys and so do the seven other defendants that it is impossible to continue as human beings with the trial of this case under the present circumstances; that it is impossible for essentially white men to sit in this room while a black man is in chains and continue—

The Court: I wish you wouldn't talk about the distinction between white and black men in this courtroom.

Mr. Kunstler: A lot of the seven white men—

The Court: I lived a long time and you are the first person who has ever suggested that I have discriminated against a black man. Come in to my chambers and I will show you on the wall what one of the great newspapers of the city said editorially about me in connection with [a] school segregation case.

Mr. Kunstler: Your Honor, this is not a time for self-praise on either side of the lectern.

The Court: It isn't self-praise, sir. It is defense. I won't let a lawyer stand before the bar and charge me with being a bigot.

Mr. Kunstler: For God's sake, your Honor, we are seeking a solution of a human problem here, not whether you feel good or bad or I feel good or bad.

\* \*

The Court: You can't solve a problem by vilifying people.

Mr. Kunstler: I haven't vilified your Honor. I have asked for a day's adjournment so we can solve a problem that must affect every sensitive human being.

The Court: That is one thing—

Mr. Kunstler: —in the United States.

The Court: Please don't raise your voice to me. I don't like that.

\* \* \*

[*Concerning Defendant Seale, currently bound and gagged*]

The Court: When the time comes when a federal judge is called a pig in open court before a hundred people, and publicized throughout the country and the Court can't do anything about it—and the contumacious conduct continues, courts whose judgment I must respect have held that that is a proper method of restraint. Now, it is the only time in my many years both in the practice of law and on the bench that I have seen anything like that happen, but it is the first time I have been called a pig.

Mr. Kunstler: Your Honor, I don't think that is really the issue, but we have argued it so many times.

The Court: Oh, of course not. I think that is just very pleasant for a judge to sit up here and be called a fascist, racist—I couldn't begin to recite all of the things that this man has said.

**November 3, 1969**

*(The following is excerpted from a letter of Charles Garry, attorney for Defendant Seale, read by Mr. Weinglass. Mr. Garry had been unable to attend the trial because of illness)*

"The crisis in this trial has been precipitated by the gross violation by the Government and the trial judge of the fundamental constitutional rights of Mr. Bobby Seale, a black American citizen and national chairman of the Black Panther Party.

"Mr. Seale's fundamental American constitutional right to counsel of his own choice was violated by the refusal of the Government and the trial judge to agree to adjourn the commencement of this trial until the seriously ill counsel of his own choice, the undersigned, Charles R. Garry, could attend. . . .

"Once the trial has started, Mr. Seale's fundamental American constitutional right to defend himself, which he demanded be afforded to him and was unlawfully and without any cause in law denied to him by the Government and the trial judge and in flagrant violation of the Constitution the Government and trial judge proceeded with the trial. . . .

"Meanwhile Mr. Seale must be immediately accorded by the Government and the trial judge his constitutional and statutory right to defend himself. He must be released forthwith from all physical bonds, gags and shackles. He must be released from all restraints upon his liberty so that he may defend himself and receive full and adequate apologies and compensation by the Government for the brutal, cruel, unusual and unconstitutional punishment inflicted upon him during the past two weeks of this trial. . . .

"[E]ven if I were physically and medically able to take part in a major trial, which I am not according to my physicians, my participation could in no way cure the fundamental constitutional infirmity with which it is already plagued. Accordingly, participation by me in this trial long after it is started would violate my basic professional responsibilities and might well be deemed malpractice."

\* \* \*

Mr. Weinglass: . . . Can't Mr. Schultz understand that a man is sitting here on trial facing the possibility of a ten-year jail sentence without his attorney being in this courtroom? And that his right is a simple question to defend himself, and there have been twenty-five witnesses called, there has been no cross-examination for him, his question has been denied by this Court, and he has requested repeatedly that he be given the right to cross-examine them; it has been denied. That isn't a ploy; that is what the Supreme Court talked about in Gideon vs. Wainright and what all of the courts I have cited have talked about. A citizen has a constitutional right to defend himself and that is not a ploy.

**November 4, 1969**

Mr. Seale: . . . I don't know all of these formalities that the lawyers know in the courtroom. I could easily learn it if you would coach me and allow me to defend myself and cross-examine the witnesses and ask pertinent questions that directly relate to these charges against me because I am very well aware of those charges.

\* \* \*

Mr. Seale: I wasn't shackled because I called you a pig and a fascist, which I still think you are, a pig, and a fascist, and a racist, but I was denied my constitutional rights. When a man is denied his constitutional rights—

The Court: Will you sit down, please.

Mr. Seale: —in the manner that you did—

The Court: Mr. Marshal, have that man sit down.

Mr. Seale: —you will still be considered a pig, and a fascist, and a racist by me. You still denied me my constitutional rights.

The Court: Miss Reporter, did you get Mr. Seale's remarks?

\* \* \*

Mr. Kunstler: Your Honor, before you bring in the jury, I want to stand with Mr. Weinglass on this. I have heard now this remark "phony" and "two-faced." It has been directed to my co-counsel. I join him in asking your Honor, and I think you have an obligation to do something about that. I just can't understand how it can go on ad infinitum here without a word coming from you from that bench. I just— you know it is not right; to call a man phony and two-faced in oral argument is not right. We both know that. You don't say anything and you are countenancing the remark.

The Court: For your information, maybe you don't know it, the word "phony" is in the dictionary.

Mr. Kunstler: So is the word "pig," your Honor.

\* \* \*

Mr. Kunstler: I am moving, your Honor—

The Court: I deny your motion.

Mr. Kunstler:   Thank you,

\* \* \*

[*Concerning the Court's contention that Mr. Kunstler is Defendant Seale's attorney*]

Mr. Seale:   I have never sat down and talked with this man before this trial at all—never, never—and I want to argue that point because you are forcing me to accept a lawyer that I have never sat down with and had anything to talk with at all about this trial whatsoever. The only man I talked to was Charles R. Garry, and you know it. I sent a motion in here one month before this trial signed by my name that Charles R. Garry was the only man that I consulted with in this trial, and you have witnesses on the stand testifying against me, and I don't have a right to defend myself. That should be clear in the record.

The Court:   Will you please sit down.

\* \* \*

Mr. Schultz:   May the record show that the Defendant Seale has been identified by the witness.

The Court:   The record may so indicate.

Mr. Seale:   And may the record show that I am a black man, too, being railroaded.

## November 5, 1969

*Cross-examination of Government Witness Bill H. Ray, a deputy sheriff in San Mateo, California*

The Court:   Mr. Kunstler, do you have any cross-examination of this witness?

Mr. Kunstler:   Just one moment, your Honor.

Your Honor, since this witness only related facts relevant to Mr. Seale who has, as your Honor knows, discharged me, I have no questions.

\* \* \*

Mr. Seale:   Well, I think I have a right to cross-examine.

The Court:   No, you have no right in the circumstances of this case.

Mr. Seale:   Why did you follow me, could you please tell me, Mr. Witness—

The Court:   Mr. Seale—

Mr. Seale:   —at the airport?

The Court:   Mr. Seale, I ask you to sit down.

Mr. Seale:   Have you ever killed a Black Panther Party member?

The Court:   Mr. Seale, I will have to ask you to sit down, please.

Mr. Seale:   Have you ever been on any raids in the Black

71

Panther Party's offices or Black Panther Party members' homes?

The Court: Mr. Seale, this is the third time I am asking you to sit down as courteously as possible.

\* \* \*

[*Colloquy between the Court and Mr. Seale*]

The Court: We are going to recess now, young man. If you keep this up—

Mr. Seale: Look, old man, if you keep up denying me my constitutional rights, you are being exposed to the public and the world that you do not care about people's constitutional rights to defend themselves.

\* \* \*

The Court: . . . [I]t is therefore order that pursuant to the authority vested in this Court by Rule 42(a) of the Federal Rules of Criminal Procedure and by Title 18, United States Code, Section 401, the Defendant Bobby Seale be punished for contempt.

. . .

The Court: Mr. Seale, you have a right to speak now. I will hear you.

Mr. Seale: For myself?

The Court: In your own behalf, yes.

Mr. Seale: How come I couldn't speak before?

The Court: This is a special occasion.

Mr. Seale: Wait a minute. Now you are going to try to— you going to attempt to punish me for attempting to speak for myself before? Now after you punish me, you sit up and say something about you can speak? What kind of jive is that? I don't understand it. What kind of court is this? Is this a court? It must be a facist operation like I see it in my mind, you know,—I don't understand you.

\* \* \*

The Court: You may speak to the matters I have discussed here today, matters dealing with your contemptuous conduct. The law obligates me to call on you to speak at this time.

. . .

I have tried to make it clear.

Mr. Seale: All you make clear to me is that you don't want me, you refuse to let me, you will not go by my persuasion, or my arguments, my motions, my requests to be, to the extent of even having to shout loud enough to get on that record for that record so that they can hear me half the time. You don't want to listen to me. You don't want to let a man

72

stand up, contend to you that that man is not my lawyer, show you and point out to you that fact, in fact, made motions and told you that I fired the man.

\* \* \*

Mr. Seale: . . . If a black man stands up and speaks, if a black man asks for his rights, if a black man demands his rights, if a black man requests and argues his rights, what do you do? You're talking about punishing. If a black man gets up and speaks in behalf of the world—

The Court: Are you addressing me, sir?

Mr. Seale: I'm talking. You can see I'm talking.

The Court: That's right, but if you address me, you'll have to stand.

Mr. Seale: Stand? Stand now. Now let's see, first you said that I couldn't stand. I got my suit. It's going to a higher court, possibly the highest court in America.

\* \* \*

*[The following is the ruling of the Court concerning Defendant Seale]*

The Court: . . . I find that the acts, statements and conduct of the Defendant Bobby Seale constituted a deliberate and willful attack upon the administration of justice, an attempt to sabotage the functioning of the federal judiciary system, and misconduct of so grave a character as to make the mere imposition of a fine a futile gesture and a wholly insignificant punishment. Accordingly, I adjudge Bobby G. Seale guilty of each and every specification referred to in my oral observations, and the Court will impose—strike that—and the Defendant Seale will be committed to the custody of the Attorney General of the United States or his authorized representative for imprisonment for a term of three months on each and every specification, the sentences to run consecutively.
. . .

The Court: . . . There will be an order in view of the disposition of this aspect of the case, there will be an order declaring a mistrial as to the Defendant Bobby G. Seale and not as to any other defendants.

Mr. Seale: Wait a minute, I got a right—what's the cat trying to pull now? . . . I can't stay?

The Court: Now I will tell you this, that since it has been said here that all of the defendants support this man in what he is doing, I over the noon hour will reflect on whether they are good risks for bail and I shall give serious consideration to the termination of their bail if you can't control your clients, and you couldn't yesterday afternoon.

Mr. Seale: I am not—I am not a defendant—he is not

my lawyer. I want my right to defend myself. I want my right
to defend myself.

Mr. Kunstler: Your Honor, they said this morning they
supported fully his right to defend himself or have his lawyer
of choice, and if that is the price of their bail, then I guess
that will have to be the price of their bail.

## November 6, 1969

[*Following the Court's severance of the Government's
prosecution of Bobby Seale from that of the other seven
defendants, Defense Attorney Weinglass made the following motion out of the presence of the jury*]

Mr. Weinglass: . . . Your Honor, I am joined in making
this motion by Mr. Kunstler who will argue following my
argument, and this motion is made on behalf of the seven
remaining defendants in the cause, and it is a motion of a
mistrial.

The Court: What?

Mr. Weinglass: A motion for a mistrial as to the remaining
seven defendants.

\* \* \*

Mr. Kunstler: [A] witness testified that he [Mr. Seale—ed.]
was here to urge people in the park, particularly black people,
to kill policemen in the city of Chicago during Convention
Week. This is something no juror can forget . . .

It is far too inflammatory and far too dramatic to ever be
forgotten by a juror hearing it in this courtroom. . . .

Mr. Kunstler: The jury knows, as Mr. Weinglass has
pointed out, what happened to Mr. Seale. They also have good
reason to believe from remarks stated in this courtroom in
their presence that this was because Mr. Seale was a bad person. . . . Well, the defendants are in association with him by
the Government's claim. They are his co-conspirators, and if he
is so terrible in the minds of the jury, then because they are
associated with him by the charge of the Government by the
indictment, then by relationship they are also terrible persons.
This severance does irreparable harm to them . . .

\* \* \*

The Court: Based on the record in this case and the appli-
cable authorities which the Court has examined prior to coming in here this morning and prior to the entry of the order on
yesterday afternoon, the motion of the defendants in this case
other than the Defendant Bobby G. Seale, that is to say, the
seven other defendants, for a mistrial will be denied . . .

[*The following are excerpts from proposed Government
Exhibits 33 and 34, audio portions of an ABC-TV News
film*]

74

Mr. Lawrence: Chicago police refused to comment on any of the charges that have been made by the Mobilization and yesterday issued a statement saying that Rennie Davis is an enemy of the American people because of your trip to North Vietnam.

What is your reaction to that kind of statement?

Mr. Davis: Well, my reaction is that I am an enemy of the police state that is being created in the city of Chicago. I am an enemy of the war in Vietnam. I am an enemy of the racist and oppressive government that refuses to deal with the problems of the American ghettos and I will continue to be this kind of enemy against these kind of injustices. . . .

. . .

Mr. Lawrence: It begins to take on the appearance of a guerilla movement.

Mr. Hayden: Well, I wouldn't say it's a guerrilla movement, simply because the Yippies and the Mobilization people are essentially unarmed. Those who have been throwing things at police are throwing rocks and bottles. They're not carrying MACE, or guns, or the kind of weapons that the police have, and they're basically fighting in a defensive way because they're being driven out of the park, hounded in the streets, and they have no alternative but to fight back at least for the purposes of survival. . . .

**November 7, 1969**

> [Francis J. McTernan, Special Attorney for Defendant Bobby Seale, arguing the illegality of the 4-year sentence imposed on his client by the Court for contempt]

Mr. McTernan: . . . It seems to me, your Honor, that although there are several incidents that occurred over a series of days, that it constituted one course of conduct and not sixteen different contempts. The one course of conduct involved Mr. Seale's attempt to defend himself, and every citation, as I read it, was related to that central theme, and I think it is a very substantial question of law where in one course of conduct, whether under one course of conduct, a man can be sentenced to sixteen different sentences to run consecutively. . . . [I]t seems to me that is just what the Supreme Court was trying to avoid.

\* \* \*

The Court: . . . [T]his defendant was not only warned and admonished each time he uttered contemptuous remarks and was guilty of contemptuous conduct—

Mr. McTernan: Your Honor—

The Court:   I beseeched him not to repeat such conduct right down to almost minutes before I imposed the sentence. . . .

. . .

Mr. McTernan:   . . . [W]e have a picture of a man who believed, your Honor, though wrongfully, but who believed, and I think who believed that he had a right to defend himself. Now, your Honor, that is the basic problem out of which this whole thing grew, and an explosion, if any, occurred.

Here is a layman, not trained as a lawyer, asking for what he considered his right to defend himself and discharge lawyers of record because the lawyer of his choice was not here. . . .

The Court:   You can disagree with the judge, laymen or lawyers—

Mr. McTernan:   A laymen is not a lawyer.

The Court:   —but you don't call him a pig and a fascist in the process of disagreeing with him.

\* \* \*

Mr. McTernan:   . . . What I wanted to get to is this: You keep referring back to how contemptuous the conduct was and I am trying to say to your Honor, and I would like to develop the argument because I didn't get it all out, that we were dealing first with a layman and not a lawyer. Secondly, we were dealing with a black man who comes out of a black ghetto.

The Court:   Oh, I don't want to hear another thing about a black man. The only person who mentioned black men in this Court for the first time was your client. You don't know me, sir, but I am as good a friend of the black people in this community as they have, and if you don't believe it, read the books.

\* \* \*

The Court:   You are the one that brings up this black man thing again. I am weary of hearing about it because he has not been discriminated against.

Mr. McTernan:   I am not suggesting, your Honor, in this phase of my argument that he was discriminated against.

The Court:   Then why mention color?

Mr. McTernan:   Because it has to do with the words he used, your Honor. It has to do with the culture from which he comes and the meaning ascribed to words. That is what I want to address myself to.

The Court:   I have known literally thousands of what we used to call Negro people, and who are now referred to as black people, and I never heard that kind of language emanate from the lips of any one of them. I have had fine Negro

76

lawyers stand at that lectern and at the lectern across in the old courthouse, and I never heard a lawyer, a Negro lawyer, use that kind of language, or any Negro defendant in a criminal case. I never did.

There is no evidence here in this case that it is part of a culture.

Mr. McTernan: Your Honor, that is precisely the point I am getting to. Of course there is no evidence here, but there should be. There should be before a man is sentenced to four years in jail for contempt for use of language. . . .

\* \* \*

Mr. Foran: . . . I would call something else to the Court's attention which again makes counsel's motion really moot and that is that Mr. Seale is not only under a charge but that he is under a charge in New Haven, Connecticut, for conspiracy to commit murder. He is not entitled to be on the street even under the Constitution.

There are other matters, your Honor, that I think you should consider. Mr. Seale is presently under conviction and sentence of three years probation from April 11, 1968, in California for a charge of carrying weapons, deadly weapons, firearms or explosives, into a prison, or having them in his possession when he was in prison.

Since that time he has been indicted on this conspiracy to commit murder in Connecticut, which is non-bailable.

Since that time he has conducted himself in this Court in a way that would indicate that if anything, he is a desperately poor risk for bail, having demonstrated his gross disrepect for the law and for the rules of this Court. . . .

. . . [T]here is no one in this courtroom that does not know that Mr. Seale is a highly intelligent and articulate man. The idea, the very idea that his gross conduct in this courtroom was due to his race is an insult to any human being who is a member of that race. His gross conduct was because he acted contemptuously in this Court, he as a human being. Sometimes I think we lose all context, all sense of the context in which these things occur when we listen to some of these arguments. . . . [T]he Court has used the patience of Job in not sentencing him to the maximum sentence on each of the individual specifications in the contempt.

. . .

The Court: Gentlemen, we have here the motion of the Defendant Seale for bail. My view is that anyone who has sat through this trial and heard the words of the defendant and watched his conduct can't but reach the conclusion that the defendant was guilty of dangerous acts of violence in open court, that he by his words intends to seek to destroy and over-turn the American judicial system. He has severely disrupted the normal trial processes of our judicial system and I think such conduct is a major threat, and I so find, to the continued existence of our democratic system. His shouting in open court, his insulting characterization of the trial judge, of the United States Attorney, the Assistant United States Attorney, the marshals, to me mean that he is a dangerous man. If he is a dangerous man, as I conclude and find, it would be gross error to permit him to be free on bail.

\* \* \*

*[From film, Government Exhibit 35, of speech by Defendant Davis in Cleveland, August 17, 1968]*
We want to say here in Cleveland that our fight is not with the policemen, our fight is not with the National Guard troops, our fight is not with the young men who are being ordered from Fort Hood in Coleman, Texas, to come to the Democratic National Convention for the protection of that convention from its own citizens. Our fight is with the policies of the United States Government that have created this situation.

### November 10, 1969

*Cross-examination of Government Witness Barbara Callender, a Chicago policewoman, by Defense Attorney Kunstler*

Q. What drew your attention first to the man you say is Jerry Rubin, which is a half hour before he spoke, as I understand it?
A. To be quite frank, I found him to be a very obnoxious man and—
Q. Go ahead. You have something else to say?
A. Yes, please. *(Continuing.)* And this drew my attention to him and I just started to follow him.
Q. Is your attention often drawn to obnoxious men?
[The Government objected to this question. The objection was sustained—ed.]

. . .

Q. Can you describe what Mr. Hayden looked like then?
A. Yes. His hair was fairly close to regular length. He has kind of a pocked face. I don't remember any mustache or anything. Kind of beady eyes.
Q. Beady eyes?
A. Yes.
Q. You don't like these defendants, do you, at all?

[The Government objected to the last question. The objection was sustained—ed.]

· · ·

Mr. Schultz: Mr. Kunstler should ask if she saw Jerry Rubin.

Mr. Kunstler: —if Mr. Schultz says he wants to replace her on the witness stand and tell this jury—

Mr. Schultz: No.

Mr. Kunstler: —what he believes she saw and did not see, let him do so, but at least do it honestly.

Mr. Schultz: I am doing it honestly.

The Court: You mean without my permission? You give your permission?

Mr. Kunstler: I give mine. If your Honor's is necessary, I would urge your Honor to give your permission.

The Court: Perhaps you want me to get down and represent your clients.

Mr. Kunstler: No, your Honor, I am not sure my clients would accept that, your Honor.

## November 12, 1969

The Court: With no objection, Government's Exhibits 44 and 45, respectively, for identification, may be admitted into evidence as Government's Exhibits bearing those numbers only as to the Defendant Rubin.

Is there anything somebody at that table wants to say?

Mr. Rubin: I was speaking to my attorney.

The Court: I will wait.

Your client wants to talk to you, Mr. Weinglass, while I am talking. I will be glad to wait.

Mr. Hoffman: We think you ought to come to Washington this Saturday and protest the trial.

\* \* \*

*Direct examination of Government Witness Irwin Bock,*
*a Chicago police officer, by Government Attorney Schultz*

Mr. Schultz: If the Court please, Mr. Hoffman, the Defendant Hoffman is not in the courtroom. He is another person who is named by the witness.

The Court: We will wait for him.

Mr. Schultz: Yes, sir.

The Court: He has returned.

Mr. Hoffman: I have a bladder problem.

· · ·

The Court: . . . I suggest to the defendants that they refrain from loud laughter. This is a trial in the United States

79

District Court, not a circus. I tried to make that clear during this trial, sometimes with great difficulty. . . .

. . .

Mr. Kunstler: I would just like the record to indicate that there was laughter at the defense, and the laughter was not out of proportion to the answers and the questions of the prosecution.

The Court: The record may indicate that you said that, and I disagree with you.

Mr. Kunstler: I know, we disagree frequently.

The Court: Not infrequently.

. . .

Mr. Kunstler: Your Honor, I object again. That is a leading question to tell him there was a meeting which he attended.

. . .

The Court: Mr. Kunstler, do a little research on this matter of leading questions. Really, evidence authorities are not very much against leading questions these days.

[But see January 6, 1970—ed.]

. . .

The Court: I direct the Marshal to go over there to the defendants' table and request them as we have done repeatedly in the past not to laugh loudly during this trial. This is a trial in the United States District Court: It is not a vaudeville theater.

Mr. Kunstler: But, your Honor, we are human beings, too, and when remarks are made from the witness stand which evoke laughter, I don't think it can be helped. You can't make automatons out of us or robots; we are human beings and we laugh occasionally, and if it comes irrepressibly, I don't really see how that really becomes a court matter.

\* \*

Mr. Schultz: Mr. Kunstler is laughing so he can influence the jury with the impression that this is absurd. That is why he is laughing aloud . . .

. . .

Mr. Kunstler: . . . [S]ometimes when the absurdity becomes too much, I laugh . . . but we are not doing it just out of some calculation so the jury sees us laugh. They are far too intelligent to be misled by an occasional—

The Court: I think they are, too.

Mr. Kunstler: Mr. Schultz is implying they are not.

The Court: I agree with you.

**November 13, 1969**
*Continued direct examination of Government Witness Bock. [Defendant Rubin explaining his absence during*

*the last half hour of previous day's testimony. The Court
had revoked his bail because of said absence.*]

Mr. Rubin:    . . . I did not walk out on the trial. That is
absolutely wrong. I like being here. It is interesting. I didn't
intend to walk out. I have been here every day at 10:00 and
2:00 and stayed here to the end.

The Court:    That is the best—

Mr. Rubin:    Let me finish.

The Court:    That is the best statement I have heard here
during the trial. You said you enjoyed being here.

Mr. Rubin:    It is good theater, your Honor.

. . .

Q. Would you relate, please, Mr. Bock, what was stated at
        that meeting?

A. . . . Tom Hayden said that "If the City doesn't give in to
        our demands, there would be war in the streets and there
        should be." . . .

. . .

A. . . . Weiner said, "A good mobile tactic would be to
        pick a target in the Loop area and bomb that target."
        He said, "Such a diversionary tactic as bombing the
        fence across the street from the federal building, the
        high wooden fence, would burn very easily, and that
        this would draw police away from the demonstrators
        in the loop." . . .
        . . . Weiner then asked me if I could obtain the bottles
        necessary to make the Molotov cocktails. . . .

. . .

Mr. Davis:    Why don't you arrest this lying police spy.
He has filed an affidavit.

Mr. Foran:    I would like to have those remarks on the
record, Miss Reporter.

Mr. Kunstler:    I suggest to you, Miss Reporter, that no one
has the authority to ask you to put those comments in the
record.

Mr. Foran:    The remark was "Why don't you arrest that
lying police spy," Miss Reporter.

Mr. Dellinger:    And that District Attorney who is teaching
him to lie.

Mr. Foran:    Take that also, Miss Reporter.

Mr. Dellinger:    That is a fine way to get to be Senator.
[Mr. Foran has been mentioned as a possible candidate
for the Senate seat from Illinois—ed.]

**November 14, 1969**

*Cross-examination of Government Witness Bock by De-
fense Counsel Kunstler*

81

Mr. Kunstler:   Your Honor, I just don't understand that objection.

The Court:   I do. I sustain it.

Mr. Schultz:   If the Court please, just for purposes of the record, I would like the record to show, if the Court would have the record so show, that the people in the audience here and at the defense table laughed at the Court's last comment.

Mr. Kunstler:   Your Honor, are we going to constantly get into this laughter business?

The Court:   When it is wrong to laugh. I don't know whether the word "constantly" is the word to use.

Mr. Kunstler: Your Honor—

The Court:   I have tried to stress here during the conduct of this trial that this is a trial in the United States District Court and we don't tolerate loud laughter—at least I don't—in the conduct of a trial which I supervise. I tried to make that clear to you.

. . .

Mr. Kunstler:   Everybody has laughed at one time in this courtroom, including your Honor, including the jury, including the defense, and including Mr. Foran and Mr. Schultz and the audience. . . .

. . .

Mr. Kunstler:   . . . Now the witness has indicated he saw him again on July 27 at a cocktail party in Evanston.

The Court:   "Cocktail party or a party."

Mr. Kunstler:   All right, I will take that modification.

The Court:   He may not have been lucky enough to have a cocktail at the party.

. . .

Mr. Kunstler:   I have made, your Honor, a request of you to let me participate in this nationwide protest—

The Court:   I make a request of you to continue with your cross-examination, sir.

. . .

The Court:   . . . The jury may disregard the requests about Washington and constitutional rights. This is a trial here; it is not in Washington.

. . .

Mr. Rubin:   I didn't laugh.

Mr. Kunstler:   Your Honor, every laugh is not at you. I think you take it very personally every time there is laughter. Every time there is laughter, it is not at you.

The Court:   I know when it is at me, Mr. Kuntsler.

Mr. Kunstler:   Kunstler, your Honor.

*Continued cross-examination of Government Witness Bock*

The Court: . . . I don't object to a smile if something humorous, in the opinion of the one who smiles, occurs, but I think in a trial loud laughter is not indicated.

Mr. Kunstler: Your Honor, I just want to correct one impression. I didn't say people want to laugh. I said laughter was irrepressible sometimes when some testimony came from the witness stand. I happen not to have heard Mr. Dellinger today at all.

The Court: I don't remember your using that word.

Mr. Kunstler: Well, irrepressible laughter, your Honor, is known to all of us. It happens to human beings.

The Court: I wouldn't say irrepressible laughter is known to all of us. Don't count me in on everything. Just confine your opinions to yourself.

Mr. Kunstler: But I have seen your Honor laugh.

The Court: Laughter is not irrespessible to me if I don't want to laugh. I don't laugh out loud in a trial being conducted in the United States District Court.

Mr. Kunstler: But, your Honor, you have in this case. I have heard you.

The Court: No, you haven't.

Mr. Kunstler: Your Honor—

The Court: Oh, but you haven't.

. . .

The Court: Mr. Kunstler, there is a great architect, Mies van der Rohe, who lately left us. He designed that lectern as well as this building and it was a lectern, not a leaning post. I have asked you to stand behind it when you question the witness.

Mr. Kunstler: Your Honor, I think the U.S. Attorney questions from this table here—

The Court: I don't permit lawyers to lean on that thing. I don't want you to do it. I have asked you before. That was put there by the Government, designed by Mr. van der Rohe, and I want you to use it for that purpose.

Mr. Kunstler: Your Honor, the U.S. Attorney questions from the back of this table and leans on his material.

The Court: I don't care about that.

Mr. Kunstler: Why am I different?

The Court: I haven't seen the United States Attorney put his elbow on that thing and lean on it as though it was a leaning post and I wouldn't permit them to do it or you.

Mr. Kunstler: Perhaps I am tired, your Honor. What is wrong about leaning on it?

The Court: If you are tired then let Mr.—

Mr. Kunstler: Weinglass.

The Court: —Weinglass take over.

Maybe I am tired, but I am sitting up here—

Mr. Kunstler: You are sitting in a comfortable chair.

The Court: I sit in the place where I should sit.

Mr. Kunstler: While I am standing up.

The Court: I will not permit you to lean on that.

Mr. Kunstler: May I place my hands like this, your Honor?

The Court: Yes. Yes. That is not leaning.

Since you are tired, we will take a recess and you can go to sleep for the afternoon.

**November 19, 1969**

The Court: . . . I have never entered a judgment in all the years I have served based on what some newspaper writer or editor wants me to do. I don't like some of the cartoon sketches that have appeared in the newspapers about me, but I don't bear them any animus because if a man assumes a public place of any kind, that is what he is exposed to.

I can't ask for a mistrial when I'm pictured in the newspapers with a whip in my hand with a title, "Justice," on the top of it.

. . .

The Court: I grant you—I saw that article of Mr. Wicker's. It was not too complimentary, but you didn't have to go all the way to New York or pay 15 cents here. You could just pay 10 cents for one of the Chicago papers and have gotten even better than Wicker's story. Paraphrasing a statement I'm sure you have heard in your day, some of my best friends are newspaper editors.

Mr. Kunstler: I have heard that in a different connotation, your Honor.

. . .

The Court: . . . I've never written to a newspaper man and thanked him for the nice things he said about me—oh, it may come as a surprise to you, but many nice things have been written about me, Mr. Kunstler—nor have I written to a newspaper or even called anyone at the newspaper and complained, nor have I ever appeared on television or spoken on the radio. Here is the place, in my opinion, where a judge should speak, and I do speak from the bench when it's necessary to speak. And I think a lawyer trying a case should speak here, too.

Mr. Kunstler: I am trying to do that, your Honor.

The Court: Well, you haven't succeeded.

Mr. Kunstler: Not for the last five minutes, anyway.

. . .

Mr. Kunstler: Can I get to my motion, your Honor?

The Court: . . . You may give everything about your grounds for a mistrial other than what appears in the newspapers.

Mr. Kunstler: Thank you, your Honor.

The Court: You don't have to thank me. You are entitled to make your motion. You are entitled to a ruling.

Mr. Kunstler: Well, I felt a certain sense of gratitude, your Honor.

The Court: What did you say?

Mr. Kunstler: I felt a certain sense of gratitude that I could get to the motion.

The Court: It is nice to have grateful lawyers.

\*   \*   \*

[*On defense motion for mistrial based on statement of
the Court while the jury was present*]

Mr. Kunstler: . . . [Y]our Honor indicated just before the luncheon recess that I was leaning on the lectern, that I should get behind the lectern, that Mies van der Rohe had intended that I be behind the lectern.

The Court: Oh, now, now, you are getting to be like some of the others. Be accurate. I happened to know Mr. van der Rohe, but he never mentioned your name. . . . A lawyer stands at that lectern, he stands erect and not leaning as though he were having a beer some place.

I don't tolerate that. I did for a while. You did it for a long time, and I finally thought I ought to take you to task for it.

. . .

The Court: I think it is slovenly, and you, yourself, recognized it by saying you were tired. You were probably tired from one of your evening speeches.

**November 21, 1969**

*Cross-examination of Government Witness Joseph Hale,
an investigator assigned to the Subversive Unit of the
Chicago Police Intelligence Divisions, by Mr. Kunstler
[Concerning demonstrations during Convention Week]*

Q. What did those officers do?

A. Well, they were ducking, ducking the missiles that were being thrown, and they couldn't do much of anything besides look out for their own welfare.

Q. Well, prior to ducking the missiles, is it not true that those officers advanced and attacked the crowd?

A. No, sir. They couldn't have possibly advanced and attacked the crowd, not a handful of uniformed police officers.

* * *

Q. Is it your testimony that the missiles just started spontaneously with no action by the police at all?

. . .

A. If you call the American flag being desecrated and the offender being placed in custody, this is what in my mind precipitated the throwing of the missiles at the police.

. . .

Q. . . . Did you ever tell any person that you had engaged in profanities yourself that day?

A. By engaging in profanity, I do remember making a statement to a cameraman for I assumed it to be a TV station, I told him to turn those censored cameras around because of that civilian brutality. That is the profanity I used.

Q. What did you say when you said censored?

A. There are ladies present.

Q. No, I want you to answer. We understand that ladies don't like to hear it, no one likes to hear it, but this is a criminal trial and it is important that we learn what you said. It has been used many times in this courtroom.

A. I don't care to use it in the presence of ladies I will tell it to you or the Judge but—

Mr. Foran: In any event, it is immaterial.

. . .

The Court: I sustain the objection.

Mr. Kunstler: Your Honor, I fail to understand that. Every obscentiy that has been ascribed to our clients has been paraded in front of this jury as if they were being tried for their swear words. When this man uses an obscenity, the police use an obscenity, we are not permitted to let the jury know what the police said.

The Court: This witness is not being tried.

Mr. Foran: . . . I am perfectly willing to confess [as] I am sure Mr. Kunstler is that he on occasion has used profanity also. That has nothing to do with this trial.

Mr. Kunstler: I think everybody in this courtroom, the

jury and everybody else has at sometime used profanity. I
don't think that is a—

The Court: I don't know about that. There are ladies on
the jury. I would not want to make that charge.

Mr. Kunstler: Well, your Honor, human life is human
life and we all fall from grace occasionally.

Q. Did the word begin with an "F"?

**November 25, 1969**

The Court: I observe, I believe, that all of the defendants
are not in attendance here.

Mr. Davis: Bobby Seale.

Mr. Kunstler: Mr. Rubin just went to the men's room.
He was here a second ago.

The Court: Lawyers would say that your observation was
a conclusion, Mr. Kunstler.

Mr. Kunstler: I can't see through the wall, your Honor,
but he had a distressed look on his face. If he comes in with
a relieved one, your Honor, I will know I was correct.

· · ·

Mr. Kunstler: [Y]ou cannot even consider the Government's motion here without at least hearing strenuous argument on the Spock issue. . . .

The Court: It would be better for your nervous system
if you don't argue strenuously. You are fond of describing
your efforts as strenuous argument.

Mr. Kunstler: We all have our own idiosyncrasies.

The Court: Ordinary argument is good enough for me.

Mr. Kunstler: No, your Honor. This case deserves better
than an ordinary argument. It's not good enough for me essentially, and I think that I have to present it in the way I
think its worth merits.

The Court: All right. You may talk strenuously then.
I certainly will not complain about the tone of your voice.
You did about me, but I wouldn't about you.

Mr. Kunstler: Well, "strenuous," always doesn't mean
tone, your Honor.

The Court: I think it does.

Mr. Kunstler: It has other aspects. I will try to keep the
tonal qualities on a non-strenuous level.

The Court: I just don't want you to get tired, as you said
you were the other day.

Mr. Kunstler: That's why your Honor wouldn't let me
lean on the lectern.

\*   \*   \*

[*Colloquy concerning Mr. Kunstler's participation in the*

*November 15, 1969, "March Against Death" in Washington, D.C.]*

The Court: What did you say on that occasion?

Mr. Kunstler: On which occasion?

The Court: In Washington, D.C., I read—

Mr. Kunstler: I sat and listened.

The Court: I read that you were on top of some kind of tractor.

Mr. Kunstler: Really? I didn't even know that.

The Court: You made a speech.

Mr. Kunstler: Your Honor, I sat on top of a tractor truck.

The Court: I wondered what you said.

Mr. Kunstler: I think I asked someone for coffee at one point.

The Court: Coffee on top of a tractor?

Mr. Kunstler: I sang once, and I listened to the speeches. But, your Honor is correct, I sat on top of a tractor-trailer, and I was thrilled by what I saw as I looked out at what seemed to me half a million people who had one thought in mind, and that was to end the war in Vietnam now and immediately. . . .

. . .

Mr. Kunstler: I am done in one minute, your Honor, because I just want to close with a statement which the defendants do adopt as their own, even, though it comes from a publication. . . . It is a study of Attorney General Mitchell and his stewardship, and the writer Richard Harris ends as follows:

"Most people no longer seem to care—if, indeed, they know—what is happening to their country. . . . When the people finally awaken, they may find their freedoms gone, because the abandonment of the rule of law must bring on tyranny. Since it is the majority's fear—fear of black men, fear of crime, fear of disorder, fear even of differences— that allows repression to flourish, those who succumb to their fears are as responsible as those who make political use of them. And in the end both will suffer equally. 'For they have sown the wind, and they shall reap the whirlwind.'"

. . .

*[The following are tape-recorded excerpts of a speech by Defendant Rubin during Convention Week, as offered in evidence by the Government]*

Mr. Rubin: . . . Another thing of significant difference between the people here at this convention and the people across town at the convention is the attitude toward money. Many of us were born in relative wealth, but we are rejecting wealth because we don't believe in the value of money, or property that comes under the individual profit system. We don't want the world run like that, we want the world to run along the principle of cooperation for we're not interested in protecting our property. The hell with property. We are not interested in becoming rich. The hell with riches. There is going to be an election coming up and people are asking themselves what that election should be. It should be one word, they'll have to disrupt that election. . . .

. . . That's why most people think this is a free country, because they never try to change the country. If they try to change it they see how free it is. . . .

* *

[*Continuation of tape*]

Mr. Rubin: . . . We've got a lot of work to do tonight and we've got to break up into small groups and go throughout the city and convince as many people as possible to try to get out of the Old Town area and try to get into the downtown area then to do whatever they think is necessary to make our point. The headline of the New York Post today was "The Battle of Chicago." See you on the streets tonight.

## November 26, 1969

*Direct examination of Richard Schaller, an intelligence analyst with the U.S. Naval Investigative Service, by Mr. Schultz. [Testimony regarding objects thrown at the police during the disorders]*

Q. Would you describe the objects that you had seen when you were on the west side of the band shell, the objects which you saw thrown?

A. Well, there were chunks of what I'd call concrete, rock aggregate mixed with mortar. There was tin cans containing garbage. The cans had been opened, the food content consumed, the top of the lid had been left so that it would hinge. There was such things as coffee grounds, lard, grease, egg shells, other materials of that type in the cans, and the lid was pushed down again so that when it hit there would be a spewing of material from the can.

There were other objects that appeared when they hit to sort of explode and spew out a colored liquid. I saw various colors, blue, yellow, green. There were some pieces of board or wood thrown also, and stones.

89

Q. Did you have occasion in any way to attempt to determine the contents of the liquid in the bags or any—

A. Not at that time, but after the rally was over, walking up the walk, I was curious to know what the objects were that contained the colored articles, and I picked one up on a stick.

It appeared to be a plastic Baggie-type container and contained the colored fluid, and in holding it up I detected the aroma of what I determined to be urine.

The Court: I didn't hear that last.

The Witness: I determined it to be urine by odor.

\* \* \*

*[Following the Court's refusal to permit John Sinclair, founder of the White Panther Party, to come from prison to testify for the defense]*

Mr. Kunstler: You may have cited all the authorities in the world. We made a decision this man is a key witness for our defense. Your Honor has made a decision in your discretion not to allow us to have this key witness.

The Court: Which the law permits me to do.

Mr. Kunstler: The law permits, but the defendants have a right to decide what they are going to do now when they have been denied a key witness to the defense. We would like a recess to discuss that.

The Court: I deny the motion for a recess. I don't take recesses—

Mr. Dellinger: Aw Jesus—fascist—

\* \*

The Court: Who is that man talking, Mr. Marshal?

Mr. Dellinger: That is Mr. David Dellinger and he is saying that that is an arbitrary denial when you say who is key to our defense. . . .

. . .

Mr. Dellinger: I think that is acting like a fascist court like Mr. Seale said when you make decisions of that kind and deprive us of our witnesses. Because he has already been persecuted in one court, now you are persecuting him and us in another one.

Mr. Davis: Why don't you gag all of us, Judge?

The Court: Who said that?

Mr. Davis: Bobby Seale said that.

. . .

The Court: I decide each motion on its own papers, sir, and I am not aware of any witnesses that the Government has sought to bring here. I don't know whether—

Mr. Hoffman: We are very confused about this. Is the

Government going to present our defense as well as our prosecution?

The Court: Have you gotten that—what is the name of that defendant speaking?

Mr. Hoffman: Just Abbie. I don't have a last name, Judge. I lost it.

* * *

*Cross-examination of Mr. Schaller, by Mr. Kunstler*

Q. Did you not report to your superiors, putting aside documents, that you feared violence from the police at that moment?

Mr. Schultz: Objection.

The Court: I sustain the objection.

Mr. Kunstler: Your Honor, could you give me the basis of the sustaining of that ruling?

The Court: When I have chosen to give you a basis, you never agree with my basis, and there is no point in my getting into arguments that I can't win.

You know, I don't like to argue when there is not a chance of winning, so I will just let my ruling stand.

Mr. Kunstler: Your Honor, I am not sure that you have lost any.

. . .

Q. On the tape during this speech particularly after the word "garbage" which appears on page 16, and after the references to Nixon, Humphrey and Wallace, which also appears on 16, there appears to be an animal sound on the tape. Was that a pig's oink?

A. Yes.

Q. And the pig oinked twice?

A. I couldn't say if he did or not, sir.

Q. You saw nothing subversive in that, did you?

Mr. Schultz: Objection.

The Court: I have to rule, so I will sustain the objection.

Mr. Kunstler: Your Honor, the word "oink" has been used several times as implying something subversive.

The Court: Yes, I know it has been used several times; so has the word "pig."

* * *

The Court: . . . Ladies and gentlemen of the jury, I deeply regret that you will not be able to spend your Thanksgiving Day in your customary manner. I hope that it will be as pleasant as it can be in the circumstances.

Mr. Kunstler: Your Honor, the defense has no objection to them spending Thanksgiving at home. We moved for that before.

Mr. Schultz:   If the defense would try to expedite this trial instead of delaying it, we wouldn't be here now.

Mr. Rubin:   We'd probably be in jail.

**November 28, 1969**
*[Testimony of Mr. Schaller on recross-examination]*
The Court:   Oh, I will let the witness tell whether he knows what an obscenity is. Do you know what an obscenity is?

The Witness:   I think I would, but I am sure counsel and I am have disagreement here and there.

. . .

By Mr. Weinglass:
Q. Mr. Schaller, is it an obscenity for the mayor of a major metropolitan area to advise his police to shoot to kill all arsonists and shoot to maim all looters?

Mr. Schultz:   Objection.

The Court:   I sustain the objection.

By Mr. Weinglass:
Q. Do you consider it an obscenity for the United States Government to use napalm in the bombing of civilians in North Vietnam?

Mr. Schultz:   Mr. Weinglass can't be serious in contending that these questions are proper on this recross-examination.

Mr. Weinglass:   That is perhaps my most serious question in this trial.

**December 1, 1969**
*Cross-examination of Government Witness Rochford, Deputy Superintendent of Chicago police, by Mr. Kunstler [During Mr. Rochford's testimony]*
Defendant Weiner:   Bill, the executioner is mumbling and I can't hear him.

Mr. Kunstler:   Your Honor, is it possible to tell the witness to keep his voice up?

The Court:   I think it is possible. I have demonstrated that because I have asked him two or three times already.

Mr. Foran:   May the record show the comment? Did you get that comment?

Defendant Dellinger:   He was speaking to his lawyer.

. . .

Mr. Kunstler:   Your Honor, Mr. Foran I don't think even heard it, but Mr. Schultz whispered in his ear and then we have this little schoolhouse episode going on of reporting to your Honor what the bad boys are doing.

The Court: You may think these are schoolhouse episodes—

Mr. Kunstler: They are, your Honor, they are what we
used to call tattletales.

The Court: If they are, you are going to be disillusioned.

. . .

The Court: Characterizing a witness in the United States
District Court out loud by one of the defendants having an
interest in the case is not a schoolhouse play.

\* \* \*

Q. Now did you see police officers leaping through the window
after people?

A. Some police officers went into the crowd to get the injured
but they didn't leap through the window.

. . .

Q. How do you know they were going through to go to the
injured?

A. Why else would they go through?

Q. They might go through to beat people with their clubs,
isn't that a possibility?

A. No, Counselor.

\* \* \*

Q. They did say they wanted to go to the Ampitheatre, didn't
they?

A. Yes.

Q. They didn't say they wanted to go to the Conrad Hilton,
did they?

A. And the police said they could not.

Q. The police said they could not and the police said they
could not because they had been ordered, had they not,
to stop any demonstrations in the vicinity of the International Ampitheatre, isn't that correct?

A. The police said they could not because to meet our total
responsibility to the delegates, to the visitors, to the
people of this city, in the judgment of the police it was
not in the interest of safety to all the citizens to permit
it.

Q. Supt. Rochford, isn't it true that you had ample police
and National Guard forces available to you to easily
control 3,000 people who wanted to march to the International Ampitheatre that night?

A. Counsel, there isn't enough manpower to control a group
of people that wants to be disorderly. There just isn't
enough manpower.

\* \* \*

Q. But isn't that almost invariably your experience, that an incident changes the character of a crowd?

A. Was the incident in this case the determination to march to the Ampitheatre? I think generally your statement is a valid one.

Q. Could it not be the gas on Congress Plaza?

A. It could be.

Q. And that after the incident occurred, is it not true then when the character of the crowd changed, as you have indicated with people leaving the park suddenly, as you put it, is it not also true that gas, the use of gas sometimes has a panicking effect on a large crowd?

A. I would say that that is a possibility. It didn't happen in this instance.

**December 2, 1969**

*Continued cross-examination of Government Witness Rochford*

Q. Is it your testimony, finally, Deputy, before this jury, that you were entirely satisfied with the performance of your policemen at the intersection of Michigan and Balbo between 7:45 and 8:15 on the evening of August 28?

A. I'm never satisfied.

Q. And could you indicate to the jury what your particular complaint about your police performance at that time was?

A. Well, my real concern—it's not a complaint. Each and every time we have a police operation, we examine it, we go to the very basic operating level, and we ask for information and evaluation reports. I feel badly and was hurt that people were injured, that in this great city of Chicago this incident occurred in the manner that it did. I have concern for anyone injured. My basic responsibility is to protect life and property.

But after reconsidering all the circumstances and all the information that I had at my fingertips, I could not be too critical of this operation.

\* \* \*

*[During examination of another witness]*

The Court: Do you want to add to those objections, Mr. Weinrob?

Mr. Weinglass: No.

\* \* \*

*[Referring to a prior comment]*

Mr. Kunstler: . . . First of all, with reference to the Ruby situation, I have a particular familiarity with that case. I argued the appeal for Jack Ruby and in that case, your Honor, there was no denial by Jack that he had killed Oswald. That was never an issue in that case.

The Court: You get awfully chummy with your clients.

Mr. Kunstler: Yes, your Honor. After living with them for a while, particularly when a man is on death row, I think it comes a time when it is not Mr. Ruby and Mr. Kunstler. There is a certain intimacy that is bred of these cases.

## December 3, 1969

[*At opening of morning session, out of presence of the jury*]

The Marshal: Your Honor, we are still missing one of the defendants, I believe.

Mr. Weinglass: Yes. I wanted to address the Court on that matter.

I have a note from—signed "Lee Weiner, Boy Defendant," and the note reads—it is dated today. I asked him to write me this note in light of his condition.

"I'm still sick, and following my doctor's advice, I will be staying home in bed, taking medicine, and trying to get better so I can get back to the trial as soon as possible. Of course I want the trial to continue even without my presence because of my illness for the next day or two.

"As we have previously discussed in these circumstances, I waive my rights to be present at the trial and agree to whatever has to be agreed to when one gets sick in the middle of a trial so that the trial may continue." . . .

## December 4, 1969

Mr. Kunstler: . . . The defendants respectfully ask the Court for an adjournment of trial today because of the murder of Fred Hampton early this morning by police officers here in Chicago. We ask this for two reasons: One, out of respect for Mr. Hampton and his dead associate, and two, because the defendants—

The Court: Will you wait just a minute? I have to send a note to somebody who is on the telephone.

You may continue.

Mr. Kunstler (*continuing*): Your Honor, we do it for two reasons: First, out of respect for Mr. Hampton who was the Chairman of the Illinois Chapter of the Black Panther Party and his associate, Mr. Clark, but, secondly, because of the emotional reaction of the defendants to what all of us at the defense table consider to be a wanton murder of an associate of many of us. . . .

It is our considered judgment that this raid searching for guns was staged in order to provoke a shoot-out and the murder of Mr. Hampton in particular and any other Black Panther that could be found in gun sight.

The Court: Why should a thing like that be presented to me?

Mr. Kunstler: We are asking for—

The Court: . . . The so-called Black Panthers, whoever they are, an organization that I have no familiarity with except as the name has been mentioned here on occasions during this trial, is no party to this indictment. . . .

* *

Mr. Kunstler: Your Honor, you are trying a case deliberately designed to destroy and kill dissent in the United States and there is no question of that, and if you want to say to me that this case has nothing to do with the Government's attempt to destroy the Black Panther Party, the Mobilization Committee Against the War in Vietnam and all shades of dissent, you are free to say that.

Of course, that is exactly what Southern judges said, that segregation was not involved in the Freedom Rider thing. We know what is involved.

* * *

The Court: . . . I don't know anything about the so-called Black Panthers. I have no knowledge of them.

Mr. Kunstler: Your Honor, we are never going to resolve that issue between us at this moment.

The Court: I have resolved it.

Mr. Kunstler: We are never going to resolve the issue—

The Court: I have resolved it as not being an issue in this case, sir.

Mr. Kunstler: It is an issue in this case, your Honor.

The Court: An issue here?

Mr. Kunstler: You may say nay, but I think most of the country knows that it is an issue in this case. But that is not the point of what my motion is.

The Court: I don't deal with the country. I deal with the courtroom, sir. I hear a case and the evidence that comes from the witness stand and in documentary form as documents are admitted.

Mr. Kunstler: Your Honor, I have heard this—you know, I tried throughout the South for eight years, and every judge I came before said, "This is not a segregation case; this is a simple breach of the peace."

The Court:   Oh, I have had segregation cases. I had the first one in the North. When I had it, I tried it as a segregation case.

\*    \*    \*

Mr. Kunstler:   Your Honor, we have an emergency motion for a mistrial based on the following facts:

Yesterday in the afternoon session Stuart Albert, who is one of the staff of the defense, was called out of court by a marshal at approximately 4:15 yesterday and the marshal told Mr. Albert who is present in court now that there were two people outside who wanted to speak to him. When he arrived outside, he found four people, one of them who told him he was under arrest, two informed him that they were agents of the Federal Bureau of Investigation.

The two who indicated they were federal agents left the elevator going down at a lower floor and did not go to the station house, police headquarters at 11th and State.

At 11th and State Mr. Albert was taken to the Police Intelligence room where his pockets were emptied. In his pockets were a multitude of documents relating to the defense of this case. Mr. Albert informed them that he was a member of the legal defense staff of the conspiracy and that the information in the documents was privileged and that the Police Intelligence officers have no right to see it, since we felt, as did Mr. Albert, that they were shown by the Police Intelligence officers to the federal officials conducting this trial and who have had intimate relationships, as your Honor knows from the people who have taken the stand here, with members of the Chicago Police Department and particularly with the so-called Red Squad.

The officers at 11th and State said to Mr. Albert, "What is privileged information? What is that?" And then they went through everything.

He was taken to a room where he asked them to return the documents or at least give him a receipt for the documents. They told him that the police were very honest and that he would get it all back. Fifteen minutes later he received back the documents but they had been out of his sight for some fifteen minutes, and it is our feeling that during that time they were photostated or xeroxed by the Chicago Police Department . . .

So I ask either for the mistrial or at least for a hearing by your Honor of what we consider a flagrant breach of our own security and a violation of the laws and the Constitution of the United States.

. . .

The Court:   The motion of the defendants, Mr. Clerk, for a mistrial will be denied, as will the alternative motion of the defendants.

Bring in the jury.

*Cross-examination of Government Witness Richard Braithwaite, a Chicago police officer, by Mr. Kunstler*

Q. Up to that time—up to the time you saw the police between 11:00 and 11:30, had you made any other arrests?

A. No, sir.

Q. Now, you did see what you have described as a couple making love in a tree, did you not?

A. I did.

Q. You saw them having intercourse in a tree, isn't that correct?

A. Yes, sir.

Q. And that was what kind of a tree, do you remember?

A. I don't know what kind of a tree it was, sir.

Q. You're sure you hadn't wandered into the zoo?

A. Quite sure.

Q. Did you arrest those people?

A. No, sir.

Q. In fact, you went right under the tree and you gazed up, isn't that correct?

A. No, sir. I was under—

Q. You weren't under the tree looking up?

A. I was under the tree. I didn't walk under. I was under there at the time.

Q. And then suddenly your attention was called to the fact that someone was making love over your head, is that correct?

A. This is right.

Q. And you looked up?

A. I did.

Q. How long did you look?

A. Two seconds.

Q. And then you walked on about your business, is that correct?

A. Yes, sir.

. . .

Q. Were you worried about their safety?

A. No, sir.

. . .

Q. Now when you went to Lincoln Park on the 26th of August, did you know that Abbie Hoffman was going to be there?

A. No, sir, I didn't.

Q. Did you ever see him before that time?

A. No. I hadn't.

Q. Did you ever see any pictures of him?

A. Not that I recall.

Q. Can you describe what he looked like when you first saw him?

A. Not really, other than the wild hair and the nose which impressed me.

Q. The nose impressed you?

A. Yes, sir.

Q. In what way did the nose impress you?

A. Its size.

   The Court:  You asked for that, Mr. Kunstler.

   Mr. Kunstler:  I am not objecting, your Honor. A nose is a nose is a nose.


## December 5, 1969

*Cross-examination of Government Witness Albert H. Baugher, Assistant Director for the Division of Community Service, Department of Human Resources, in Chicago, by Mr. Kunstler [Concerning a meeting between Abbie Hoffman, Chicago Deputy Mayor Stahl, and the witness]*

Q. Did Abbie Hoffman indicate—state to you at that meeting that Spiro Agnew had offered him $200,000 to come to Chicago? Did that come up?

A. I don't recall that, sir. He might have.

Q. Did you laugh when he said that?

. . .

Q. At any time did you or Deputy Mayor Stahl contact Spiro Agnew and ask him whether he had made a serious offer of $200,000?

   Mr. Foran:  Your Honor. I object to that, and I ask Mr. Kunstler to refrain from playing to his gallery.

   Mr. Kunstler:  Your Honor, I think he said he took a serious offer, and he said Abbie Hoffman might have said Spiro Agnew offered him $200,000 to come to Chicago, and I asked whether he contacted Spiro Agnew.

   The Court:  I would ask that you don't waste our time. I sustain the objection, sir.

. . .

Q. Now, you indicated that it was sometime around this time, that you met Lee Weiner, is that correct?

A. Yes, sir.

Q. And about what time was that?

A. Four o'clock, five o'clock.
Q. I think you describe the conversation something like this. You said you said, "Hi," right?
A. Something to that effect, "Hello."

. . .

Q. . . . Mr. Rubin then said, "Fascist pig"?
A. Yes, sir.
Q. Did he say "Hi" first?
A. No, sir.
Q. And then I think you resorted to a classic American expression, "Shove it."
A. I believe so, sir, yes.

\* \* \*

[*On direct examination, regarding a conversation with Abbie Hoffman*]
Q. What was the conversation?
A. Mr. Hoffman approached me, and we talked generally for a while. He gave me a copy of a booklet which he had printed in New York called "Fuck the System," which he said he was giving me free. He said that the city of New York had paid for it through an OEO grant that they had received from the city.

He then suggested that Chicago would be wise to co-operate, that they had first run into trouble in New York. I think he mentioned the Grand Central Station incident in March and said that since that time the city had been very cooperative and there had been no trouble, and they've gotten this money just to keep things cool.
Q. Did he give any explanation of how they got the money or for what purpose?
A. He said that they had applied for a grant of venereal disease clinic, to the best of my recollection, and that they had used the money to print the booklet which had a small part on venereal disease, operate a free store, and use the money whichever way they saw fit.

**December 8, 1969**
*Extend arguments by opposing counsel on defense contention that the Government had failed in its affirmative duty to prove the defendants guilty beyond a reasonable doubt, thus obviating the need for the defendants to present their evidence*
Mr. Kunstler: . . . The main statute involved is 2101 and the defendants are accused of a conspiracy to travel in interstate commerce, to use the facilities of interstate commerce, with an intent to incite a riot and commit acts of violence in connection with or furtherance of such a riot and to aid and

abet persons in committing acts of violence in furtherance of a riot, and to perform certain overt acts in furtherance thereof. . . .

Conspiracies are what Learned Hand called the "Darling of the Prosecutor's Nursery," because in so many cases, the courts have permitted conspiracies to be proved by a bootstrap operation. The Government proves only acts of the defendants, and then lets the jury presume or speculate that the defendants must have met and must have conspired together else these acts would not have occurred. This is what I have termed a bootstrap operation. This is the reason that conspiracy prosecutions have been so favored by the Government and no more favored than in what I have called in the past political cases. . . .

Conspiracies are so easy to prove in the general sense because you don't have to prove anything. You never have had to prove the conspiracy in the routine case; all you have to prove is that the defendants had committed certain acts or one or two of them did and that they had some access to each other. Therefore this is why conspiracy is so often used, particularly in cases like this.

The crime of conspiracy evolved in the court of star chamber crime as we know it today. It was formulated in the court of star chamber and used by that infamous court in order to prove in political cases primarily that acts of a certain type meant there must be agreement. But when you get into the type of case we have before your Honor, we are no longer in the routine conspiracy case . . . We are in the case of a so-called conspiracy in the First Amendment area . . . and the Government must be held to a standard of strictissimi juris which means that they must have established a prima facie case in the light of the rule of strictissimi juris—that is, they must be held to the strictest standard of the law in so establishing such a case.

\* \*

In this particular case where we have a statute which is so suspect itself and and which does involve First Amendment rights to an enormous degree, I don't think there is a legal scholar in the United States who, reading the statutes, would not say that it raises First Amendment problems. . . .

. [T]he use or the evidence of public meetings, what they call mere public meetings, are not enough to prove a conspiracy. . . . Well, that is what we have in this case. You have mere meetings, all open. . . .

These defendants or some of them, according to the proof submitted in this case, were meeting in Lincoln Park, in Grant

101

Park, speaking to thousands of people from platforms in both places They had open meetings in the Mobilization office, in Noble Hall and elsewhere. These were meetings at which anyone could walk in and anyone did, as the evidence indicates, everyone from informers to people who were training as marshals to the press .

. That doesn t mean, of course, that every conspiracy has to be done in the dead of night in a room three floors underneath the street level Everyone realizes that. . . . But where you have open air meetings, the law requires something else . .

. [T]here is nothing illegal about giving a speech There is nothing illegal about conducting a self-defense marshals' session There is nothing illegal about meeting in the Mobilization office or anywhere else. In fact, it is very difficult to find a single illegal act here attributable to any defendant. It is highly remarkable that in all of the illegality which was put on allegedly committed in Chicago, that with two exceptions you have no arrests of any defendant. . . .

\* \* \*

. . . If anything, the Government has proved one thing in presentation of its evidence. that it has put together a mass of meetings, mainly public, a mass of speeches, all of which were public, a mass of statements in an earnest effort to prove that the defendants in this case committed some sort of a crime.

What they have really proved is essentially what we have argued throughout this case. What they have really proved is that the Government of the United States is out by any means necessary to destroy the First Amendent to the Constitution, and I think in that they have succeeded in so proving, and your Honor's judgment of acquittal granting our motion will be, I think, a refreshing breath of air in what is a case which has such onerous possibilities and dangers for the right of free speech in the United States.

\* \* \*

[*Mr. Schultz, responding to Mr Kunstler's argument*]
Mr. Schultz. . . . First, with regard to Count I. Mr. Kunstler has argued Count I. and Mr Kunstler said that the Government had failed to prove an agreement He said that that was the basic thing that we had failed to prove. He did not analyze in any way what the evidence was regarding an agreement. He just made the statement I propose to just very, very briefly. in a matter of a few minutes. go through some

of the meetings in the evidence which do establish an agreement.

The first one would be August 9, which is the first marshals' meeting where we had a meeting with Davis, Hoffman, Hayden, Weiner, Dellinger, and Froines present at the meeting in planning the marshal activities, and their programs for the demonstrations during the Convention. [The defendants] talked about having a mill-in, disrupting traffic, running through stores, streets and setting fire alarms off, setting small fires, stopping people from moving around in the Loop. They discussed that. They discussed holding Lincoln Park. The Defendant Hoffman said the Yippies would aid in the diversionary tactics on the 28th, and he wanted the park held by the marshals. They discussed building barricades in the park if they were ever unable to leave it. They discussed at that meeting having a march to the Amphitheatre, knowing all the dangers involved. In unison, they were discussing their plans.

. . .

Mr. Kunstler touched on none of them [the meetings—ed.]. The point is the defendants prior to the Convention and during the Convention were meeting together, discussing together their plans, what they were going to do. It was very difficult to have absolute, concrete plans because you don't know what the police are going to do. They had alternative plans, many of them, which the evidence has shown were carried out, and many were not. They were together. They were the organizers of the demonstrators. They were bringing the demonstrators here, and these were some of the discussions they had relating to plans of violence and acts that would result in riots during the Convention . . .

\* \*

. . . I think the last point that I want to comment on, because I think I have covered all of the points that were raised, the last point that I want to comment on is Mr. Kunstler's statement that the Government by this prosecuion, by any means necessary, is trying to destroy the First Amendment. . . .

. . . We have the obligation to prove the statements of incitement to riot like "Get them. Kill them," right in the middle of a riot or just before a riot, which certainly are not statements protected by the First Amendment. We have proven these statements over and over again and are in no way—in any way emasculating the First Amendment right. The rights that we are—I don't think there is anybody who says that the First Amendment protects those kinds of speeches. . . .

. .

Mr Kunstler: . . . Now with reference to the last point

103

raised by Mr. Schultz, the destruction of First Amendent, I don't think that there is any need for me to comment further on that except to indicate . . .that what really is the victim and the intended victim is dissent against Governmental policies with reference to racism, the war in Vietnam, poverty, and youth culture . . .

[*Ruling of the Court, and explanation*]

The Court:   As has been said here by one of the lawyers for the defendants, the Court must at this time for the purposes of the motion made for a judgment of acquittal consider the evidence most favorably to the Government. That is not to say that there might [not] later be introduced or rather offered and admitted into evidence proof that might conclusively dissipate the effect of some of the evidence of the Government.

But at this time, Mr. Clerk, the several oral motions made by the respective defendants, through their attorneys, Mr. Kunstler and Mr. Weinglass, for a judgment of acquittal at the close of the Government's case in chief will be denied. We will expect the defense to go forward with its evidence at two o'clock, at which time, the Court has already directed the jury to return.

# III

# Case for the Defense

Transcript pages 97-64-20430

Officer of the Court:

> THEREUPON the defendants, to main-
> tain the issues in their behalf, presented
> the following evidence, to-wit:

[With these words the case for the defense officially begins.
In the ensuing pages you will read the highlights of that presentation. We remind the reader that the dialogue which follows
is the verbatim language of the participants in the trial—ed.]

*[Argument by Defense Attorney Kunstler urging admis-
sion into evidence of "Dissent and Disorder," a report on
the April 27, 1968, peace parade in Chicago]*

Mr. Kunstler: . . .The reason for that, your Honor, is that
the document then came to the attention of these defendants
and indicated that the police were brutal in their treatment of
demonstrators on April 27, 1968. Whether that is true or not
is immaterial. . . . [T]hey would then make necessary prepa-
rations for medical help and the use of helmets, and the like—
and the use of vaseline for Mace which the report found was
used by the police on demonstrators.

The purpose of this, of course, is to show the reason or
motivation of the defendants in utilizing certain defense tactics in preparation for the August march. . . . They talked
about wearing helmets and the like, which, if taken in one way
might mean they were there for offense instead of defense, but
if they were influenced by the report, that would go to their
motivation in taking those defensive measures.

Therefore, introducing the document not for the truth of
it but to show the influence it had on the defendants would be
vital for the defense case. . . .

\* \* \*

*Direct examination of Edward Sparling, a member of the commission which wrote the report mentioned above, by Mr. Kunstler*

Mr. Kunstler: Your Honor, we are not going to be permitted to have this witness introduce the report?

The Court: That is my ruling.

Mr. Kunstler: Is your Honor—I just don't understand it. The hearsay rule is—

The Court: You will have to see a lawyer, Mr. Kunstler, if you don't understand it.

Mr. Kunstler: I don't understand it. I wish you would explain it to me.

The Court: I am not obligated to sit up here and to compel a lawyer to understand it. I am here to rule according to law of evidence.

Mr. Kunstler: Your Honor—

The Court: I will rule accordingly, sir. Ask your next question.

Mr. Kunstler: You won't let me question this man. I have no questions. What can I do?

The Court: You have no further questions?

Mr. Kunstler: What can I do? I can't have him testify.

The Court: I know what you can do. Is there any cross-examination?

\* \* \*

Mr. Kunstler: Your Honor, might we have a brief recess? We expected—

The Court: No, no recess. We just started.

Mr. Kunstler: Let me finish my statement.

The Court: We are not going to have a recess when we just started.

Mr. Kunstler: We expected this man to be able to testify before this jury.

The Court: You are an accomplished and experienced lawyer. You know that you must anticipate that a court might rule against you on occasion.

Mr. Kunstler: When the law is this clear, we did not think it would be ruled against us.

The Court: More than ever now. You may call your next witness.

Mr. Kunstler: We need time, your Honor, in any event.

The Court: Call your next witness.

Mr. Kunstler: Your Honor—

The Court: I have waited for these defendants, and I have waited for counsel to come in here. Call your next witness.

Mr. Kunstler: Let me finish my statement. I am not going

to call anyone unless you let me finish my statement. My statement is we need some time to set up a projector.

The Court: Why didn't you say so. You said you needed some time to call your next witness. If your next witness is a projector, I will give you time to set it up. . . .

**December 9, 1969**

*[Following Court's refusal to allow Mr. Kunstler to leave the courtroom to speak to a newly arrived witness]*

Mr. Kunstler: . . . Then, your Honor, I am going to have the witness come to the counsel table and sit with the attorneys.

The Court: You are not going to have witnesses at the counsel table.

Mr. Kunstler: Your Honor, how can you be so inhumane as to not permit the lawyers to sit with the witnesses? I just don't understand it. It is with the consent of the defendants.

The Court: That is a very serious word to apply to a judge and I make a special ruling—

Mr. Foran: Your Honor, there is a motion to exclude witnesses from this courtroom that was made by that man a long time ago.

Mr. Kunstler: I am not "that man," Mr. Foran. I have a name, William M. Kunstler.

Mr. Foran: Do you really? Do you really?

Mr. Kunstler: And use my name. You use my name when you call me and not "that man."

Mr. Foran: What I think of calling you I won't say before ladies.

**December 10, 1969**

*Conversation between the Court and Defense Witness Anne Kerr, a member of Parliament*

The Court: Just a minute, please. What do they call a member of Parliament in England? I want to address you properly.

The Witness: Just call me Anne.

The Court: Well, now, we call our Senators here Senator. We call our Congressmen, Congressman.

The Witness: You can call me the Honorable Member for Rochester and Chatham.

The Court: That is a little long. I will just have to call you Madame Witness. Read her last answer.

The Witness: I was trying to make it easy for you.

The Court: Don't make it easy for me. That is not your responsibility.

The Witness: Mine is to tell the truth.

\* \* \*

107

*Direct examination of Defense Witness Sarah Diamant, a teaching fellow at Cornell University, by Defense Attorney Weinglass*

Q. Can you describe for the jury how they felt after the Macing?

A. My eyes and the skin all around the top of my face were burning. I tried—I put my hand up because it hurt, and, you know, sort of clawed at it, and a boy took my hand away and said, "Don't touch it." I realized what he meant because the moment I put my hand on the skin and pulled it down, the burning followed my hand right down my face, and I wanted to throw up, and I couldn't, I just kept gagging.

\* \* \*

The Court: . . . The film is offered as Defendants' 145 for identification. I don't know what five minutes means. You say you are going to edit something. Actually you are not offering what was shown, isn't that true?

Mr. Weinglass: No. The Government used this procedure with many of its films. We went back and we edited out—

The Court: I wish you would confine your reply to me to the question I am asking about now, not what the Government did.

Mr. Weinglass: Well, in making my reply—

The Court: I am asking you whether you offered Defendants' Exhibit 145 for identification.

Mr. Weinglass: When I make my answer to the Court I borrow on what has gone before in this case with the expectation that the same rules will apply to us in that area.

The Court: Don't borrow on that. Your credit isn't good in that area. . . .

. . .

Mr. Foran: Your Honor, if we could edit that film to eliminate the kind of title scenes, those line drawings and those individual pictures like the shot of a poster which I think is purely editorial and comment. The shot of the young man who looks like either Christ or Joshua, depending on which side we are standing on here.

The Court: I so hoped you would say Moses.

Mr. Foran: All right, Judge, I will throw in Moses.

If we could edit out those things, the Government would have no objection.

. . .

Mr. Foran: We will limit it [our objection—ed.] to the poster shot of Mayor Daley. That should go out. That is editorial and comment.

Mr. Weinglass: Another Biblical figure.

*Continued cross-examination of Defense Witness Diamant*

Q. Well, from the time that the Poor People's wagon went through the police line, there were continuous chants from the crowd?

A. That is right.

Q. And did you hear anything of those chants?

A. Sure.

Q. Do you remember what they were?

. . .

A. They were yelling, "Dump the Humph," which I think referred to Hubert Humphrey.

Then there was, I am trying to remember what the "LBJ" one was. It wasn't that. "Hey, hey, LBJ, how many kids did you kill today?"

\* \* \*

*Direct examination of Defense Witness Phil Ochs, folksinger, by Mr. Kunstler*

Mr. Foran: Your Honor, may we refer to the defendants by their proper names so we will have a proper identification in the record?

The Court: Yes.

Mr. Kunstler: I think Mr. Hoffman has dropped his last name

The Court: What did you say?

Mr. Kunstler: I think that Mr. Hoffman has dropped his last name as a protest against this court.

The Court: He will have to do that in law. Here he is indicted as Abbie Hoffman. I know that he said that in court, Mr. Kunstler, but his mere saying of that doesn't deprive him of a last name.

Mr. Kunstler: I know, but legally, your Honor, there is no requirement that you do have a formal change of name at all. A person can drop his last name.

The Court: That is not an issue here. I do not share your view about that, but I think I will ask you to refer to your clients by their surnames.

Mr. Kunstler: All right, I will rephrase the question, to change Abbie and Jerry to Abbie Hoffman and Jerry Rubin.

\* \* \*

*[Concerning testimony describing events occurring in February, 1968]*

Mr. Foran: I object to that for about a dozen—

Late winter of '68 was after the Convention. The rest of the question was leading and suggestive.

Mr. Kunstler: Late winter of '68 was after the Convention? I don't understand that.

The Court: When was the Convention?

Mr. Kunstler: The Convention was in the summer of '68, so late winter of '68 would seem to me to be before August of '68.

Mr. Rubin: February.

The Court: I don't get that, Mr. Kunstler.

Mr. Kunstler: Your Honor, late winter and early spring of '68 indicate the winter of '67-'68.

I will rephrase it.

The Court: You didn't say '67.

Mr. Kunstler: I will rephrase the question.

The Court: You said "late winter of '68." Late winter of '68 means to me from September 21 to December 31. That is winter.

Mr. Kunstler: I think that is fall.

The Court: What do you say? Through December 31, isn't that winter?

Mr. Kunstler: Well, winter starts on December 21, but I will rephrase the question.

The Court: All right. At any rate you have got your dates wrong.

\* \* \*

[*Concerning a speech by Defendant Rubin in Chicago's Civic Center*]

Q. To the best of your recollection, what did he say?

A. Something to the effect, "Why take half a hog when you can have the whole thing?" He announced the pig's name, pigasis. He said—the opening sentence was something like "I, pigasis, hereby announce my candidacy for the Presidency of the United States." He was interrupted in his talk by the police who arrested us.

Q. What was the pig doing during this announcement?

Mr. Foran: Objection.

\* \* \*

The Court: If you think I should tell the jury why this witness was directed to leave the stand, I will do it.

Mr. Kunstler: I think they would be confused when the defense puts a witness up on the stand—

The Court: Oh, trust me. You use that word so often. I shall not confuse the jury, Mr. Kunstler. Don't worry about it.

Mr. Kunstler: Your Honor, every remark you take as a personal affront. I am not saying that you would confuse them. I think without an explanation they would be confused.

\* \* \*

Mr. Schultz:   [Speaking to the Court] . . . [I]f you would simply tell the witness to listen carefully to the question so he can answer the questions, so we can move on to something else.

The Court:   I did that this morning. You are a singer, but you are a smart fellow, I am sure.

The Witness:   Thank you very much. You are a judge and you are a smart fellow.

\*    \*    \*

The Court:   I note some finger pointing by the Defendant Rubin.

Mr. Weiner:   No.

The Court:   Defendant Weiner. I called you by your right name, didn't I, that time?

Mr. Weiner:   Thank you.

The Court:   No more of that, sir.

Mr. Kunstler:   Your Honor, I think the record should also indicate for the last few interchanges, there has been laughter in the court joined in by the Court.

The Court:   Laughter has nothing to do with what I was talking about.

Mr. Kunstler:   We have a lot of defendants here who have been accused of laughter.

\*    \*    \*

Q. . . . Now would you stand and sing that song so the jury can hear the song that the audience heard that day?

Mr. Schultz:   If the Court please, this is a trial in the Federal District Court. It is not a theater. The jury is sequestered. We don't want to take too much time. We don't have to sit and listen to the witness sing a song. Let's get on with the trial. Let's get to the issues and let's try to get through with the case.

I object.

Mr. Kunstler:   Your Honor, this is definitely an issue in the case. Jerry Rubin has asked for a particular song to be sung.

The Court:   And the witness has testified that he sang it.

Mr. Kunstler:   Right. But the point is that there has been testimony in this court that Jerry Rubin gave an inflammatory speech to a group of people at that audience during that day and this is one of the acts which the Government has laid before this jury. What he asked the witness to sing and what he sang to the audience reflects both on his intent and on the mood of the crowd. . . .

\*    \*    \*

Q. Mr. Ochs, I would then ask you to recite to the jury the words which you sang on that day to the audience."

111

A. The words? Okay. . . .

"It is always the old to lead us to the wars; it is always the young to fall. Now look at all we've won with the sabre and the gun. Tell me, is it worth it all?"

. . .

"Now the labor leaders screaming when they close a missile plant; United Fruit screams at the Cuban shore. Call it peace or call it treason, call it love or call it reason, but I ain't marching any more. No, I ain't marching any more."

\* \* \*

*Cross-examination of Mr. Ochs by Mr. Schultz*

Q. Now, in your plans for Chicago, did you plan for public fornication in the park?

A. I didn't.

Q. No, I am talking about your plans. In your discussions with either Rubin or Hoffman, did you plan for public fornication in the park?

A. That might have been a phrase. I mean, no, we did not seriously sit down and plan public fornication in the park.

. . .

Q. And at those discussions did you—when I say the word "you" I mean you people who were participating in the discussion—you is used in the plural—did you at the discussion discuss having nude-ins at the beaches on Lake Michigan?

A. I think that was mentioned.

Q. At the same discussions did you discuss body painting?

A. I think that was mentioned.

\* \* \*

Mr. Schultz:   He was holding back a laugh. I thought that either I was very homely and he was laughing at me or I said something that was amusing to him. I wanted to know.

Mr. Kunstler:   Mr. Ochs is a very gentle man, Mr. Schultz, and he will not laugh at your face.

\* \* \*

Q. Were you also told there was an exclusion of witness rule in this court and that the testimony of prior witnesses—

A. No, I wasn't told anything like that.

Q. You weren't told that. Who told you all these things?

A. Mr. Kunstler told me the one thing, not all these things, the one thing I said which I repeated, that—something that Jerry was accused of something in the park on Sunday night and that's all I was told, nothing else.

Q. You are certain of that?

112

A. Yes.

Q. You don't want to get Mr. Kunstler into trouble, do you?

Mr. Kunstler: Your Honor, first of all—

Mr. Schultz: Suddenly he backs off—suddenly he backs off. It is too patent, your Honor.

Mr. Kunstler: Your Honor, that is the most flagrant statement I have heard in the courtroom. He is sitting in front of this jury—

The Court: Will the record show that Mr. Kunstler—

Mr. Kunstler: Yes, I did, your Honor. I think it is a disgraceful statement in front of a jury.

The Court: —threw a block of papers noisily to the floor.

Mr. Kunstler: All right. I dropped papers noisily to the floor.

The Court: I shall not hear from you in that tone, sir.

. . .

Mr. Kunstler: I am sorry for putting the paper on the table and it fell off onto the floor, but I still repeat that his statement—First of all, I didn't object to his going into discussing with a lawyer—what a lawyer is discussing with a prospective witness. The witness has told him what we discussed. But then to say in front of a jury "that is too patent" and "what are you backing off for?" — I think, your Honor, any court in the land would hold that that is unconscionable conduct and I think we are entitled to a direction to the jury that Mr. Schultz is admonished, and if I am angry, I think I am righteously so in this instance.

Mr. Schultz: Your Honor, I don't think my statement was that improper, but I move to withdraw the statement as it apparently offends Mr. Kunstler greatly. . . .

\* \* \*

Mr. Kunstler: The episode is not over, your Honor. I am not offended. I am angry, that is true, but I am not offended personally. I have an obligation as does Mr. Weinglass to certain clients, and we have an obligation when the United States Attorney makes an improper remark which he has wisely withdrawn in front of this jury—I think you ought to do something about it.

The Court: I don't permit a lawyer's obligation to clients, as he puts it, to act as you have acted.

Mr. Kunstler: Oh, your Honor, I got angry for a moment. Your Honor has gotten angry, too.

The Court: Oh, not angry. I have taken you to task when you deserved it.

Mr. Kunstler: I know, your Honor, but I am taking the

U. S. Attorney to task when he deserves it, and I ask your Honor to do that for me.

The Court. You haven't any authority to.

Mr. Kunstler: I know. That is why I have to ask your Honor. We have no alternative. I can't do it

\* \* \*

*Direct examination of Defense Witness Allen Ginsberg, poet, by Mr. Weinglass*

Q. Could you indicate for the Court and jury what the area of your studies consisted of?

A. Mantra Yoga, meditation exercises, chanting, and sitting quietly, stilling the mind and breathing exercises to calm the body and to calm the mind, but mainly a branch called Mantra Yoga, which is a yoga which involves prayer and chanting.

\* \* \*

Q. Now, calling your attention to the month of February 1968, did you have occasion in that month to meet with Abbie Hoffman?

A. Yeah.

. . .

Q. Do you recall what Mr. Hoffman said in the course of that conversation?

A. Yippie—among other things. He said that politics had become theater and magic; that it was the manipulation of imagery through mass media that was confusing and hypnotizing the people in the United States and making them accept a war which they did not really believe in; that people were involved in a life style which was intolerable to the younger folk, which involved brutality and police violence as well as a larger violence in Vietnam, and that ourselves might be able to get together in Chicago and invite teachers to present different ideas of what is wrong with the planet, what we can do to solve the pollution crisis, what we can do to solve the Vietnam war, to present different ideas for making the society more sacred and less commercial, less materialistic, what we could do to uplevel or improve the whole tone of the trap that we all felt ourselves in as the population grew and as politics became more and more violent and chaotic.

\* \* \*

Q. After he spoke to you, what, if anything, was your response to his suggestion?

A. I was worried as to whether or not the whole scene would get violent. I was worried whether we would be allowed

114

to put on such a situation. I was worried whether, you know, the Government would let us do something that was funnier or prettier or more charming than what was going to be going on in the convention hall.

\* \* \*

Q. Would you explain what your statement was.

A. My statement was that the planet Earth at the present moment was endangered by violence, overpopulation, pollution, ecological destruction brought about by our own greed; that the younger children in America and other countries of the world might not survive the next 30 years, that it was a planetary crisis that had not been recognized by any government of the world . . . [T]he more selfish elder politicians . . . were not thinking in terms of what their children would need in future generations or even in the generation immediately coming or even for themselves in their own life-time and were continuing to threaten the planet with violence, with war, with mass murder, with germ warfare. . . . The desire for preservation of the planet and the planet's form, that we do continue to be, to exist on this planet instead of destroy the planet, was manifested to my mind by the great Mantra from India to the preserver God Vishnu whose Mantra is Hare Krishna, and then I chanted the Hare Krishna Mantra for ten minutes to the television cameras and it goes:

"Hare Krishna, Hare Krishna, Krishna, Krishna, Hare, Hare, Rama, Hare, Rama, Rama, Rama, Hare, Hare."

\* \* \*

Mr. Kunstler: Your Honor, I object to the laughter of the Court on this. I think this is a serious presentation of a religious concept.

The Court: I don't understand it. I don't understand it because it was—the language of the United States District Court is English.

Mr. Kunstler: I know, but you don't laugh at all languages.

The Witness: I would be glad to explain it, sir.

The Court: I didn't laugh. I didn't laugh.

The Witness: I would be happy to explain it.

The Court: I didn't laugh at all. I wish I could tell you how I feel. Laugh, I didn't even smile.

. . .

Mr. Foran: Your Honor, of course the laughter came from everybody that Mr. Kunstler is usually defending for laughing.

115

Mr. Kunstler: Your Honor, I would say—You mean from the press?

The Witness: Might we go on to an explanation.

The Court: Will you keep quiet, Mr. Witness, while I am talking to the lawyers?

* * *

Q. Mr. Ginsberg, I show you an object marked 150 for identification, and I ask you to examine that object.

A. Yes.

Mr. Foran: All right.

Your Honor, that is enough. I object to it, your Honor. I think that it is outrageous for counsel to—

The Court: You asked him to examine it and instead of that he played a tune on it.

Mr. Foran: I mean, counsel is so clearly—

The Court: I sustain the objection.

Mr. Foran: —talking about things that have no conceivable materiality to this case, and it is improper, your Honor.

The Witness: It adds spirituality to this case, sir.

**December 12, 1969**

*Continued direct testimony of Defense Witness Allen
Ginsberg by Defense Attorney Weinglass*

Q. Did you hear the defendant, Jerry Rubin, say anything at this meeting?

A. Jerry Rubin said that he didn't think the police would attack the kids who were in the park at night if there were enough kids there, that he didn't think it would be a good thing to fight over the park if the police started fighting with the kids, if the police attacked the kids and tried to drive them out of the park as the police had announced at 11 o'clock, that as far as he was concerned, he wanted to leave the park at 9:00 and would not encourage anybody to fight and get hurt that evening if the police did physically try to force every-body out of the park. That was on Saturday night, the first night when the people would be in the park.

* *

Q. Did the defendant, Abbie Hoffman, say anything at this meeting?

A. Abbie Hoffman said the park wasn't worth fighting for, that we had on our responsibility invited many thou-sands of kids to Chicago for a happy festival of life, for an alternative proposition to the festival of death that the politicians were putting on, and that it wasn't right to lead them or encourage them to get into a violent

116

argument with the police over staying in the park overnight. He didn't know, he said he didn't know what to say to those who wanted to stay and fight for what they felt was their liberty, but he wasn't going to encourage anybody to fight, and he was going to leave when forced himself.

. . .

Q. Now, do you recall what, if anything, occurred at 10:30?
A. There was a sudden burst of lights in the center of the park, and a group of policemen moved in fast to where the bonfires were and kicked over the bonfires.
Q. That what—
A. There was a great deal of consternation and movement and shouting among the crowd in the park, and I turned, surprised, because it was early. . . .

. . .

Q. Without relating what you said to another person, Mr. Ginsberg, what did you do at the time you saw the police do this?
A. I started the chant, O-o-m-m-m-m-m-m-m, O-o-m-m-m-m-m-m.

Mr. Foran:    All right, we have had a demonstration.
The Court:    All right.
Mr. Foran:    From here on, I object.
The Court:    You haven't said that you objected.
Mr. Foran:    I do after the second one.
The Court:    After two of them? I sustain the objection.

\*    \*

Mr. Weinglass:   If the Court please, there has been much testimony by the Government's witnesses as to this Om technique which was used in the park. Are we only going to hear whether there were stones or people throwing things, or shouting things, or using obscenities? Why do we draw the line here? Why can't we also hear what is being said in the area of calming the crowd?

Mr. Foran:   I have no objection to the two Om's that we have had. However, I just didn't want it to go on all morning.

\*    \*    \*

*By Mr. Weinglass*
Q. Did you finish your answer?
A. I am afraid I will be in contempt if I continue to Om. . . .

. . .

Q. What did you do when you saw the policemen in the center of the crowd?
A. Adrenalin ran through my body. I sat down on a green hillside with a group of younger people that were walk-

117

ing with me at about 3:30 in the afternoon, 4 o'clock,
sat, crossed my leg and began chanting O-o-m—O-o-m-
m-m, O-o-m-m-m, O-o-m-m-m.

Mr. Foran:  I gave him four that time.

The Witness:  I continued chanting for seven hours.

Mr. Weinglass:  I am sorry, I did not hear the answer.

The Court:  He said he continued chanting for seven hours.
Seven hours, was it, sir?

The Witness:  Until 10:30.

The Court:  I wanted to know what your answer was. Did
you say you continued chanting for seven hours?

The Witness:  Seven hours, yes.

. . .

Q. Now, when you left the Coliseum, where, if anywhere, did
you go?

A. The group I was with, Mr. Genet, Mr. Burroughs and
Mr. Seaver, and Terry Southern, all went back to
Lincoln Park.

Q. What time did you arrive in the park?

A. 11:00, 11:30.

Q. What was occurring at the park as you got there?

A. There was a great crowd lining the outskirts of the park
and a little way into the park on the inner roads, and
there was a larger crowd moving in toward the center.
We all moved in toward the center and at the center
of the park, there was a group of ministers and rabbis
who had elevated a great cross about ten-foot high in
the middle of a circle of people who were sitting around,
quietly, listening to the ministers conduct a ceremony.

. . .

Q. After the ministers moved the cross to another location
which you have indicated, what happened?

A. After, I don't know, a short period of time, there was a
burst of smoke and tear gas around the cross, and the
cross was enveloped with tear gas, and the people who
were carrying the cross were enveloped with tear gas
which began slowly drifting over the crowd.

. . .

Q. And when you saw the persons with the cross and the cross
being gassed, what if anything did you do?

A. I turned to Burroughs and said, "They have gassed the
cross of Christ."

Mr. Foran:  Objection, if the Court please. I ask that the
answer be stricken.

The Court:  I sustain the objection.

*By Mr. Weinglass:*

118

Q. Without relating what you said, Mr. Ginsberg, what did you do at that time?

A. I took Bill Burroughs' hand and took Terry Southern's hand, and we turned from the cross which was covered with gas in the glary lights that were coming from the police lights that were shining through the tear gas on the cross, and walked slowly out of the park.

. . .

Q. Do you recall when in the course of the rally you heard Mr. Abolafia speak?

A. Oh, I think toward the end of the rally before the formation of the parade.

Q. Was he introduced?

A. No, he just appeared from nowhere and got up to the microphone and started yelling into it.

Q. Do you recall hearing what he was yelling?

A. "The police out there are armed and violent. You are walking into a death trap."

Q. When you heard him yelling that over the microphone, what, if anything, did you do?

A. I went down and sat next to him and grabbed his leg and started tickling him and said, "Hare Krishna, Louis." . . .

. . .

Q. How were you walking?

A. Slowly.

Q. Were your arms—

A. Our arms were all linked together and we were carrying flowers. Someone had brought flowers up to the back of the stage and so we distributed them around to the first rows of marchers so all of the marchers had flowers.

Q. Now how far did you walk?

. . .

A. We came to a halt in front of a large guard of armed human beings in uniform who were blocking our way, people with machine guns, jeeps, I believe, police, and what looked to me like soldiers on our side and in front of us.

Q. And what happened at that point?

A. Mr. Dellinger—the march stopped and we waited, not quite knowing what to do. I heard—all along I had heard Dave Dellinger saying, "This is a peaceful march. All those who want to participate in a peaceful march please join our line. All those who are not peaceful, please go away and don't join our line." . . .

. . .

Q. Now, Mr. Ginsberg, you have indicated you have known Jerry Rubin since 1965?

A. Yes.

Q. Would you indicate to the Court and jury whether or not you have ever seen him smoke a cigarette?

A. I don't remember.

The Court:     I didn't hear the answer.

Miss Reporter, will you read the answer.

*(Answer read)*

*By Mr. Weinglass:*

Q. I mean a tobacco cigarette.

\* \* \*

*Cross-examination of Defense Witness Ginsberg by Government Attorney Foran*

Q. Now when you went out to the Coliseum and you met Abbie Hoffman, you said when you met him you kissed him?

A. Yes.

Q. Is he an intimate friend of yours?

A. I felt very intimate with him. I saw he was struggling to manifest a beautiful thing, and I felt very good towards him.

Q. And you do consider him an intimate friend of yours?

A. I don't see him that often, but I see him often enough and have worked with him often enough to feel intimate with him, yes.

\* \* \*

Q. I call your attention to page 32 of that exhibit. Does that have on page 32 the poem, "The Night-Apple"?

A. Yes.

Q. When you look at that page, Mr. Ginsberg, does it refresh your recollection of the poem, itself?

A. Yes. I wrote it in 1950. That was nineteen years ago. It still looks good.

Q. After refreshing your recollection, Mr. Ginsberg, could you recite that poem to the jury?

A. Yes. "The Night-Apple."

> "Last night I dreamed
> of one I loved
> for seven long years,
> but I saw no face,
> only the familiar
> presence of the body:
> sweat skin eyes
> faces urine sperm
> saliva all one
> odor and mortal taste."

120

Q. Could you explain to the jury what the religious significance of that poem is?
A. If you would take a wet dream as a religious experience, I
could. It is a description of a wet dream, sir.

\* \* \*

*[During direct examination of Defense Witness William
Styron, an author, by Mr. Kunstler]*

Mr. Kunstler:  —one of the defenses in this case is that if
there were any riots in Chicago during the Democratic Convention Week, they were caused solely and exclusively by the
police. The defense maintains that the police brutalized the
crowd, and that, in effect, this trial that is going on here is an
attempt by the Government to justify what the police did in
the streets of Chicago during Convention Week, and if this
witness can testify that the police broke what he considers
existing rules, and regulations, and methods of handling
crowds to go out of Lincoln Park on Tuesday night and chase
the crowd, and beat them in the streets of Chicago, that is
part of our defense, and I don't think that we could present
that part of the defense unless we can ask a witness who has
had considerable experience in crowd control a type of question which goes something like this: In your opinion, did the
police follow established procedures, and from that, to raise
the inference that in breaking established procedures, if the
jury believes this witness, the police were motivated by a desire not to really control the crowds in Lincoln Park, but to
beat them to the ground so that they would never come back
to Lincoln Park, they would never come back to Chicago, and
they would never demonstrate in front of the Democratic
National Convention or anywhere else in the city of Chicago,
that the mayor of this city thought they should not demonstrate in the city, and I think we should be permitted to show
that.

\* \* \*

*Cross-examination of Mr. Styron by Mr. Schultz*

Mr. Schultz:  He has testified that he smelled gas
Mr. Kunstler:  Gas is gas.
Mr. Schultz:  I am trying to establish that he smelled stink
bombs that were in the Hilton as well.
Mr. Kunstler can't have one and not the other. If he smelled,
we are going to find out what he smelled.
Mr. Kunstler:  He might have smelled Chanel No. 5, for
all of me, your Honor. I am not answering one or the other.
Mr. Schultz:  But the defendants—
The Court:  Do you use that Mr. Kunstler?
Mr. Kunstler:  What, Aerosol No. 5?
The Court:  Chanel No. 5?

Mr. Kunstler: Only on special occasions, your Honor.

The Court: You asked for that one, you know.

Mr. Kunstler: I didn't make any serious objection.

The Court: No, I didn't think you would.

Mr. Kunstler: I have found that Brut is very good, though.

## December 15, 1969

*Direct examination of Defense Witness Dick Gregory, comedian and politician, by Mr. Kunstler*

Q. All right, I will ask you this, Mr. Gregory.
After this moment that you have just described, did you see Abbie Hoffman?

A. Yes.

Q. And would you describe to the jury where you saw him and what you saw him do.

A. At 18th Street, lying under or directly in front of what I believe to have been a tank.

. . .

A. . . .[W]hen I looked at Abbie, before we got to the crowd that started moving, I said, "Where are you going?" He said, "I don't know. The police is leading it." I said, "What do you mean by that?" He said, "The guy on the bullhorn." He said, "There is an undercover agent. He is leading it, so let him take them back to the park." . . .

\* \* \*

*[Out of the presence of the jury]*

The Court: . . . [O]ne of the defendants who we all remember, I think—he is no longer here—charged me with being a racist with absolutely no basis in fact.

Mr. Kunstler: He said if your Honor didn't permit him to act as his own attorney you were—

The Court: I would want this very nice witness [Mr. Gregory—ed.] to know that I am not, that he has made me laugh often and heartily.

Mr. Kunstler: Your Honor, white people have always laughed at black people for a long time as entertainers.

The Court: I want him to know I was the first judge in the North to enter a decree desegregating schools. But that is beside the point. There is no issue of racism in this case. . . .

\* \* \*

*[Cross-examination] by Mr. Foran*

Q. Mr. Gregory, you mentioned that Abbie Hoffman was lying down in the street out near 18th and Michigan on that afternoon?

A. Right.

122

Q. You said he had his finger up in the air. What was he doing?

A. Like this (*indicating*).

Q. His middle finger stuck up in the air?

A. Yes.

\* \* \*

*Direct examination of Defense Witness Ruth Migdal, an artist and art professor, by Defense Attorney Weinglass*

Mr. Schultz: I have never heard a lawyer present a legal argument the way Mr. Weinglass does. He says, "You haven't let me do this, you haven't let me do that," as though he is really being oppressed.

If Mr. Weinglass would follow the rules of evidence instead of trying to alter them and then say, "Oh, but you are not letting me do this"—if he would follow the rules of evidence, the probative rules, instead of asking the silly questions, trying to make it appear that poor Mr. Weinglass is being taken advantage of, we could proceed with this trial. . . .

. . .

Mr. Schultz: I want Mr. Weinglass' two statements that were made to be stricken. The word "glibly" is not appropriate. And that we asked the question and it was answered was also inappropriate. In fact, the record is we withdrew the question on the defendants' objection of Mr. Rochford [deputy and Government Witness—ed.].

I ask both of those statements be stricken because both are inaccurate.

Mr. Kunstler: Your Honor, the word "silly" to characterize a lawyer's statement is just as inaccurate and inappropriate. If we are going to withdraw "glibly" I think the world "silly" should be withdrawn and that the jury should be instructed that the word "silly" is improper for one lawyer to use to characterize another lawyer's questions. . . .

. . .

The Court: I don't know what you are trying to say. If you want me to strike the word "silly," I will strike it.

Mr. Kunstler: It is just as inappropriate and improper as "glibly."

The Court: I direct the jury to disregard the use of a different word to characterize your notion of your adversary's conduct. . . .

. . .

Q. What, if anything, did you see after the bus pulled up and stopped?

A. I saw the door open and I saw red faces angry, very angry police coming out with their clubs up.

Mr. Schultz: Objection to the description. If their faces were red, she can describe it, but angry—

The Court: Yes. "Their faces were red," that, I think, is proper, but "very angry," those words I think are improper to use. I strike them and I direct the jury to disregard the words "very angry."

By Mr. Weinglass:

Q. Could you describe that you saw without using a descriptive word such as that?

A. Yes. I saw red faced, blue helmeted, blue shirted or short-sleeve shirted men, their arms up, a club in one arm, coming out of the bus at full speed chanting, "Kill, kill, kill" and then go across the street and charge into the crowd and start beating heads.

\* \* \*

*Direct examination of Defense Witness James Wright, a self-employed operator of a barbecue business in Chicago, by Defense Attorney Weinglass*

Q. Now while you were standing there and waiting with the other marchers, did you hear any sounds aside from speeches?

A. Yes.

Q. What did you hear?

A. This Om-ing.

Q. Om?

A. Yes.

Q. Were a number of people Om-ing?

A. Oh, yes, everybody.

Q. Were you Om-ing?

A. Yes.

\* \* \*

[*The following colloquies occurred during the direct examination of Defense Witness Angus MacKenzie*]

The Court: . . . Mr. Marshal, will you remove that man sitting there? Ask him to leave. This man right here

Mr. Weinglass: Your Honor, I don't believe Mr Ball was—

The Court: He was laughing right at me while I was speaking.

Mr. Weinglass: I was standing here Mr Ball did not laugh.

The Court: Mr. Ball was laughing right at me.

Mr. Davis: Your Honor—

The Court: I ask Mr. Ball to leave.

Mr. Hoffman: I was laughing.

Mr. Davis: It was me that was laughing, your Honor.

The Court: I can't order you to leave. You are at trial.

* * *

The Court: Mr. Marshal, take Mr. Ball out.

Mr. Dellinger: That is an injustice.

Mr. Kunstler: That is a lawyer who is part of our defense team.

The Court: He is not a lawyer admitted to practice in this Court.

Mr. Kunstler: You are removing a lawyer from the defense table.

The Court: No, he is not a lawyer admitted to practice here.

Mr. Kunstler: That doesn't matter, your Honor. He is—

Mr. Dellinger: He wasn't laughing.

Mr. Kunstler: You have given him permission to sit here.

The Court: I withdraw the permission.

* * *

Mr. Kunstler: Your Honor, this is the second time you have picked the wrong man.

Mr. Dellinger: Your Honor—

Mr. Kunstler: Mr. Davis has admitted he laughed.

The Court: That will be all, sir. Now I am making a ruling.

Mr. Hoffman: I was laughing.

* * *

Mr. Kunstler: . . . [Y]ou are depriving us of a lawyer at our defense table.

The Court: That is just too bad. You will have to suffer through without him. He is not a lawyer admitted to practice here.

Mr. Kunstler: He is a member of the bar of the District of Columbia. He has been assisting us for three months through this trial.

The Court: Let him go back to the District of Columbia. I will not have him here laughing at me while I am trying to rule—

Mr. Kunstler: But he didn't laugh, your Honor If he laughed, that is one thing, perhaps, but two defendants have admitted laughing.

The Court: My eyesight is good and my hearing is good.

Mr. Kunstler: You were wrong about Mr. Dellinger. You thought he made a noise. We have submitted an affidavit as to that.

The Court: I suppose I didn't hear him call me a liar in open court.

125

Mr. Kunstler: That is a different matter, your Honor.

The Court: Oh—

Mr. Dellinger: I said if you said I was talking, that that was a lie, that you were calling me a liar.

The Court: You didn't—you said, "You are a liar."

Mr. Kunstler: No. Read the transcript.

Mr. Dellinger: You accused me of being a liar and I said that was a lie.

Mr. Dellinger: And you are very prejudiced and unfair and I state that in open court. It is not a fair trial and you had no intention of giving us a fair trial and when I speak throughout the country, I say that you are the Assistant Prosecutor or maybe the Chief Prosecutor and it is true and the people of this country will come to learn that about you and about some other judges in this Court.

A Spectator: RIGHT ON!

Mr. Dellinger: That's why I called it a fascist court before.

A Spectator: RIGHT ON!

\* \* \*

Mr. Kunstler: Your Honor, what is happening? The marshals are taking people out.

A Spectator: Why don't you clear the whole courtroom?

The Court: Will you—

Mr. Dellinger: You see, we are interested in the truth and you are not and the Government is not and that is what the conflict is here.

\* \* \*

The Court: No, Mr. Ball will not be readmitted. He is not admitted to practice here and for good and sufficient reasons I order him out.

Mr. Kunstler: Your Honor, put him on the stand and ask him whether he laughed.

The Court: Will you sit down, please?

Mr. Kunstler: He wouldn't lie under oath.

The Court: Will you sit down, please?

Mr. Kunstler: I guess I have no alternative, your Honor.

The Court: That is right. . . .

\* \* \*

Mr. Schultz: Your Honor, this tactic of one jumping up and then the other, this disruption that is slowly escalating is becoming quite eviden[t] and I would ask your Honor to order these—

Mr: Hoffman: Why don't you call out the National Guard.

\* \* \*

The Witness: Could I ask a question about court procedure?

126

The Court:  You ask the lawyers when you go out that brought you here.

The Witness:  It is too late.

The Court:  I am not permitted to practice law under the law.

The Witness:  I thought you were the judge.

The Court:  I am. That is why I am not permitted to practice law.

## December 16, 1969

*Direct examination of Defense Witness Linda Morse, a former office manager of the Fifth Avenue Peace Parade Committee, by Defense Attorney Kunstler*

The Court:  . . . Miss Morse, please listen to the question of Mr. Kunstler.

The Witness:  O.K. I am sorry.

The Court:  Reflect on your answer. Take all the time you need. Then answer the question without making any independent observations that are not responsive to the question.

The Witness:  I am sorry, your Honor. It is the first time I have ever testified. It is very confusing.

Mr. Kunstler: I know it is difficult.

Mr. Schultz:  It is not difficult at all, and Mr. Kunstler has so very carefully told all his witnesses say what you please, and when you are cut off, say your Honor, this is the first time. . . .

Mr. Kunstler:  Your Honor, Mr. Schultz has made a statement, which I think is quite a serious one. . . .

He has implied that I have coached a witness to come into this courtroom and make statements that will be objectionable.
. . .

Mr. Kunstler:  I think the jury ought to be told that is an improper statement, to imply that counsel has in some way coached a witness that she will make statements that will be objectionable.

The Court:  I will direct the jury that the statement of Mr. Schultz is not well founded in fact, and to disregard it.

Mr. Kunstler:  All right.

\* \* \*

*Cross-examination of Miss Morse by Government Attorney Schultz*

The Witness:  . . . [T]he Government of the United States has lost its credibility today; there is fighting in the United States today going on in cities in this country today. People's Park in Berkeley, the policemen shot at us when people were unarmed, were fighting, if you wish, with rocks, the policemen used double-load buckshot and rifles, and pistols against un-

127

armed demonstrators. That is fighting. OK? There is fighting
going on in the United States right now. People are fighting to
regain their liberty, fighting to regain their freedom, fighting
for a totally different society, people in the black community,
people in the Puerto Rican community, people in the Mexican-
American community and people in the white communities.
They are fighting by political means as well as defending themselves.

Mr. Schultz: Your Honor, that is not an answer to my
question. . . .

Mr. Kunstler: Your Honor, they are intensely political
questions and she is trying to give a political answer to a
political question.

The Court: This is not a political case as far as I am concerned.

Mr. Kunstler: Well, your Honor, as far as some of the
rest of us are concerned, it is quite a political case.

The Court: It is a criminal case. There is an indictment
here. I have the indictment right up here. I can't go into
politics here in this Court.

Mr. Kunstler: Your Honor, Jesus was accused criminally,
too, and we understand really that was not truly a criminal
case in the sense that it is just an ordinary—

The Court: I didn't live at that time. I don't know. Some
people think I go back that far, but I really didn't.

Mr. Kunstler: Well, I was assuming your Honor had
read of the incident.

\* \* \*

Q. With regard to the revolution that we are talking about,
you are prepared, aren't you, both to die and to kill
for it, isn't that right?

A. Yes.

. . .

Q. And the more you realize our system is sick, the more
you want to tear it from limb to limb, isn't that right?

A. The more that I see the horrors that are perpetrated by
this Government, the more that I read about things like
troop trains full of nerve gas traveling across the country where one accident could wipe out thousands and
thousands of people, the more that I see things like companies just pouring waste into lakes and into rivers and
just destroying them, the more I see things like the oil
fields in the ocean off Santa Barbara coast where the
Secretary of the Interior and the oil companies got together and agreed to continue producing oil from those
off-shore oil fields and ruined a whole section of the

coast; the more that I see things like an educational system which teaches black people and Puerto Rican people and Mexican-Americans that they are only fit to be domestics and dishwashers, if that; the more that I see a system that teaches middle-class whites like me that we are supposed to be technological brains to continue producing CBW warfare, to continue working on computers and things like that to learn how to kill people better, to learn how to control people better, yes, the more I want to see that system torn down and replaced by a totally different one; one that cares about people learning real things in school; one that cares about people going to college for free; one that cares about people living adult lives that are responsible, fulfilled adult lives, not just drudgery, day after day after day going to a job; one that gives people a chance to express themselves artistically and politically, and religiously, and philosophically. That is the kind of system I want to see in its stead.

Mr. Schultz: Your Honor, the answer is not responsive. I move it be stricken.

Mr. Kunstler: The answer could not have been more responsive to his question.

The Court: Not much more, I strike the answer and direct the jury to disregard it as being unresponsive to the question.

. . .

*By Mr. Kunstler:*

Q. Miss Morse, I want to read you something from the Declaration of Independence, which I think the Court can take judicial notice of, and then ask you a question about it.

Mr. Schultz: Objection to reading from the Declaration of Independence.

. . .

The Court: I can think of nothing in the cross-examination that makes the Declaration of Independence relevant on redirect examination.

Mr. Kunstler: Your Honor, if the Declaration of Independence isn't relative to what is going on in the courtroom here, I can hardly think of anything more relevant.

The Court: I didn't say that. I said to the redirect examination. I wouldn't let you read the entire Constitution or one of Mr. Ginsberg's poems. It must be relevant to the examination which precedes it.

Mr. Kunstler: But your Honor, the cross-examination went into great lengths on Miss Morse's philosophy of change of government, of change of the way a society exists, and since the Declaration has relevant statements on that, I wanted to read them to her and have her comments on them.

The Court: I will not permit you to read from the Declaration of Independence. I sustain the objection.

## December 17, 1969

*Direct examination of Defense Witness Richard H. Perez, a CBS-TV News cameraman, by Defense Attorney Kunstler*

Mr. Kunstler: Your Honor, before the film is shown I would just like to ask your Honor's assistance. We have a young man outside, Robert Loeb, who has been denied admission to the Court because he is wearing a yarmulke which he traditionally wears.

The Court: Oh, that is a subject not to be discussed in the presence of the jury, Mr. Kunstler. I came out here in connection with this exhibit.

Mr. Kunstler: It is a simple matter to let him—there was room and this is about the eighth time it has occurred and we would like to move the Court to have him admitted with his yarmulke.

The Court: The matter of who is admitted to the Court is a matter for the marshals and the rule of Court is that gentlemen take their hats off. This is not a church.

Mr. Kunstler: I know, but a man wears his yarmulke regularly and I think he should be admitted.

The Court: We conduct trials here under the laws of the United States and not under ecclesiastical law. . . .

. . .

The Court: Mr. Kunstler, I have had a prince of the Catholic Church in this courtroom who didn't wear a head-covering.

Mr. Kunstler: That may not have been his religious obligation, your Honor.

The Court: And we do not permit in this Court a man to come in with his head covered. Now I will let you or any lawyer who represents him make a record on it.

Mr. Kunstler: I am only interested in our public trial, your Honor, and we thought that this interfered with a public trial.

The Court: This is a public trial. If you don't know it, why read the newspapers, Mr. Kunstler.

\* \* \*

*Cross-examination of Defense Witness Thomas W. Pew, Jr., editor and publisher of the Troy (Ohio) Daily News, by Mr. Schultz*

Mr. Schultz: Your Honor, it is really very difficult to examine a witness when constantly the defendants are muttering to me, muttering under their breath, laughing. Maybe they can't restrain themselves. It is quite difficult, but perhaps with a court admonition it will help. It is distracting. I think they do it for that reason, so it will be distracting.

Mr. Kunstler: Your Honor, I didn't hear any muttering. Mr. Schultz, I have always thought had very finely attuned ears, particularly to what happens on our side of the table, but I did not hear muttering. I am sure your Honor did not hear muttering.

The Court: You speak for yourself, sir.

Mr. Kunstler: I will ask you, your Honor, did you hear muttering?

The Court: I will accept your statement that you did not hear muttering.

Mr. Kunstler: I am asking whether your Honor heard any muttering.

The Court: You weren't asking, you told me I didn't.

Mr. Kunstler: I withdraw that question and ask another.

The Court: That wasn't a question. That was a statement.

Mr. Kunstler: I am asking a question.

\* \* \*

*Redirect examination by Mr. Kunstler*

Q. Mr. Pew, after you sent your letter to Mayor Daley on September 25, 1968, do you know whether he sent it to the FBI?

Mr. Schultz: Objection.

The Court: I sustain the objection. You know I sustained the objection?

Mr. Kunstler: Do I know why you did, or that you did sustain it?

The Court: You know I sustained the objection. You did hear that?

Mr. Kunstler: Yes, I sensed that.

. . .

*By Mr. Kunstler:*

Q. Just one last question. Mr. Pew, do you know whether any Chicago officials, officials of the city of Chicago, or any officials of the Democratic Party have been indicted for conspiracy to promote a police riot?

Mr. Schultz: Objection.

The Court: I sustain the objection.

Mr. Kunstler: I have no further questions.

**December 18, 1969**

*[Excerpts from sound track of Defense Exhibit 187 for*

131

*identification, a news film of the confrontation in front of the Hilton Hotel, shown in court out of the presence of the jury*]

They are forcing, the police are forcing the crowd back and now, and it is going to be a difficult job. A big police van has pulled into the intersection, and its role, I assume its role is just to clear a way. Here come the police. Step up here. The police are pushing and shoving. Here they come. We're going to get it. We're going to get it. They are clear, and we are out of the way. Watch the wire.

Now the police are clubbing this young man, clubbing him. This is a real police charge. Now I have seen them club at least three young people. Now they are moving into the crowd and beating them with the night sticks. The beatings are going on. Here they come. There are glasses and bottles being thrown. These police mean business. Watch the wire. Here come the police. There are a lot of young people on the ground now. This is a real bedlam.

This is the worst it has been so far in Chicago. Police running across here. There's another one hit the ground, and he is screaming. They are really letting them have it now. Here they come.

There the police go. They are clubbing these young people. Our truck is down there. They are dragging them across the intersection. They are dragging them across the intersection.

This is the most amazing thing that has ever occurred in the Loop of Chicago in modern history. A firecracker went off there. They have just turned Michigan and Balbo into a war zone.

They have cleared part of the intersection. They have young people off on the sidewalk now. I have seen dozens of them being beaten, and the police really mean business here in front of the Hilton Hotel.

The whole world watches. The whole world watches.

They are shouting, 'The whole world watches.' The police are regrouping.

The whole world watches.

As you can see now, the police are regrouping in the street here on Michigan Avenue and they are forming up in squad formation.

Here comes another skirmish on the other side. They are moving these people back, chasing them up the bridge, moving them in full force. As you can see, they are chasing them up the bridge, across the bridge, back into the Grant Park area.

## THE PEOPLE AND
## THE COURTROOM — SCENES
## FROM THE CHICAGO
## CONSPIRACY TRIAL

No cameras were allowed inside the courtroom during this dramatic trial. Newspapers, magazines and television networks sent skilled artists to sketch the action as it happened. The sketches that follow in this special section, and those on the covers of this book, were done on the scene by Verna Sadock for NBC-TV. They will appear in her book, *Four Months and Fifteen Days — A Picture Story of the Chicago Trial*, published by The Third Press — Joseph Okpaku Publishing Co., Inc.

The Courtroom

Jerry Rubin

John Froines

Rennie Davis

Lee Weiner

Tom Hayden

abbie Hoffman

David Dellinger

Bobby Seale

Because of the ban on
Cameras, the media mobbed
the press Conferences.

U. S. Attorney Thomas Foran
questions a witness.

Chicago's Mayor Daley
takes the stand.

Prose

Richard
Schultz

Table

Cubbage

Thomas
Foran

Huddle at the Prosecution table.

Tom
Hayden

David Dellinger

John Froines

The defendants rest during a quiet moment in the trial.

Counsel for the defense,
William Kunstler.

A wide range of witnesses
appeared before the Court.

A tense moment for the defense.

Nancy

Jerry Rubin's girlfriend, Nancy,
answers questions for the press.

Controversial films were part of
the evidence presented to the jury.

Lee Weiner

Tom Hayden

A long day in Court.

Foran cross-examines a
witness for the defense.

Out bursts from spectators were frequently silenced by U. S. Marshals.

The jury: ten women and two men,
selected after much debate.

The eighth defendant.

Debris is flying here. It is really flying. Here comes a bottle. It is a film can of some kind, a metal can.

Now the police are going to hold the line right here by our cameras, and it is truly amazing here. There's some young people fallen into the street now by the Hilton Hotel. Some of the Red Cross Peace people are picking them up and moving them on to the sidewalk, and the police van is now moving back to the west, away from Michigan Avenue.

Now there are some things being thrown out of the hotel window of the Sheraton-Blackstone just north of the Hilton, and these young people mean business, and so do the police, and it's not over yet.

**December 19, 1969**

*Direct examination of Defense Witness, Dr. Timothy Leary, former Harvard professor, by Mr. Kunstler*

Q. Prior to this press conference had you had any other meetings with Jerry and Abbie?

A. Yes, we had met two or three times during the spring in which we were planning the Chicago Convention love-in.

Mr. Foran: Your Honor, I object to the constant use of the diminutives in the references to the defendants.

The Court: Yes, I think it is better courtroom form, Mr. Kunstler, to refer to the defendants by their surnames.

Mr. Kunstler: Your Honor, sometimes it is hard because we work together in this case, we use first names constantly.

The Court: I know, but if I knew you that well, and I don't, how would it seem for me to say, "Now Billy . . ."
. . .

Mr. Kunstler: I was just thinking I hadn't been called "Billy" since my mother used that word the first time.

The Court: I haven't called you that.

Mr. Kunstler: I know, but you used it.

The Court: I used it . . .

Mr. Kunstler: It evokes some memories.

The Court: I was trying to point out to you how absurd it sounds in a courtroom.

Mr. Kunstler: It didn't sound . . .

The Court: Oh, let's get on. Let's examine this witness. He seems eager to get away.

\* \* \*

Q. Dr. Leary, tell what people said.

A. Yes. Mr. Hoffman continued to say that we should set up a series of political meetings throughout the country, not just for the coming summer but for the coming

133

years. Mr. Hoffman suggested that we have love-ins or be-ins in which thousands of young people and freedom-loving people throughout the country could get together on Sunday afternoons, listen to music which represented the new point of view, the music of love and peace and harmony, and try to bring about a political change in this country that would be nonviolent in people's minds and in their hearts, and this is the concept of the love-in which Mr. Hoffman was urging upon us and this was the first time that the coming to Chicago was mentioned.

. . .

I also told Jerry that my wife and I had had a press conference about the Yippie meetings and the Convention the day we were in Chicago. I told Jerry we had that press conference at the Model Farm, I think it is in Lincoln Park, where my wife, whose name is Mrs. Leary, had a lantern by a cow, and we were announcing that we were going to come to Chicago in August, not with fire, but to bring light and peace.

\* \* \*

[Dr. Leary testifying to another conversation]

Dr. Leary: . . . Both Mr. Hoffman and Mr. Rubin at that time said to me before I left that they were not sure whether we should come to Chicago, and that we would watch what happened politically. At that time, Jerry Rubin pointed out that Robert Kennedy was still alive, and many of us felt that he represented the aspirations of young people, so we thought we would wait. I remember Mr. Rubin saying, "Let's wait and see what Robert Kennedy come out with as far as peace in concerned. Let's wait to see if Robert Kennedy does speak to young people, and if Robert Kennedy does seek to represent the peaceful, joyous, erotic feelings of young people . . ."

The Court:  "Erotic," did you say?

The Witness:  Erotic.

The Court:  E-r-o-t-i-c?

The Witness:  Eros. That means love, your Honor.

The Court:  I know; I know. I wanted to be sure I didn't mishear you.

The Witness:  Because Mr. Rubin pointed out that Mr. Robert Kennedy did represent a youthful, healthy, masculine approach that was lacking in most of our other politicians, and we felt that young people would respond to a person like Mr. Kennedy, who seemed to enjoy life as opposed to the pessimistic uptight older politicians.

So Mr. Rubin suggested that we hold off the decision as to whether we come to Chicago until we saw how Mr. Kennedy's campaign developed, and at that point, I think most of us would have gladly, joyously called off the Chicago meeting.

Mr. Foran: Oh, I object to this, your Honor.

\* \* \*

*Direct testimony of Defense Witness Elizabeth J. Snod-grass, a nurse who was giving medical assistance to those injured during Convention Week, by Mr. Weinglass.*

Q. Directing your attention to approximately eight p.m. on Wednesday night, August 28, 1968, where were you?
A. I was at the intersection of Michigan and Balbo.

. . .

Q. Were you struck by a rock?
A. Yes, I was.
Q. And do you recall what the police said to the group?
A. Yes.
Q. Will you tell the court and jury what the police said?
A. The police picked up the rock, and he said, "Medical aids, my ass. If it weren't for you fucking bastards, the rest of the group wouldn't be here."

\* \* \*

[*The following concerns the acquittal after trial of Chicago policemen indicted for their actions during Convention Week*]

Mr. Kunstler: The defendants have contended that the prosecution of the police was a sham prosecution.

Mr. Schultz: Just a minute.

Mr. Kunstler: Will you let me finish?

Mr. Schultz: I will not let him finish. We prosecuted those cases as vigorously as we could. The First Assistant of our office prosecuted those three policemen. We have done everything we could, and, certainly, Mr. Kunstler is not going to try to establish before this jury that the Government fell down on a case by retrying a case here.

. . .

The Court: [talking to the jury] . . . I direct you now also to disregard the statement of Mr. Kunstler that the prosecution to which he referred was a sham prosecution. There is no evidence of that here.

Mr. Kunstler: Your Honor, they ought to know that the policemen conceded the assault in that case . . .

. . .

Mr. Kunstler: What the jury does not know, and actually the false impression that has been raised here, is that the defense in the case of the policemen concerned conceded the assault. Their defense was that they didn't interfere with civil rights of an American citizen under the Federal Statute 241 or 242, but they conceded the assaults, and that is what this witness is being questioned about.

. . .

Mr. Foran: Your Honor, any lawyer in the world would have, before this witness took the stand, advised the court that he was presenting evidence in this kind of a context, and asked for a hearing outside of the presence of the jury. If he was even a decent man he would do that.

Mr. Kunstler: Oh, your Honor.

(Whereupon, at this point the court was in disorder.)

\* \* \*

[*After order was restored in the courtroom*]

Mr. Kunstler: Your Honor, can we beg to admonish once —we have never had a single admonishment . . .

The Court: I will admonish the marshal to direct all of those people at that table who shouted not to do that again.

Mr. Kunstler: Well, your Honor, that is begging the question I am asking. The United States Attorney now says that I am indecent . . .

The Court: Don't lounge on that lectern and tell me that I am begging the question.

### December 22, 1969

*Direct examination of Paul Sequeira, a photographer, by Defense Attorney Kunstler*

Q. By the way, Mr. Sequeira, was that the exact language he used in telling you to get out?

A. He either said, "Get the hell out of here," or—I was told it on two or three occasions to "Get the fuck out of here."

Q. By police officers?

A. By police officers, yes.

\* \* \*

*Cross-examination of Mr. Sequeira by Government Attorney Schultz*

Q. Did you hear anybody, any of the demonstrators, shouting "Pig, fascist, s.o.b.," and other profanities?

A. At this particular time?

Q. At the time you were at the squadrol.

A. No, sir, I do not recall.

Mr. Kunstler: Your Honor, I object to the characterization of "fascist" as a profanity. He has lumped together a lot of things. I don't think "pig" is a profanity. He said "and other profanities."

136

The Court:   He said "s.o.b." and other profanities.

Mr. Kunstler:   No, he said "pig, fascist—"

The Court:   "s.o.b. and other profanities."

Mr. Kunstler:   Right, but I am not sure that the word "pig" or the word "fascist" is a profanity.

The Court:   Well, I don't know. We went through a long war about—

Mr. Kunstler:   Fascist as a definite meaning.

The Court:   To call a man a fascist is a pretty serious thing.

Mr. Kunstler:   That is not a profanity, your Honor.

The Court:   I am not sure. I am not sure about that, Mr. Kunstler. I never looked up the word in that connotation.

Mr. Kunstler:   It is a common word. It is in the dictionary, your Honor. It is in any dictionary.

Mr. Schultz:   I didn't call it a profanity. I said "pig, fascist, s.o.b., and other profanities."

The Court:   I am not prepared to rule on that at this time, Mr. Kunstler.

Mr. Kunstler:   If Mr. Schultz is relating that the only word he classified as a profanity among those is s.o.b., then I have no objection.

The Court:   To call a man a fascist may be contemptuous, but it may not be profane.

Mr. Kunstler:   But it may be accurate.

The Court:   What do you say?

Mr. Kunstler:   But it may be accurate.

Mr. Schultz:   I don't think Mr. Kunstler is very funny. He is trying to be very humorous.

The Court:   Oh, he is trying to be humorous? I thought he was making a legal argument.

Mr. Kunstler:   I am making an argument. Mr. Schultz is categorizing it, and I am not going to argue about his feelings.

Mr. Schultz:   Your Honor was obviously referring to having been called a fascist and Mr. Kunstler is saying it might be accurate.

Mr. Kunstler:   I wasn't referring to that at all. I was saying that the word "fascist"—

The Court:   Oh, I have been called worse than that. We will take care of that. I am not sure but that the word "fascist" used as it has been used on occasions is not even worse than profanity.

Mr. Kunstler:   Your Honor, it is used in many contexts every day. It is used in the newspaper one way or another. That is what I am referring to.

The Court:   Not every day. I read the newspapers every day. I can't remember when I have seen the word "fascist" in the newspapers except in connection with this trial.

137

Mr. Kunstler: Then I recommend today's New York Times to your Honor.

The Court: What do you say?

Mr. Kunstler: I call to your Honor's attention today's New York Times.

The Court: Am I called a fascist in that paper?

Mr. Kunstler: No, your Honor. Every time the word "fascist" is used it doesn't necessarily mean Judge Julius Hoffman.

The Court: Well, that is reassuring. That is so reassuring.

Mr. Kunstler: You are taking it so personally every time it is used—

The Court: Oh, no, not at all. I haven't said anything about myself personally.

Mr. Kunstler: Well, your Honor, I got the strong drift that you were taking it quite personally this time. If I am wrong, I am sorry.

The Court: Don't drift so easily.

Mr. Kunstler: I will fight against the tide winds.

Mr. Schultz: Since Mr. Kunstler has made the big issue of profanities, I will ask more detailed questions. I tried to avoid it.

## December 23, 1969

*Cross-examination of Defense Witness Duane R. Hall, press photographer for the Chicago Sun-Times, by Government Attorney Foran*

Mr. Weinglass: I object to Mr. Foran—I think he is reading from a document that hasn't even been marked for identification.

· · ·

The Court: I know of nothing in the law of evidence that prevents a lawyer from reading from whatever notes he has. I do it constantly.

Mr. Weinglass: A lawyer can read from a document that is not in evidence?

Mr. Foran: As long as he doesn't identify it as a document.

The Court: There is nothing identified.

Mr. Weinglass: That is permissible procedure?

The Court: I said it was. You don't have to ask me after I said it.

Mr. Weinglass: I am sorry. I object to it.

The Court: Sometime I am going to take an oath before I talk to you, you ask me so many questions.

\* \* \*

*Colloquy between attorneys and Judge Hoffman during direct testimony of Defense Witness, the Reverend Bruce Young*

Mr. Kunstler: Your Honor, there is an old maxim in law that if the police are brutal to one group, there is an inference they may be brutal to other groups, and that is a—

The Court: That is a maxim of the law I never heard of, and I sustain the objection.

Mr. Kunstler: You heard the maxim that "False in one thing, false in all." That is what I am saying:

"Falsus in uno, falsus in omnibus."

That is the maxim.

The Court: You ought to put on your striped trousers and be a professor.

Mr. Kunstler: Your Honor, I am afraid I don't have striped trousers.

The Court: I didn't ask you for a lecture. I just ruled on one objection. That is all.

Mr. Kunstler: I am giving an answer, that is all.

The Court: I do the best I can.

Mr. Kunstler: The prosecution have claimed—

The Court: I don't know all of those fancy phrases that you used.

Mr. Kunstler: I think your Honor does.

The Court: But I will let my ruling stand.

\* \* \*

[*Without jury present*]

The Court: You have no right to know why I came in here at 2:30. You never tell me when you are late. The defendants have never told me when they are late.

Mr. Kunstler: Your Honor, we just noticed that both the Court and the United States Attorney came in almost simultaneously after we waited here until 2:30, and I think that perhaps the defense would be entitled to an explanation.

The Court: Perhaps they are not.

Mr. Schultz: If the Court please—

The Court: They will not have any explanation from me. I am not obligated to advise counsel. For your information, my calendar and I don't say this boastfully, but by way of information for you, it may be of interest to you even though you don't practice in this jurisdiction regularly, is the—

Mr. Kunstler: That is not true any longer.

The Court: What did you say?

Mr. Kunstler: That is not true any longer. I am practicing here fairly regularly since September.

139

The Court: No, you made a serious observation. I am trying to treat it seriously.

Mr. Kunstler: I am just trying to clear up the record.

The Court: —my civil and criminal calendars are more current than any in the building, so don't you worry about a half an hour, sir.

. . .

Don't keep track of my time, sir. I will keep track of yours, but don't you keep track of mine.

Mr. Kunstler: Well, that seems equitable.

\* \* \*

Mr. Foran: Your Honor, excuse me just a moment, there are four defendants missing.

Mr. Weinglass: If the Court please, Mr. Rubin is in the men's room.

Mr. Kunstler: Your Honor, the understanding was that the defendants without interrupting the trial could occasionally go to the rest room.

I would like to get on with it.

The Court: I would like to get on with it but it seems to me an awkward thing to try a case with seven defendants and only two sitting at the table as there were, and I notice that a few moments ago three of the defendants came in at the same time. Now we are waiting for the other one.

Mr. Kunstler: They share certain obligations in common, your Honor, that are hard to resist sometimes. But I don't think we really ought to be a slave to the gastric system and go on now at least.

Shall I go on, your Honor, or—

The Court: We will wait. We will wait for the defendants.

\* \* \*

*Direct examination of Defendant Abbott H. Hoffman by Defense Attorney Weinglass.*

Q. Will you please identify yourself for the record.

A. My name is Abbie. I am an orphan of America.

. . .

Q. Where do you reside?

A. I live in Woodstock Nation.

Q. Will you tell the Court and jury where it is.

A. Yes. It is a nation of alienated young people. We carry it around with us as a state of mind in the same way the Sioux Indians carried the Sioux nation around with them. It is a nation dedicated to cooperation versus competition, to the idea that people should have better means of exchange than property or money, that there

140

should be some other basis for human interaction. It is
a nation dedicated to—

The Court:  Excuse me, sir.

Read the question to the witness, please.

(*Question read*)

The Court:  Just where it is, that is all.

The Witness:  It is in my mind and in the minds of my
brothers and sisters. We carry it around with us in the same
way that the Sioux Indians carried around the Sioux nation.
It does not consist of property or material but, rather, of ideas
and certain values, those values being cooperation versus competition, and that we believe in a society—

Mr. Schultz:  This doesn't say where Woodstock Nation,
whatever that is, is.

Mr. Weinglass:  Your Honor, the witness has identified it
as being a state of mind and he has, I think, a right to define
that state of mind.

The Court:  No, we want the place of residence, if he has
one, place of doing business, if you have a business, or both if
you desire to tell them both. One address will be sufficient.
Nothing about philosophy or India, sir. Just where you live,
if you have a place to live.

Now you said Woodstock. In what state is Woodstock?

The Witness:  It is in the state of mind, in the mind of
myself and my brothers and sisters. It is a conspiracy.

. . .

Q.  Can you tell the Court and jury your present age?

A.  My age is 33. I am a child of the 60's.

Q.  When were you born?

A.  Psychologically, 1960.

. . .

Q.  Can you tell the Court and jury what is your present occupation?

A.  I am a cultural revolutionary. Well, I am really a defendant—

Q.  What do you mean?

A.  —full time.

\*     \*     \*

The Court:  . . . Will you remain quiet while I am making
a ruling. I know you have no respect for me.

Mr. Kunstler:  Your Honor, that is totally unwarranted.

Mr. Schultz:  That is not unwarranted. Mr. Kunstler here
in the presence of the jury the other day said the Defendant
Hoffman had changed his name from Hoffman because it was
the same name, indicating it was the same name. Mr. Kunstler
is the one who initiated this, and now he takes great offense
that your Honor—

141

The Court: I am mindful of that.

Mr. Kunstler: I think your remarks call for a motion for a mistrial.

The Court: And your motion calls for a denial of the motion. Mr. Weinglass, continue with your examination.

Mr. Kunstler: You denied my motion? I hadn't even started to argue it.

The Court: I don't need any argument on that one.

\* \* \*

The Court: The witness turned his back on me while he was on the witness stand.

Mr. Kunstler: Oh, your Honor, aren't—

Mr. Schultz: Mr. Kunstler went out of his way, out of his way the other day to explain to the jury that the defendant Hoffman had eliminated his last name.

The Court: I will have no further argument on your motion. I will ask you to sit down.

The Witness: I was just looking at the pictures of the long-hairs up on the wall.

\* \* \*

Q. During the year 1967, were you living a totally private life?

Mr. Schultz: Objection to the form of the question.

The Witness: I understand that one.

The Court: I sustain the objection.

The Witness: I didn't understand the other one, but I understand that question.

The Court: I heard the objection. I sustain the objection. I relieve you of the obligation of answering it.

The Witness: Oh, thanks. Gee.

\* \* \*

*[Testimony by Defendant Hoffman regarding previous Yippie activity]*

A. The money that I got from that job two weeks later I threw it out in the Stock Exchange in New York City on Wall Street, meaning to the other people who were in the money, we wanted to make a statement that we weren't doing it for money, and that, in fact, money should be abolished. We didn't believe in a society that people had to interact with money and property, but should be on more humanitarian bases. That was what the community was about.

\* \* \*

*By Mr. Weinglass:*

Q. Now in exorcising the Pentagon, were there any plans for the building to raise up off the ground?

A. Yes. When we were arrested they asked us what we were

142

doing We said it was to measure the Pentagon and we wanted a permit to raise it 300 feet in the air, and they said "How about 10?" So we said "OK." And they threw us out of the Pentagon and we went back to New York and had a press conference, told them what it was about.

. . .

Mr. Schultz. I would ask Mr. Weinglass please get on with the trial of this case and stop playing around with raising the Pentagon 10 or 300 feet off the ground.

The Witness: They are going to bring it up.

Mr. Schultz: There are serious issues here and if we could get to them so that he can examine the witness, I can cross-examine the witness, and we can move on.

Mr. Kunstler: Your Honor, this is not playing around. This is a deadly serious business. The whole issue in this case is language, what is meant by—

Mr. Schultz: This is not—

The Court: Let Mr. Weinglass defend himself.

Mr. Weinglass: Your honor, I am glad to see Mr. Schultz finally concedes that things like levitating the Pentagon building, putting LSD in the water, 10,000 people walking nude on Lake Michigan, a $200,000 bribe attempt are all playing around. I am willing to concede that fact, that was all playing around, it was a play idea of the witness, and if he is willing to concede it, we can all go home.

The Court: I sustain—

Mr Weinglass: Because he is treating all these things as deadly serious.

. .

Q  What equipment, if any, did you personally plan to use in the exorcism of the Pentagon?

A  I brought a number of noisemakers—

Mr. Schultz: Objection if the Court please.

The Court: I sustain the objection.

\* \* \*

[*Testimony by Defendant Hoffman concerning remarks made by Jerry Rubin at a pre-Convention meeting*]

A  . . Jerry Rubin. I believe, said that it would be a good idea to call it the Festival of Life in contrast to the Convention of Death, and to have it in some kind of public area, like a park or something, in Chicago. . . .

At one point, I believe it was Mr. Krassner, when we were talking about the Hippie community, Mr. Rubin asked how come we are called Hippies when we never called each other that, but we look in the papers and read day and night about this thing, and we are called

143

Hippie, and I said that was a myth, that myths are created by media, by people communicating to each other, but it wasn't an accurate description of the phenomenon that was taking place, and the phenomenon had to be experienced itself, and I described to Mr. Rubin my attitude about communication.

## December 24, 1969

*[Colloquy between Judge Hoffman and Mr. Kunstler]*

Mr. Kunstler: . . . [I]n the years I have practiced in both federal and state courts, I have never accused, if I can recall at all, either judge or prosecutor of using intimidating tactics on me. This is my first time.

The Court: This may come as a surprise to you. In all the years I have sat on both benches, no lawyer, no lawyer has ever charged me with intimidation.

Mr. Kunstler: Well, your Honor, this is an unusual case. There have been unusual things done and said by many people.

The Court: In many respects, it is unusual.

Mr. Kunstler: Your Honor has for the first time found lawyers in contempt.

The Court: I didn't ask for this case to be assigned to my calendar, and if you think that I recommend it to any other judge for a summer vacation, you are mistaken.

Mr. Kunstler: I think we all agree on that.

\* \* \*

*[Colloquy concerning absence of Defendant Hoffman]*

Mr. Weinglass: . . . I ask the Court to adjourn to Room 406A of Michael Reese [Hospital—ed.] where your Honor could for yourself talk to Abbie and see his condition with doctors present and make a determination right at that point.

The Court: You know despite the complaints that have been made by representatives of the defendants about the size of this courtroom, I find it pretty nice. I don't feel that I am living in squalor here. I think I will refrain from going to Michael Reese. It is really very depressing, hospitals are depressing, especially in their crowded conditions now.

Present my compliments to Mr. Hoffman and thank him for the invitation. Tell him that I decline it with regrets.

## December 29, 1969

*Continued direct examination of Defendant Hoffman.*
*[Testimony by A. Hoffman about founding of Yippies]*

A. . . . Anita said at that time that although "Yippie" would be understood by our generation, that straight newspapers like the New York Times and the U.S. Govern-

144

ment and the courts and everything wouldn't take it seriously unless it had a kind of formal name, so she came up with the name of the "Youth International Party." She said that we could play a lot of jokes on the concept of party because everybody would think that we were this huge international conspiracy, but that in actuality we were a party that you had fun at.

\* \* \*

[*Colloquy concerning admission of "flyer" as evidence*]
Mr. Schultz: . . . The identical sheet is already in evidence. It was put in by the Government. It is marked Government Exhibit C-2.

I don't see any reason for there being two of them.
Mr. Rubin: Ours is in color.

\* \* \*

[*Speaking to Judge Hoffman*]
Mr. Weinglass: We have attempted to lay a foundation that the Festival of Life was a further conceptualization of guerrilla theater and to give an idea of what their intent was in coming to Chicago to have a festival, you have to go back and see how the Yippie concept developed and grew through these guerrilla theater activities, starting with the money at the stock exchange and coming through this mock raid at Stony Brook, right up through Grand Central Station and Central Park be-in and on to Chicago. It's part and parcel of the whole history and pattern of why and how the Yippies came to Chicago and what they had in mind when they came here, so I think it is essential and critical to an understanding of precisely what's on trial, and what is their intent in coming here.

\* \* \*

*By Mr. Weinglass:*
Q. Directing your attention to Sunday, May 13, which is Mother's Day, 1968, where were you on that day?
A. I was in Lincoln Park in Chicago.
Q. What was occurring in the park at that time?
A. There was what we might call a mini festival of life, a rock concert, I believe. Rev. Tuttle was marrying people. There were marriages taking place and there was a preparation—everybody had pies, apple pies and cherry pies and were going to march to the 18th—there was the beginning of a march to the police station to present the police who were on duty that Sunday, Mother's Day, with pies, apple pies.
Q. Do you know that this was done?
A. There were about 300 people—

Mr. Schultz:    Objection. Marching to the police station on Mother's Day with pies is irrelevant.

. . .

Mr. Weinglass:    It is irrelevant by Government standards. If they went to the police station carrying bombs, they would say that was relevant.

**December 30, 1969**

[*Continued direct examination of Defendant A. Hoffman*]

The Court:    Bring in the jury, please, Mr. Marshal.

Defendant Hoffman:    Wait a second. We have a matter—

The Court:    Who was that waving and talking at me, one of the lawyers?

Mr. Schultz:    He is acting as his own lawyer, I think, your Honor. Abbie Hoffman. He is doing a pretty good job of it. He shows Mr. Weinglass up.

Defendant Hoffman:    Wait until you get your chance.

\* \* \*

Q. Could you relate to the Court and to the jury the substance of your conversation with David Stahl [Deputy Mayor of Chicago—ed.] at that time.

A. Well, I said, "Hi, Dave. How's it going?" I said, "Your police got to be the dumbest—the dumbest and the most brutal in the country," that the decision to drive people out of the park in order to protect the city was about the dumbest military tactic since the Trojans first let the Trojan horse inside the gate and that there was nothing that compared with that stupidity. I again pleaded with him to let people stay in the park the following night. I said that there were more people coming to Chicago. There would be more people coming Monday, Tuesday, and subsequently Wednesday night, and that they should be allowed to sleep, that there was no place to sleep, that the hotels are all booked up, that people were getting thrown out of hotels, that they were getting thrown out of restaurants, and that he ought to intercede with the police department. I told him that the city officials, in particular his boss, Daley, were totally out of their minds, that I had read in the paper the day before that they had 2,000 troops surrounding the reservoirs in order to protect against the Yippie plot to dump LSD in the drinking water. I said that there wasn't a kid in the country, never mind a Yippie, who thought that such a thing could even be done, that why didn't he check with all the scientists at the University of Chicago—he owned them all. I said that it couldn't in fact be done.

146

He said that he knew it couldn't be done, but they weren't taking any chances anyway. I thought it was about the weirdest thing I had ever heard. I said, "Well, it was good advice, that he could withdraw those troops, that that couldn't be done, but maybe Mayor Daley was taking a little acid," and I told him—I told him that he could get in touch with me through the Seed office but that really if he just wanted to contact me, he knew where to reach me any minute since there were two policemen and sometimes four from the Chicago Intelligence office following me all day . . .

\* \* \*

*By Mr. Weinglass:*

Q. Did you speak for an hour, Abbie, on this speech?

Mr. Schultz:  It isn't Abbie, it is a 33-year-old man. His name is Mr. Hoffman.

The Court:  Oh, yes, but that has been gone into. If a lawyer persists in that, there is nothing very much I can do about it at this time.

*By Mr. Weinglass:*

Q. Could you relate to the Court as much as you can of your speech?

A. I think I can, Len.

The Court:  What did he call you?

The Witness:  Len.

Mr. Weinglass:  Len. It is the approriate name.

\* \* \*

*[Defendant Hoffman testifying about his arrest]*

A. They grabbed me by the jacket and pulled me across the bacon and eggs and Anita over the table, threw me on the floor and out the door and threw me against the car, and they handcuffed me. I was just eating the bacon and going, "Oink, oink."

Q. Did they tell you why you were arrested?

A. They said they arrested me because I had the word "fuck" on my forehead.

Q. Now, will you explain—

A. They called it an "obscenary," they said it was an "obscenary."

Q. Can you explain to the court and the jury how that word got on your forehead that day.

A. I had it put on with this magic marker before we left the house.

Q. And why did you do that?

A. Well, there were a couple of reasons. One was that I was tired of seeing my picture in the paper and having news-

147

men come around, and I know if you got that word, they aren't going to print your picture in the paper, and secondly, it sort of summed up my attitude about the whole—what was going on in Chicago. It was a four-letter word for which—I liked that four-letter word. I thought it was kind of holy, actually.

\* \* \*

*[Testimony describing a speech in Grant Park]*

Q. Do you recall what you said to the group that had gathered there at that time?

A. I described to them the experience that had happened to me in the jails of Chicago. I said that there were young people in the jails being beaten up, that they weren't being allowed to have their lawyers. I said it was typical of what took place in jails all around the country. I described the experience in the courtroom and the attitude of the Judge and I said it was particularly common among judges in this country. I said that Lenny Bruce had once said, "In the halls of justice the only justice is in the halls." And I said that the judicial system was as corrupt as the political system.

\* \* \*

*[The Court answering Mr. Weinglass]*

The Court: . . . I have ruled on that, Mr. Weinramer— Weinglass, rather.

\* \* \*

*By Mr. Weinglass:*

Q. Prior to coming to Chicago, from April 12, 1968, on to the week of the convention, did you enter into an agreement with David Dellinger, John Froines, Tom Hayden, Jerry Rubin, Lee Weiner, or Rennie Davis to come to the city of Chicago for the purpose of encouraging and promoting violence during the Convention Week?

A. An agreement?

Q. Yes.

A. We couldn't agree on lunch.

\* \* \*

*Cross-examination of Defendant Hoffman by Government Attorney Schultz. [Colloquy concerning a book written by Defendant Hoffman]*

Mr. Weinglass: I will have fourteen copies of the book for the jury in the morning, and they can read the entire book. We are not ashamed of a word in this book.

The Court: No, you will not. You may have fourteen copies, but they will not go to the jury.

Mr. Weinglass: Mr. Schultz is indicating to the jury that we are afraid of this book, and—

The Court: If you will listen to me, sir. I am the one who determines what the jury sees. Those books are not in evidence.

Mr. Weinglass: Then you should admonish the U.S. Attorney not to say that we are afraid of this book.

The Court: I will admonish the jury—the United States Attorney—

The Witness: Wait until you see the movie.

The Court: if it is required that he be admonished.

The Witness: Wait until you see the movie.

The Court: And you be quiet.

The Witness: Well—the movie's going to be better.

* * *

By Mr. Schultz:

Q. Did you see some people urinate on the Pentagon?

A. On the Pentagon itself?

Q. Or at the Pentagon?

A. In that general area in Washington?

Q. Yes.

A. There were in all over 100,000 people. That is, people have that biological habit.

Q. And did you?

A. Yes.

Q. Did you symbolically—

A. Did I go and look?

Q. Did you symbolically and did you—did you symbolically urinate on the Pentagon, Mr. Hoffman?

A. I symbolically urinate on the Pentagon?

Q. Yes.

A. Nearby yes, in the bushes, there, maybe 3,000 feet away from the Pentagon. I didn't get that close. Pee on the walls of the Pentagon?

You are getting to be out of sight actually. You think there is a law against it?

Q. Are you done, Mr. Hoffman?

A. I am done when you are.

Q. Did you ever on a prior occasion state that a sense of integration possesses you and comes from pissing on the Pentagon?

A. I said from combining political attitudes with biological necessity, there is a sense of integration, yes I think I said it that way, not the way you said it, but—

Q. You had a good time at the Pentagon, didn't you, Mr. Hoffman?

A. Yes, I did. I am having a good time now.

Could I—I feel that biological necessity now Could I be excused for a slight recess?

The Court: We will take a brief recess, ladies and gentlemen of the jury.

Ladies and gentlemen of the jury, we will take a brief recess.

The Witness: Just a brief—

The Court: We will take a brief recess with my usual orders. The Court will be in recess for a brief period.

*(Brief recess)*

\* \* \*

Q. At this meeting on the evening of August 7, you told Mr. Stahl that you were going to have nude-ins in your liberated zone, didn't you?

A. A nude-in? I don't believe I would use that phrase, no.

Q. You told him you were going to have public fornication?

A. I might have told him that ten thousand people were going to walk naked on the waters of Lake Michigan, something like that.

Q. No, you told him specifically, didn't you, Mr. Hoffman, that you were going to have nude-ins, didn't you?

A. No. I don't—No, I don't recall using that phrase or that I ever used it. I do now. It's—I don't think it's very poetic, frankly.

Q. You told him, did you not, Mr. Hoffman, that in your liberated zone you would have—

A. I'm not even sure what it is, a nude-in.

Q. Public fornication?

A. If it means ten thousand people, naked people, walking on Lake Michigan, yes.

Mr. Kunstler: I object to this because Mr. Schultz is acting like a dirty old man.

Mr. Schultz: We are not going into dirty old men. If they wanted to have 500,000 people in the park and are telling the city officials they going to have nude-ins and public fornication, the city officials react to that, and I am establishing through this witness that that's what he did, that and many more things.

The Court: There is no objection. Do you object?

Mr. Kunstler: I am just remarking, your Honor, that a young man can be a dirty old man.

The Witness: I don't mind talking—

The Court: I could make an observation. I have seen some exhibits here that are not exactly exemplary documents.

Mr. Kunstler: But they are, from your point of view, your Honor—making a dirty word of something that can be beautiful and lovely, and that's what's being done.

The Court: I don't know that they have been written by the United States Attorney.

Mr. Schultz: We are not litigating here, your Honor, whether sexual intercourse is beautiful or not. We are litigating whether or not the city could permit tens of thousands of people to come in and do in their parks what this man said they were going to do.

The Court Oh, you needn't argue that.

Mr. Schultz Yes, your Honor.

Mr. Kunstler: The city permitted them to do it in trees, your Honor, as I recall some of the testimony. The policeman was right under the tree

The Court The last observation of Mr. Kunstler may be stricken from the record.

\* \* \*

Q By the way, was there any acid in Lincoln Park in Chicago?

A. In the reservoir, in the lake?

Q. No, among the people

A. Among the people was there LSD? Well, there might have been. I don't know It is colorless, odorless and tasteless. One can never tell.

Q. What about the honey, was there anything special about any honey in Lincoln Park?

A. There was honey, there was—I was told there was honey, that there was—I was getting stoned eating brownies. Honey, yes. Lots of people were—

Q. There was LSD to your knowledge in both the honey and in some brownies? Isn't that right?

A. I would have to be a chemist to know that for a fact. It is colorless, odorless and tasteless.

Q. Didn't you state on a prior occasion that Ed Sanders passed out from too much honey?

A. Yes. People passed out

The Court: You have answered the question.

The Witness: Yes. Passed out from honey? Sure. Is that illegal?

*By Mr Schultz*

Q. And that a man named Spade passed out on honey?

A. Yes. I made up that name. Frankie Spade, wasn't it?

It must have been strong honey

The Court: The last observation of the witness may go out and the jury is directed to disregard it and the witness is directed again not to make gratuitous observations.

\* \* \*

Q. It was part of your myth in getting people to Chicago, Mr. Hoffman, that it was announced that the Yippies would block traffic, isn't that right?

151

A. That I said that people would block traffic?

Q. No, not what you said but that it was part of the Yippie myth created early in 1968, a statement that they would block traffic?

A. Yes, I believe I heard it from Sheriff Joseph Woods.

\* \* \*

Q. Now, prior to the beginning of the convention, Mr. Hoffman, that is, on August 22 at about five in the morning, do you recall having coffee with some police officers? I think August 22 was the day that you later went into court before Judge Lynch, so that it would be that morning, if that helps you.

A. With the policemen that were trailing me from the Chicago Red Squad? Yes. They bought me breakfast every morning and drove me around. It could have been—yes. Do you want to go further and then maybe I can recall what was said?

Q. Do you recall while having coffee with—

A. I don't drink coffee so—I haven't drank coffee for three years, so—

Q. While having breakfast—

A. It is one of the drugs I refrain from using.

. . .

Q. It was your Yippie myth, Mr. Hoffman, was it not, that people will among other things in Chicago smoke dope and fuck and fight cops?

A. Yes. I wrote that as a prediction. So did Norman Mailer, I might add.

**December 31, 1969**
*Continued cross-examination of Defendant A. Hoffman by Government Attorney Schultz*

Q. In fact, you thought it was a great boon to you that your case [requesting a permit to use city park—ed.] had been assigned to Judge Lynch because you could make a lot of hay out of it, isn't that right, Mr. Hoffman?

A. No. No, I had learned at that time that they had turned down the McCarthy people's request for a permit, and I thought if they weren't going to get it, we sure as hell weren't, either, and that was one of the decisions.

The Court: Mr. Witness, we don't allow profanity from the witness stand.

The Witness: Well, I wouldn't want—all right.

*By Mr. Schultz:*

Q. When did you prepare, Mr. Hoffman, your—

The Court: And I don't like being laughed at by the witness—by a witness in this court, sir.

The Witness:   I know that laughing is a crime. I already—

The Court:   I direct you not to laugh at an observation by the Court. I don't laugh at you.

The Witness:   Are you sure?

The Court:   I should?

The Witness:   I said, "Are you sure?"

The Court:   I haven't laughed at you during all of the many weeks and months of this trial.

The Witness:   Well—

Mr. Schultz:   May I proceed, your Honor?

The Court:   Yes, you may.

Mr. Kunstler:   I am not sure, your Honor, "hell" is classified as profanity, and I think from what has been circulated in this courtroom it's hardly profane language.

The Court:   Oh, I will concede that it is a lesser degree of—

Mr. Kunstler:   I am not even sure it is classified as profanity.

The Court:   You don't think so.

Mr. Kunstler:   I don't think—

The Court:   Well, probably not among your clients, but I—

Mr. Kunstler:   I take it among your friends, too, Judge, and I would say you have used it and everyone else has used it.

The Court:   I don't allow a witness to testify that way on the witness stand, if you don't mind, sir.

Mr. Kunstler:   I object to the dictionary—

The Court:   We strive here to conduct this Court in the traditional—

Mr. Kunstler:   You say my clients are habituated to using "hell," you know, which is a categorization of my clients. My clients use lots of words, and your friends use lots of words—

The Court:   I don't think you know any of my friends.

Mr. Kunstler:   You'd be surprised, your Honor.

The Court:   Please don't—

Mr. Kunstler:   The father of one of our staff men is a close friend of yours.

The Court:   If they know you, they haven't told me about it.

Mr. Schultz:   Your Honor, may we proceed?

The Court:   Yes.

The Witness:   I know your chauffeur.

*By Mr. Schultz:*

Q. Mr. Hoffman, when did you prepare your original—I'll wait until you're finished laughing, Mr. Hoffman.

A. I was just laughing at your profanity.

Q. Are you ready, Mr. Hoffman?

A. Yes, ready.

\*     \*     \*

Q. Are you finished, Mr. Hoffman?

A. Yes, I'm finished.

Q. Do you want to do any headstands for us?

A. No, but I think I might like to go to the bathroom, if I could.

Mr. Schultz: Your Honor, we only have about ten more minutes. I'd like very much to get this finished.

The Witness: Ten more minutes?

*By Mr. Schultz:*

Q. Can you wait ten more minutes, Mr. Hoffman?

Mr. Schultz: Your Honor, can we go for ten more minutes?

*By The Witness:*

A. Yes. Yes, I'll wait.

*By Mr. Schultz:*

Q. Did you hear Davis say that on the last day of the—on the last day of the Democratic National Convention there was going to be a march if there was anybody left? Did you hear him say that?

A. Was the last question— Did you ask me to do a headstance?

The Court: Answer this question, please.

The Witness: Oh. I was going to oblige.

The Court: If you can.

The Witness: Go ahead.

*By Mr. Schultz:*

Q. Did you hear the question?

A. No, sorry. I was thinking about the last one.

The Court: Read it to the witness.

Mr. Weinglass: Your Honor, he is indicating he would like to answer the question before. Mr. Schultz has expressed a request that he do a headstand, and I think he should have, in answer, an opportunity to comply with that request if that is what the witness wants to do.

The Court: I don't think that was put in the form of a question.

Mr. Schultz: I didn't intend it to be.

Mr. Weinglass: He is stating—

Mr. Schultz: He is clowning for us, and I thought maybe in his clowning he would want to do a headstand or a cartwheel or something.

The Court: You don't want to do that, do you. You don't, do you?

The Witness: I want to comply with Mr. Schultz' request, if he wants to see such a thing.

The Court: You want to answer the question. All right. He says no, in effect.

The Witness: I think it might start a riot.

The Court: That question has been answered.

. . .

The Witness: Could you hurry it up a little? O.K. Sorry.
*By Mr. Schultz:*
Q. Mr. Hoffman—
Mr. Schultz: Well, maybe we ought to take a break now.
Mr. Hoffman is uncomfortable.
The Witness: Well, is it five more minutes?
The Court: Well, I don't know whether "uncomfortable"
is the proper characterization.
The Witness: Just two minutes.
*[The Court then recessed.]*

\* \* \*

*[Concerning Judge's ruling that Witness Hoffman must
answer a prosecution question]*
The Witness: I consider that an unfair ruling and I am
not going to answer. I can't answer.
The Court: I direct you to answer.
The Witness: Well, I take the Fifth Amendment, then.
Mr. Schultz: Your Honor, the witness has taken the stand
to defend the charges here. He has testified on direct examin-
ation and he has waived his Fifth Amendment right.
The Court: I order you to answer, sir.
The Witness: What does that mean?
The Court: I order you to answer the question, sir. You
are required to under the law.

. . .

The Court: I order you to answer the question. Do you
refuse?
Mr. Weinglass: Your Honor, could we have a recess?
The Court: No, no. We just had a recess for that purpose.
Mr. Weinglass: For another question—
The Court: No, no. No further recesses. And I ask you to
sit down.
Mr. Schultz: Your Honor, may the court reporter repeat
the question.
The Court: Yes. Read the question to the witness.
*(Question read.)*
The Court: You may answer. I order you to answer.
The Witness: I just get yes or no, huh? Yes. I was there.
All my years on the witness stand, I never heard anything
like that ruling.

**January 2, 1970**
*Continued cross-examination of Defendant A. Hoffman
by Government Attorney*
Q. I show you Government's Exhibit 18 for identification,

which is a photograph. Do you recognize the photograph?

A. Do I recognize the general scene?

Q. Yes.

A. Yes.

Q. Do you see yourself in the photograph?

A. Well, we all look alike. . . .

\* \* \*

Mr. Weinglass: When we were cross-examining on grand jury testimony—

The Court: Mr. Weingrass, I must caution you again when there is a ruling, the argument ceases. That is good courtroom procedure.

The Witness: Weingrass?

\* \* \*

Q. Mr. Hoffman, isn't it a fact that one of the reasons why you came to Chicago was simply to wreck American society?

A. No.

Q. Isn't it a fact, Mr. Hoffman, that—

A. Do you consider the Democratic Party part of American society?

The Court: Mr. Witness, you are not interrogating the lawyer; he is asking you questions.

\* \* \*

By Mr. Schultz:

Q. As you watched on Thursday, you knew you had won the battle of Chicago. You knew you had smashed the Democrats' chances and destroyed the two party system in this country and perhaps with it electoral politics, isn't that a fact?

A. I knew it had destroyed itself and that the whole world would see, and that was the sense of the victory.

**January 6, 1970**

[*Colloquy between Defense Counsel and the Judge concerning admissibility of a document offered as evidence by Government Counsel*]

Mr. Kunstler: . . . Your Honor, this is apparently a Yippie document rather than a conspiracy document. We have no objection to the Court seeing it. It calls for a public demonstration.

The Court: Is it a document distribution of which has been participated in by one or more of the defendants?

Mr. Kunstler: No, no. I didn't say that at all. It is apparently a Yippie document—

The Court: That means nothing to me. Despite the fact that I have been on trial here for more than three months, I still don't know what a Yippie is, so I wouldn't know what a Yippie document—

Mr. Kunstler: I think if there had been more questions permitted on that, your Honor, your Honor would be more erudite in that field by this time.

The Court: I'd hate to think my erudition depended on my—

Mr. Kunstler: Erudition in one field, anyway.

The Court: I'd hate to think my erudition in any field depended on that . . .

* * *

The Court: I don't listen to the broadcasts of the defendants for a variety of reasons. First, I don't expect to hear anything nice about myself on the air . . .

[But see November 12, *supra.*—ed.]

* * *

*Direct examination of Chicago Mayor Richard Daley, called as a witness by the Defense, by Defense Attorney Kunstler*

Q. Mayor Daley, on the 28th of August, 1968, did you say to Senator Ribicoff—

Mr. Foran: Oh, your Honor, I object.

*By Mr. Kunstler:*

Q. (*continuing*)—"Fuck you, you Jew son-of-a-bitch, you lousy mother fucker, go home"?

Mr. Foran: Listen to that, I object to that kind of conduct in a courtroom. Of all of the improper, foolish questions, typical, your Honor, of making up questions that have nothing to do with the lawsuit.

Mr. Kunstler: That is not a made up question, your Honor. We can prove that.

Mr. Foran: Oh, they can? That is so improper. I ask that counsel be admonished, your Honor.

. . .

Mr. Kunstler: I have the source, your Honor.

The Court: May I suggest to you, sir, that this witness is your witness and you may not ask him any leading questions even of the sort that you proposed—especially, rather, of the sort that I heard a part of a moment ago.

[But see November 12, *supra*—ed.]

* * *

[*Colloquy concerning Judge's ruling that Mayor Daley was not a hostile witness.*]

Mr. Kunstler: The Court ruled adversely.

157

The Court: Don't make it appear that I used some kind of club. I am trying to rule according to the law, based on years of experience on this bench, Mr. Kunstler. I didn't club you into anything.

Mr. Kunstler: Well, your Honor, it had some of that feeling as far as I was concerned, because I thought your Honor was wrong, and your Honor has been ruled wrong in the past. There's nothing sacrosanct about either one of us in the fact of whether we interpret the law—

The Court: I only do my honest best, Mr. Kunstler. I know of no judge who has been on the bench, especially as long as I have, who hasn't been ruled wrong, and I think that's an unkind remark—

Mr. Kunstler: No, I am only saying we are not infallible—

The Court: —for a lawyer to make—

Mr. Kunstler: —either one of us.

The Court: I resent it, and I told a lawyer who made that kind of a remark to me once that it was a cheap sort of remark. I repeat it, sir.

Mr. Kunstler: Well, your Honor, I am saying it because, your Honor—there is no infallibility on either side, and I am trying to persuade your Honor—that's my job, to persuade your Honor—

The Court: Well, you will never persuade me by insulting me.

Mr. Kunstler: That is not an insult.

The Court: Yes, it is.

Mr. Kunstler: That is a little ultra sensitivity.

The Court: You have done it during this trial before, and you are not going to continue to do it, and if you do—

Mr. Kunstler: You have taken as insults a lot of things which I don't think were insults in any sense of the word.

The Court: All right.

Mr. Kunstler: You have an ultra sensitivity in a lot of areas, I know that.

The Court: I have no ultra sensitivity, but I have good ears.

Mr. Kunstler: Well, they lead to an area of ultra sensitivity, I think, in some fields.

The Court: Well, you leave my personality and my hearing and my sensitivity to me. That is not the function of a partisan advocate in the trial of a lawsuit.

Mr. Kunstler: Well, your Honor has engaged in some references to hearing, et cetera, but I think we are probably wasting some time here.

The Court: Oh, I think you are.

Mr Kunstler    Well, I said 'we"

The Court    I think you are  When you call a man as
your witness, he is your witness until he s proved hostile.
This witness has not been proven hostile.

* * *

Mr. Foran.    Your Honor, may we suspend until the Defendant Davis returns to the courtroom?

Mr. Kunstler    Your Honor, the defendants have permission to leave for necessary purposes.

The Court:    For a necessary purpose—

Mr Kunstler    We can't look through the wall so I assume
he is fulfilling that necessary purpose.

* * *

*By Mr. Kunstler:*

Q. I direct your attention, Mayor Daley, to March 28, 1968;
do you recall having any conversation or meeting with
Mr. Stahl on that day?

A. Well, being the Deputy Mayor, I would meet with him
several times a day.

Q. Do you recall any conversation or meeting with him with
reference to the Youth International Party?

A. I gave Mr. Stahl the same instructions I gave any other
department, certainly, to meet with them, to try to co-
operate with them, and do everything they could to
make sure that they would be given every courtesy
and hospitality while they were in the city of Chicago.

· ·

*[After a brief recess] By Mr. Kunstler:*

Q. Mayor Daley, in one of your answers to my previous
questions, you stated something about your instructions
to offer hospitality to people coming to Chicago.

Mr. Foran:    I object to the form of the question, your
Honor, as leading.

Mr. Kunstler:    It's not even a question, your Honor. It's a
statement, a predicate for—

The Court.    Well, ask the question. Don't summarize the
previous evidence. I sustain the objection.

*By Mr. Kunstler:*

Q. In view of what you said, did you consider that the use
of night sticks on the heads of demonstrators was
hospitable?

Mr. Foran:    Objection, your Honor.

The Court    I sustain the objection.

* * *

*[The following is illustrative of Defense Counsel's diffi-
culty in questioning Mayor Daley due to the Court's rul-*

159

*ing that he was a hostile witness. Were he declared a hostile witness by the Court, the defense would be accorded wider latitude in the scope and form of its questions*] *By Mr. Kunstler:*

Q. Mayor Daley, do you believe that people have the right to demonstrate against the war in Vietnam?

Mr. Foran: Your Honor, I object to the form of the question. It's an improper form of a question.

The Court: I sustain the objection to the question.

*By Mr. Kunstler:*

Q. Now, Mayor Daley, you've testified that you were at the Democratic National Convention on Wednesday, August 28, and I questioned you about a statement with reference to Senator Ribicoff.

Can you indicate what you did say to Senator Ribicoff on that day.

Mr. Foran: Your Honor, I object to the form of the question, and again I ask that counsel be admonished. Those are improper questions under the law of evidence.

The Court: I sustain the objection, and I remind you again and admonish you, Mr. Kunstler, of my order.

Mr. Kunstler: Your Honor, I have tried to reiterate ten times that in view of the nature of this witness, it is impossible to examine him and get to the truth of anything with these restrictions—

The Court: This witness is no different from any other witness.

Mr. Kunstler: But, your Honor, that isn't so. He is different from any other witness. He is the Mayor of the city—

The Court: The fact that he happens to occupy a high public place—other than that, he is a witness. In this court he is just a witness.

Mr. Kunstler: But, your Honor, the defendants—

The Court: Your witness.

Mr. Kunstler: —have publicly stated that they believe he is the real culprit here.

The Court: You procured him to come to a court through a writ which was issued out of this Court. He is here.

If you ask him proper questions—

Mr. Kunstler: We are trying, your Honor, to get to the truth of what happened during Convention Week.

The Court: You must get at the truth through proper questions, sir.

Mr. Foran: Through the law of evidence, your Honor, that it has taken five hundred years to achieve.

*By Mr. Kunstler:*

Q. Mayor Daley, have you been familiar at all with the report of President Johnson's Commission to investigate the causes of violence at the Democratic National Convention?

Mr. Foran: I object, your Honor.

The Court: I sustain the objection.

Q. Do you agree with that Commission's finding that a police riot took place in the city of Chicago?

Mr. Foran: Your Honor, now I object to that. The law of evidence, your Honor, has grown up because it helps—with five hundred years of the adversary system, it helps to reach the truth if you obey the law of evidence, and I object to that question.

I ask the jury be instructed to disregard it, and I ask that counsel be admonished for asking an intentionally improper question.

The Court: I do sustain the objection, because it is grossly improper. I direct the jury to disregard the last question put to the witness by Mr. Kunstler.

\* \* \*

[*In the absence of the jury*]

Mr. Kunstler: . . . In view of the Court's ruling refusing to declare Mayor Daley a hostile witness, defendants are unable to cross-examine him adequately.

Had the Mayor been designated a hostile witness, the defendants would have offered proof through his testimony to show the following:

1. That there was a conspiracy, overt or tacit, between Mayor Daley and the Democratic Administration of Lyndon B. Johnson to prevent or crush any significant demonstrations against war, poverty, imperialism, and racism, and in support of alternative cultures at the 1968 Democratic National Convention.

2. That the members of this conspiracy planned and executed the use of every means at their disposal, including calculated official inertia, in the processing of necessary permit applications, the deliberate intimidation of potential demonstrators, in order to deter their participation in the Democratic National Convention . . . the open and blatant encouragement of violence toward demonstrators by police and other military forces, and the employment of savage, brutal, and inhuman tactics to intimidate, deter, or prevent the exercise by the people of their most fundamental constitutional rights, all in order to prevent or crush such public exhibition of dissatisfaction with American domestic and foreign policies.

3. That in so doing the conspirators were determined to

continue the fraudulent myth that the people of the United States had a real voice in their Government and that they would have a significant choice in the national election of 1968 . . .

4. That Mayor Daley obtained and maintains in power in Chicago by the creation and maintenance of a corrupt political machine . . .

5. That this political machine by its control or influence over national, state, and local legislatures, the judiciary, and executive offices at every level of government, is determined, whatever the cost, to, through democratic and representative government, prevent the exploration, determination and effectuation of meaningful solutions to the awesome problems presently facing the people of the United States and those of the rest of the world.

6. That the conspirators, in order to continue and even accelerate their oppressive and inhuman policies, have embarked on a program of intense and brutal repression against all those who are seeking such solution . . .

7. That in furtherance of this conspiracy, Mayor Daley among other things:

(a) On April 15, 1968, ordered his police to respond to the assassination of Dr. Martin Luther King, Jr., with orders to shoot to kill arsonists and shoot to maim or cripple looters in the black community.

(b) Attempted first to obstruct the peace parade of the Chicago Peace Council on April 27, 1968, and then brutalized the marchers therein as a warning to peace demonstrators to stay away from the Democratic National Convention.

(c) Attempted first to obstruct the demonstrations at the Democratic National Convention in August of 1968 and then harassed, victimized, and brutalized the participants therein, and

(d) Attempted to mislead the people of Chicago and the United States as to the nature and cause of such obstructive and brutal tactics.

8. That in furtherance of this conspiracy, Mayor Daley utilized the services of members of his political machine, including those of Thomas Foran, the United States Attorney for the Eastern District of Illinois and a former Assistant Corporation Counsel of the city of Chicago.

9. That the indictment in this case was procured as a result of the said conspiracy in order to (a) shift the deserved blame for the disorders surrounding the Democratic Convention from the real conspirators or some of them to deliberately

selected individuals symbolizing various categories and degrees of dissent from American foreign and domestic policies.

(b) punish those individuals for their role in leading and articulating such dissents, and

(c) deter others from supporting or expressing such dissent in the future. . . .

. . .

14. That behind the Mayor are powerful corporate interests who determine broad public policy in Chicago but are responsible to no elected or public body. . . . which no group of citizens can effectively check or reverse without dislodging these private interests of their control over public officials and institutions.

Voice: Right on.

Mr. Kunstler: This is our offer of proof. This is what we would have hoped to have proved had we been able to have the Mayor declared, as we think he ought to be, a hostile witness and thus give us the ability to ask leading questions and under the guise of cross-examination of a hostile witness.

The Court: Mr. United States Attorney, what is the position of the Government in respect to what has been described here as an offer of proof?

Mr. Foran: First of all, an offer of proof under the law has certain requirements of specificity, none of which that offer of proof implies.

Secondly, that the basis of the offer of proof that they were unable to prove these conclusionary statements by reason of the fact that they could not question the witness with leading questions is a clear misstatement of the law. The rule of evidence that has grown up over hundreds and hundreds of years was designed as it was to ask proper questions, because it was most likely thereby to elicit the truth, rather than have a counsel be permitted to testify, as it were, by question. The classic one that lawyers always use to demonstrate the leading question is, "Did you hit your wife with an axe?" If the witness says no, you say, "What did you hit her with?" And that is what the character has been of question after question that Mr. Kunstler has proposed to this witness.

Every single proper question and many that were leading and suggestive that the Government did not object to this witness answered directly and clearly, giving every indication that any proper question he was asked and that the Court held was proper or to which the Government did not object he would have answered and he would answer.

Some of the questions—the structures of some of those questions were so obviously improper that it was a clear

163

demonstration that the whole purpose of the call of this witness was to permit a conclusionary speech as this offer of proof was. It was not in any sense a proper offer of proof and the Government for that reason and for the reason of the Court's proper rulings on the questions that were proposed by Mr. Kunstler which in no way keep these defendants from eliciting the truth from this witness, the Government objects to the offer of proof on that ground.

The Court: The United States Attorney has characterized the offer as a speech.

Without agreeing or disagreeing with that statement, certainly it is not an offer of proof and was obviously carefully prepared before the questions were even put to the witness.

The proper method of making an offer is to place a witness on the stand, ask the question, and upon the sustaining of an objection, state with particularity what the witness would answer if permitted to do so. Nothing less constitutes an offer.

The objection of the Government to the so-called offer of proof of the defendants will be sustained.

\* \* \*

*Direct examination of Defense Witness Cunningham by Defense Attorney Weinglass*

Mr. Schultz: Your Honor, before we proceed with the examination, may we have the defendants present? We are missing three of them now. It is improper that the defendants aren't here during an examination of one of their witnesses.

The Court: Yes. We will wait until they come in.

The Marshal: One is in the rest room, your Honor.

The Court: We will wait for him.

*By Mr. Weinglass:*

Q. Now after the police chased you this length of four or five blocks—

Mr. Schultz: Objection to summarizing the witness' answer.

The Court: No, that is not proper, Mr. Weinglass. You do that, I know.

Mr. Weinglass: Well, your Honor—

The Court: This summarizing of what the witness—the summary of what the witness' answer to a preceding question was is not proper examination. I sustain the objection. The jury has heard the answer of the witness. You needn't repeat it.

Mr. Weinglass: I was using approximately seven or eight words to introduce the next question for the sake of continuity, but I know we are in a hurry, and we can't afford that kind of time.

The Court: We are not in a hurry. You take all the time

you want to examine this witness. No one has ever said we are in a hurry.

Mr. Weinglass:   I am sorry. I thought that was the thrust of Mr. Schultz's comment before.

The Court:   Except you.

Mr. Schultz:   We are in a hurry, your Honor.

. . .

. . . Because the jury has had to sit here and listen to nonsensical questions, direct and cross, wasting all of our time. We want to get it out of the way, ask pertinent questions, determine the facts, get the trial over so that the jury can go home. That's the hurry we're in.

Mr. Weinglass:   I know Mr. Schultz believes in summary executions, but unfortunately the Constitution allows for a defense, and if he is a little impatient with it, we have a right to put it on.

The Court:   Ask your next question, if you have one.

\* \* \*

[*Government Attorney Schultz on Defense Attorneys' contention regarding the admissibility of defense evidence*]

Mr. Schultz:   . . . Mr. Weinglass knows that if this Court makes a mistake in the rules of evidence, he has the appropriate recourse and he should not, nor should Mr. Kunstler on his examination of the Mayor, state that, "Well, if you are going to oppress me, this is what I am going to have to do." Lawyers don't act that way. Lawyers ask the question and when an objection is made if it is sustained, he has a record, he has made a record. And if he is right he can prevail at another time. But he does not say in front of the jury or imply in front of the jury that he is being treated unfairly.

## January 7, 1970

*Continued direct examination of Carl Oglesby, a New Left writer, by Defense Attorney Weinglass*

Mr. Foran:   Your Honor, may that answer be stricken, the volunteered statement?

The Court:   Yes. . . .

The Witness:   May I ask why?

The Court:   I am under no obligation to explain my rulings to witnesses, sir.

The Witness:   Oh, well, I wouldn't imagine that you were. I am curious, however, as to why an answer to a question is stricken.

The Court:   Well, you see the lawyers after court who brought you to court.

The Witness:   I think they would be as mystified as myself, sir.

The Court:   I don't explain my rulings. I am not conducting a class here. I am here to try this case.

* * *

*Direct examination of Defense Witness Paul Bradley, Asssistant Public Defender for Cook County, by Defense Attorney Kunstler*

Q. Now after you had communicated the information to Sgt. Larson which was either that week or the successive week, were you ever visited by any member of the IID?

A. No, I was not.

Q. Were you ever contacted with reference to giving testimony or further information?

Mr. Schultz:   I object to that. That is improper. He doesn't know what the IID did in its investigation. He was interviewed by the IID and to ask him what did the IID do, did you ever testify, is improper at this point.

Mr. Kunstler:   I don't know if Mr. Schultz is in the same courtroom I am, your Honor, but I asked the question only whether they interviewed him.

The Court:   Look around and see if you don't know.

Mr. Kunstler:   I see physically, but I just don't see that he is mentally here.

The Court:   I don't want to sit here and have a lawyer say he doesn't know whether his adversary is in the courtroom or not.

Mr. Kunstler:   I see him.

The Court:   I don't want to take advantage of you.

Mr. Kunstler:   My statement is, your Honor, that if Mr. Schultz is here with us today he is not hearing what the questions are because if the question is read back I think your Honor will see I merely asked him whether they had interviewed him. He would know that.

* * *

[*Colloquy with jury out of room*]

The Court: . . . —I deny you the right to call Mr. Ball [an attorney—ed.].

Mr. Kunstler:   Your Honor, I hope you are not denying it because you appear to be somewhat upset at some laughter in the courtroom.

The Court:   I am not upset—I don't upset very easily. I try to discipline people who are indecent in their courtroom conduct on occasions, Mr. Kunstler.

Mr. Kunstler:   I know, but—

The Court:   I think you must have noticed over three

months plus that I am not easily upset. I sometimes am embarrassed for those who participate in demonstrations here in the United States District Court, but I—even with the assistance of marshals, I am not always able to do away with them. No, I am not upset. Put it out of your mind.

Mr. Kunstler: It was obvious to me that your demeanor had suddenly changed.

The Court: Nobody at that table upsets me, but I shall continue to the end of this trial to act as the governor of the trial, as I have been directed to do by the United States District Court, and I will do it in the best fashion possible.

## January 8, 1970

*Cross-examination of Defense Witness David Evans, a graduate student at Northwestern University, by Government Attorney Foran*

Mr. Foran: Your Honor, may we suspend again? Mr. Kunstler is gone. Three of the defendants are unrepresented. Mr. Kunstler is not here.

Mr. Weinglass: Your Honor, Mr. Kunstler is temporarily out of the room as he and I have been—

The Court: I will wait for him.

Mr. Weinglass: —periodically in order to—

The Court: I will wait for him. From here on a lawyer will have to get my permission to leave the trial.

Mr. Weinglass: We have asked the Court for that permission and you denied it, your Honor, so the case can go on without interruption. It is not necessary to have both attorneys present.

Mr. Foran: That is not true and—

Mr. Weinglass: We specifically made a motion on that point.

The Court: If you will permit me, this trial will not go on at this time without the attendance of Mr. Kunstler.

And here he is.

Mr. Kunstler, hereafter when you wish to leave during the progress of the trial, please ask the permission of the Court.

Mr. Kunstler: Right. Someone had come and asked for me and wanted to know—

The Court: I don't know what happened. I wasn't told. Hereafter, please ask the permission of the Court.

Mr. Kunstler: Right. I just didn't want to interrupt.

The Court: I am just telling you what to do in the future.

Mr. Kunstler: Right.

The Court: That is just common courtesy, good manners.

\* \* \*

167

The Court: Now, you are going to stop arguing after a ruling. I have tried for weeks, Mr. Weinglass, to tell you what the rules are. You have disregarded them. I tell you now again, there will be no argument after a ruling.

Mr. Kunstler: That should be for both sides of the table, your Honor, because there has been argument after ruling by the Government.

The Court: I didn't invite you to tell me how to conduct this trial.

Mr. Kunstler: I just want you to be fair. That's all.

\* \* \*

Mr. Kunstler: Your Honor, the prosecution table—Mr. Cubbage has left the room without asking your Honor's permission. Mr. Stanley leaves almost after every one of our witnesses.

The Court: They have only one client, United States of America, and there has always been a lawyer there—

Mr. Marshal.

Mr. Kunstler: And we don't tattle every time they leave the room and run up as Mr. Schultz does to let you know that I was outside for a minute.

The Court: You don't—

Mr. Kunstler: Because we are not little babies and doing things like that. We are above that kind of ridiculous aspects in a courtroom of whispering to Mr. Foran that I'm not in the room when I happen to be helping a witness who is lost in the corridor here to get to the witness room. It's ridiculous. There is no way we can conduct a defense under those circumstances.

The Court: You are conducting—

Mr. Kunstler: Over great hardships, your Honor.

The Court: I don't know about a defense, but you are doing some conducting, and you are being—

Mr. Kunstler: I know, but under some great hardships.

\* \* \*

*Direct examination of Defense Witness Jan Linfield, a social worker, by Defense Attorney Kunstler.*

Mr. Kunstler: Your Honor, I want you to notice that Mr. Stanley is now leaving the room. No request was made of your Honor, no courtesy was made of your Honor. He goes after every one of our witnesses to check his FBI files on our witnesses.

\* \* \*

The Court: Call your next witness, please.

Mr. Weinglass: Your Honor, without excusing the jury, our next witness is waiting for his shoes and if I may have a few minutes—

The Court:   Well, I have seen people come in here almost without shoes so he may come in without his shoes. I will excuse him.

Mr. Kunstler:   I just want to see if they have arrived.

Mr. Foran:   Your Honor—

Mr. Kunstler:   Your Honor, may I have the Court's permission to attend the men's room?

The Court:   To attend the—

Mr. Kunstler:   Well, I am being very delicate. I want to phrase it delicately.

The Court:   I think you used the wrong verb, Mr. Kunstler. If you want to visit—

Mr. Kunstler:   I will accept that substitution, your Honor.

The Court:   You may go.

Mr. Kunstler:   Thank you.

*(Brief intermission.)*

Mr. Kunstler:   I have returned, your Honor.

The Court:   Oh, let's be done with that. Really that doesn't amuse me at all.

Mr. Kunstler:   Your Honor, I am just trying to live up to what Mr. Schultz apparently thinks we ought to do like in a schoolhouse, check in and check out.

The Court:   My eyesight is not impaired. When you walk in here, I can see, sir.

Bring your next witness to the stand.

\* \* \*

*Direct examination of Defense Witness Ed Sanders, leader of the rock group "The Fugs," by Defense Attorney Weinglass*

Q. Mr. Sanders, could you indicate to the Court and to the jury what your present occupation is.

A. I am a poet, songwriter, leader of a rock and roll band, publisher, editor, recording artist, peace-creep—

Mr. Schultz:   What was the last one, please. I didn't hear the last one.

The Court:   Miss Reporter, read the last words of the witness. I think there were two words and they were hyphenated.

*(Record read by the reporter.)*

The Court:   Peace-creep?

The Witness:   Yes, sir.

The Court:   Will you please spell it for the reporter.

The Witness:   P-e-a-c-e, hyphen, c-r-e-e-p.

The Court:   Peace-creep, Mr. Schultz.

*By the Witness:*

A. *(continuing)* And yodeler.

169

*By Mr. Weinglass:*

Q. Now in connection with your yodeling activities—

Mr. Schultz: Your Honor, this is all very entertaining but it is a waste of time. We don't have to do anything in connection with his yodeling to get to the issues in this case.

I ask you to ask Mr. Weinglass to stop making this a funny thing which will last much longer and to get to the issues.

If he will testify as to what he knows—

The Court: Beyond mere lasting longer, I will let you ask a question. I am obligated to let him ask a question.

Mr. Weinglass: Your Honor, quite frankly I thought seizing the Federal Building this morning was quite funny. It is just a question of taste in humor.

Mr. Schultz: Yes, it was quite funny. It was quite funny.

Mr. Kunstler: I might indicate, your Honor, Mr. Cubbage is not at the prosecutor's table.

The Court: I think I told you that I wasn't amused by any of your observations. There is no obligation for Mr. Cubbage to be there.

Mr. Kunstler: They have three lawyers for the government. We have two for eight clients—seven clients.

The Court: The government is represented by two lawyers and they are both here.

Mr. Kunstler: Three lawyers.

The Court: I say it is represented at the table. And don't you be concerned about their representation.

Mr. Kunstler: Well, they are concerned about our representation.

Mr. Schultz: We are concerned about these defendants' rights. We are concerned about the record we are making in this courtroom.

The Court: That is right. That is right. I am, too.

Mr. Kunstler: They are very concerned about our rights, your Honor. That is—I had better sit down.

The Court: I think you had better. That is the best decision you have made.

Mr. Kunstler: I was so overwhelmed by their concern, your Honor—

The Court: I thought you said you were going to sit down.

Mr. Kunstler: But your Honor made another comment so I thought that I would answer it.

The Court: You may finish your question.

\* \* \*

The Court: Please let me tell you that, Mr. Witness. It is conceivable that the Government lawyer who has just sat down may make an objection to a question put to you by Mr. —

Mr. Weinglass:  Weinglass.

\*   \*   \*

Mr. Schultz:  But, Your Honor, there is a problem. Most of the questions are leading, and we don't object to all of them but we keep on getting up and getting up. As I said before, it becomes embarrassing. For people who don't know the legal rules, it looks very bad for the Government to constantly be getting up. Now if these questions are constantly asked and the Government has to constantly get up, it makes it appear that we are trying to hide certain things and we just want him to conform—

The Court:  I appreciate that, Mr. Schultz. The record is replete with the Court's admonitions to both lawyers for the defendants not to—

Mr. Kunstler:  Your Honor, is this an objection or a speech, because we don't understand it.

Mr. Schultz:  I am begging—I am begging defense counsel to ask questions properly.

The Court:  Don't beg.

Mr. Schultz:  That is what it is.

The Court:  Don't beg. You needn't beg. I will order them not to ask leading questions.

I order you not to ask any further leading questions.

Mr. Weinglass:  Your Honor, I am prepared to submit to this Court tomorrow morning a memorandum of law justifying the position we are taking in asking these questions. I invite the Government to prepare an answering memorandum.

. . .

The Court:  I sustain the objection to the question.

Mr. Weinglass:  May I submit a brief or memorandum of law to the Court?

The Court:  I don't want briefs on the subject of leading questions.

Mr. Kunstler:  Your Honor, you sustained the beg— there is no objection. As I understand it, Mr. Schultz made his speech and then there was no objection, as I understood it. He made a beg, whatever a beg is.

Mr. Schultz:  That is the position we are put in, your Honor, when we are the recipients of this kind of conduct. We have to plead with the Court to plead with them and they turn around and laugh at us.

The Court:  You do not want me to interpret what you said as an objection to the question?

Mr. Schultz:  I asked your Honor to instruct defense counsel and you did so instruct.

The Court:  I did.

Mr. Kunstler: Then you sustained a nonexistent objection, because it was—

The Court: Mr. Kunstler, I will not hear you and Mr. Weinglass at the same time on the same question. I will ask you to sit down.

\* \* \*

*[Colloquy between Mr. Kunstler and Judge Hoffman during cross-examination of Ed Sanders]*

Mr. Kunstler: Your Honor, I would like to know why we are having people removed from the courtroom again. We were promised an explanation yesterday by your Honor from the marshals, or two days ago.

The Court: You just leave the management of the courtroom to the managers of the courtroom.

Mr. Kunstler: We can't do that, your Honor. This is a public trial. We have a right when people with beards and long hair are thrown out to know why and we want to know why.

The Court: If you will excuse me, sir—

Mr. Kunstler: No. I am arguing. I am making an argument.

The Court: You won't excuse me? Then I won't hear you.

Mr. Kunstler: Your Honor, you have told me 40 times never to interrupt you and we have refrained from this. Now you are interrupting me.

The Court: Yes, and I will continue to do so when you say things you are not entitled to say.

. . .

Mr. Kunstler: . . . We are entitled to a public trial and if people are removed—

The Court: You are getting a public trial. The doors have been open ever since September 24, sir.

Mr. Kunstler: The doors being opened doesn't mean anything, your Honor, if people are thrown out of the courtroom.

The Court: It does to me. It does to me.

That will be all, sir.

## January 9, 1970

*Direct examination of Defense Witness Donald Kalish, professor of philosophy at UCLA, by Defense Attorney Kunstler*

The Marshal: Excuse me, Mr. Kunstler. [Next sentence addressed to Mr. Rubin—ed.] Will you sit down, sir.

Mr. Kunstler: Your Honor, Mr. Rubin is, I think, seeking to go to the men's room.

The Court: We made an order on that yesterday.

172

Mr. Kunstler: But that's a jail cell, your Honor, with an open, uncovered toilet.

The Court: I know. That was my order, and that order will be in effect.

Mr. Kunstler: But, your Honor, they are not convicted yet. They don't have to go into a jail cell.

The Court: That is not a jail cell. It's a men's room, and he may use that.

Mr. Kunstler: It's the first men's room I ever saw with bars, your Honor.

The Court: There are locks on the doors.

Mr. Kunstler: But—

The Court: They will use that, Mr. Kunstler.

Mr. Kunstler: It is an open, unseated toilet in a cell.

The Court: He may use that because they violated the privilege I have given them before. The marshals report that they have gone out and held conferences in the hall, they've gone places other than the regular public men's room. That is a place they will use when they have to go.

Mr. Kunstler: Your Honor—

The Court: There will be no argument about it.

Mr. Kunstler: —there is something ignominious about being in a jail cell.

The Court: There will be no argument about it.

. . .

The Court: Mr. Marshal, will you have those men at the table remain quiet. Their lawyer—

The Marshal: Sit down, Mr. Rubin.

Mr. Rubin: I want to go to the bathroom. That's a jail. I spent time in there when I was in jail. That is going behind locked doors, bars.

The Court: Then you may sit down if you don't want to use the facilities there.

Mr. Rubin: I want to go to the bathroom.

Mr. Dellinger: Convicted us already.

Mr. Davis: Guilty until proven innocent.

Mr. Kunstler: There is no argument on that, your Honor?

\* \* \*

Mr. Rubin: Your Honor, could Mr. Schultz be directed not to make remarks? He sarcastically pointed to the bathroom in there and said "Go to the bathroom" to me.

Mr. Schultz: As I walked back to the counsel table, your Honor. Mr. Rubin was laughing at me and snickering at me, and I pointed to the bathroom. I did that, you Honor—

Mr. Rubin: He said, "Go to the bathroom."

173

Mr. Schultz:  Your Honor—

Mr. Rubin:  —like it was a victory for you to force us to go to the bathroom in jail.

Mr. Schultz:  I said that. It was not very professional of me, your Honor. Apparently I succumbed a little bit to Mr. Rubin's harassment that started four months ago and of the defendants that started four months ago, a procedure and technique they have been using on authorities and policemen all of their lives. They have been trying it on your Honor and on Mr. Foran and myself, and I did, I succumbed, and pointed to the bathroom, and that was improper, and I'm sorry, very sorry, that I did that.

Mr. Kunstler:  Do you want to be a witness? You can sit up there.

Your Honor, can I call Mr. Schultz for a few moments? If he'd like to testify, I have no objection.

The Court:  No, you may not. You may not, and we won't have—

Mr. Kunstler:  Then I would like to have the record contain a motion for a mistrial at this time. Mr. Schultz—

The Court:  And the record may contain the Court's order denying it, Mr. Kunstler.

Mr. Kunstler:  You haven't even heard my argument.

The Court:  What did you say?

Mr. Kunstler:  You haven't even heard my argument.

The Court:  Oh, it had so little basis—

Mr. Kunstler:  No basis when a prosecutor stands in front of a jury and accuses us of harassing everybody?

The Court:  I don't want to hear anything further. Will you be quiet, sir.

\*   \*   \*

*Discussion, with the jury out of the room, concerning the defense's motion for a mistrial based on Mr. Schultz' statement to Defendant Rubin.*

Mr. Schultz:  . . . Today as I walked back to the counsel table—this morning as I walked back Rubin was making additional comments to me and I did as I stated to your Honor simply pointed out the bathroom, and then he told me that he was going to do it on me. That is what he said. Then we— instead of going to the bathroom. That was the colloquy. said nothing.

The Court:  Mr. Marshal, will you maintain order, please at the table.

Mr. Schultz:  I said nothing and I sat down and then Mr. Rubin said what he said to your Honor and I responded and in my response I made this reference.

174

The Marshal: Sit up, Mr. Davis. Sit up.

A Defendant: Don't touch him.

The Marshal: Nobody is touching him. You shut up, too, Mr. Dellinger.

Mr. Dellinger: You don't have to say shut up.

The Marshal: I have been telling you all day.

Mr. Schultz: That little colloquy is typical of what has been happening here and it builds and it builds and as I said to your Honor, perhaps it shouldn't have been said in front of the jury. That is the device they use, that is the device they use against authorities and they have been trying it on your Honor for the last three and a half months and have found it very unsuccessful. They succeeded with me momentarily this morning.

\* \* \*

The Court: The motion of the defendants for a mistrial will be denied and in denying that motion let me say that yesterday I entered an order here forbidding the defendants from going out at their pleasure ostensibly to what has been referred to not infrequently by counsel as the bathroom. I have never sat in a case where lawyers mention that word as often. I wonder if you, Mr. Marshal, can keep that man quiet while I am speaking. I am trying to decide his lawyer's motion. Please go to him and tell him to keep quit.

The Marshal: Mr. Dellinger—

The Court: Let the record show that after I requested the Marshal to keep Mr. Dellinger quiet he laughed right out loud again. The record may so indicate.

Mr. Dellinger: And he is laughing now, too.

The Marshal: And the Defendant Hayden, your Honor.

The Court: Mr. Hayden also.

Mr. Kunstler: Oh, your Honor, there is a certain amount of humor when talking about a bathroom—

The Court: Oh, I know that is your favorite reply.

Mr. Hoffman: I laughed, too.

Mr. Kunstler: But people can't help it sometimes, your Honor. You have laughed yourself.

The Court: I have really come to believe you can't help yourself. I have come to believe it.

Mr. Kunstler: But that is true. A whole courtroom full of people laugh when I say something and when you say something.

The Court: What I am saying is not very funny.

Mr. Kunstler: I know, but you are so ultra-sensitive to laughter.

The Court: Will you sit down and not interrupt the Court when a decision is being made?

\* \* \*

The Court: . . . [Y]esterday I entered an order directing that if the defendants had to make use of the toilet facilities, they use the one to my left, over there where the door is.

This morning Mr. Rubin, flagrantly violating the order, got up and started to walk out, and it became necessary for the Marshal to bring him back, and it is more than passing strange that he didn't use the facilities that were offered him by the Court.

Mr. Rubin: I have to go to the bathroom.

The Court: Let the record show that Mr. Rubin immediately got up and walked into the facilities that were offered him by the Court.

Oh, I've been through something like this before, but not often, not in many years on the bench have I seen such circus behavior.

Now, that was as I say, a flagrant violation of the Court order.

I repeat, I deny the motion for a mistrial, and when the jury comes in, I shall direct the jury to disregard the remarks of Mr. Schultz.

\* \* \*

*Direct examination of Defense Witness Mark Lane, author and unsuccessful Vice-Presidential candidate, by Defense Attorney Kunstler*

Q. Now, Mr. Lane, just one thing I forgot to ask you before, and in all fairness to the prosecutor, I have represented you, have I not in the past?

A. Yes, you represented me—

Mr. Schultz: Objection. That is not relevant.

The Court: We won't hold that against you.

Mr. Kunstler: Your Honor, I represented him in Mississippi as a freedom rider, and I wanted—

The Court: Wholly irrelevant. I know you have another client. I can tell you two or three more of them.

Mr. Kunstler: I think, your Honor, you could ten thousand of them over the years. Freedom riders were the first.

The Court: I know who your clients are.

Mr. Weiner: What does he mean?

Mr. Kunstler: Your Honor, I hope you are not meaning any slur by my clients.

The Court: Oh, no. You are the one who opened the professional discussion. Wholly irrelevant.

176

Mr. Kunstler: I know, but I know your Honor means it in good spirit, I hope.

The Court: Oh, yes, good spirit.

\* \* \*

Q. I take it you were not a successful candidate.

A. We peaked a little too early, I'd say.

The Court: You don't want me to strike that, do you, as being—it's not responsive to the question.

Mr. Schultz: No, it's not responsive.

The Court: You have the right to so move, Mr. Kunstler.

Mr. Kunstler: No. He said they peaked a little too early, your Honor, and I accepted that as an answer.

The Court: You do accept it.

Mr. Schultz: Mr. Kunstler likes to spend our time with a lot of levity. We would like to spend our time with relevant things so we can get done.

Mr. Kunstler: Your Honor, it is not my answer, but if it makes a little levity, I can't see where that is a great crime in this world.

The Court: Well, a waste of time. It is not a crime, but it is expensive.

Mr. Kunstler: I think there is more time wasted by the observation of Mr. Schultz than the six seconds it took him to say he peaked a little early.

Mr. Schultz: There's more time wasted on improper questions to which we have to object that your Honor has to rule on and then the same questions are asked again.

The Court: Go ahead.

Mr. Schultz: That is what time is wasted on.

The Court: Go on with the examination.

Mr. Kunstler: That is another fifteen seconds down the drain, your Honor.

Mr. Schultz: It was only in the hopes that we could save time in the future.

Mr. Kunstler: Four more.

\* \* \*

### January 12, 1970

*Continued cross-examination of Defense Witness Lane by Mr. Schultz*

Q. What did the leaflets say, to the best of your recollection?

A. I don't recall them precisely. It's been a long time since then, but I think the leaflets said that "A march is not authorized and arrests may be made if you participate in the march," something of that nature.

Q. When the march formed up, you heard police officers on

177

a bull horn in an automobile announcing "No march
will be permitted" in substance, did you not?

A. Yes, I heard that in Jackson, Mississippi, also. I heard i
in Chicago.

\* \* \*

Mr. Kunstler: . . . I think Mr. Lane can take care o
himself.

The Court: Oh, I am sure that he can. I am sure that h
can. He can be taken care of, too.

Mr. Kunstler: Well, that is threat No. 96, I guess, agains
lawyers.

\* \* \*

*Direct examination of Defense Witness Christophe
Chandler, senior editor of the Chicago Journalism Re
view, by Mr. Kunstler*

The Court: Just a minute, Mr. Kunstler. Mr. Weinglas
is not here. His clients are unrepresented by counsel.

Mr. Kunstler: Your Honor, I think that they would b
perfectly willing to waive that and do that on the record.

The Court: I will insist on Mr. Weinglass being here.

. . .

The Court: Mr. Marshal, will you go out—where is Mr
Weinglass, do you know?

Mr. Kunstler: I think he is with a witness, your Honor

The Court: Have you been able to find him?

Marshal Joneson: Yes. He is in the washroom, you
Honor.

Mr. Kunstler: Then I am wrong.

The Court: Is that where he interviews his witnesses
There is no law against that.

Mr. Kunstler: It may be the only place that isn't bugged
your Honor.

\* \* \*

*By Mr. Kunstler:*

Q. Would you state what—go through the interview, what di
Mr. Davis say and what did you say, what questions di
you ask him, and what did he respond?

A. I asked Mr. Davis about his background, first of all. H
said that he was raised in Virginia, that he first came t
Chicago as a member of a 4-H Club as a chicken judger
that he won fourth prize in a chicken judging contes

\* \* \*

The Court: The objection of the Government to Defen
dants' Exhibit 279 for identification will be sustained.

Mr. Dellinger. Oh, ridiculous.

178

The Court:   Who said "ridiculous"?

Mr. Dellinger:   I did. It was ridiculous. I stand on that fact. You don't want us to have a defense.

The Court:   I just wanted to know who said that.

. . .

Mr. Dellinger:   I stand by them too. You earned them. It really brings the whole system of justice under discredit when you act that way. What Mayor Daley and the police did for the electoral process in its present form you are now doing for the judicial process.

\* \* \*

Mr. Weinglass:   I want my motion clearly stated and the two grounds for it are the two comments by the Court in the presence of the jury that this defense—this case should be gotten rid of—this defense should be gotten rid of or this case, and, secondly, that we have a defense "if you can call it that." And I think the Court is familiar with the fact that you are not permitted to comment in front of the jury on the quality or the caliber or the length of the defense and you have done it twice.

The Court:   Mr. Weinrass—

Mr. Weinglass:   Weinglass, your Honor.

Mr. Davis:   Weinstein.

A Defendant:   Weinfeld.

## January 13, 1970

Mr. Schultz:   Your Honor, will your Honor explain to the jury that we have been working for the last hour? I am sure they were wondering.

The Court:   I certainly will.

Mr. Schultz:   Thank you.

The Court:   I sometimes wonder what juries think of us, all of us, including the Court.

\* \* \*

*Direct testimony of Defense Witness Mark Simons, a University of Chicago law student, by Mr. Weinglass.*
*[Testifying to a conversation with Defendant Weiner]*

A. . . . He [Mr. Weiner—ed.] also said that one particular problem that existed at all demonstrations was that when a problem happened in the demonstrations, that when the police saw something that they thought should be stopped and an undercover policeman went to stop it, the marshals and the rest of the marchers wouldn't know that the undercover policeman was a policeman and would assume that he was a bystander opposed to the policies of the people who were marching. They would

179

move in, attempting to separate the two, regular policemen guarding the march would see the marshals and
the other marchers attacking—apparently attacking this
undercover policeman and would join in, making what
could have been a minor problem into a major battle,
and so it was requested that not only would undercover
policemen not be used . . .

* * *

*Direct examination of Defense Witness Julian Bond,
member of the Georgia House of Representatives, by Mr.
Kunstler*

. . .

Q. Before I leave your background, could you state what organizations you are presently a member of?

Mr. Foran:   Objection, your Honor.

The Court:   Presently a member of?

Mr. Kunstler:   Yes, your Honor, presently a member.

The Court:   I don't know what you mean.

Mr. Foran:   It is irrelevant.

The Court:   I don't know what you mean by that, what
kind of organizations.

Mr. Kunstler:   Well, your Honor . . .

The Court:   Member of B'nai B'rith or the Knights of
Columbus or—

Mr. Kunstler:   I will ask him if he is a member of B'nai
B'rith.

* * *

[*Regarding a meeting with Defendant Hayden in a Nashville, Tennessee, motel*]

Q. Would you describe what conversation, what Mr. Hayden
said and what you did?

A. He mentioned he was interested in demonstrations at the
Democratic National Convention which was then some
months away, and as we were speaking, this was the day
after the murder of Martin Luther King. As we were
speaking there was gunfire and sirens, police sirens in
the streets of the city of Nashville. Looking out the
window you could see flashes from what we assumed
to be guns. An extremely tense situation. The city was
cordoned off into sections, the black neighborhoods
had been segregated by the police in the city. Tom said
that he was afraid that the same sort of thing might
happen in the city of Chicago. He was afraid that police
violence in this city might occur in the city of Chicago
during the Democratic National Convention and ex-

pressed time and time again his fear that such violence
might result. . . .

\* \* \*

Q. At that time did you have any conversation with Dave
Dellinger?

. . .

A. Well, he talked generally about trying to get permission to
march in the streets of the city of Chicago. He talked
about marshals, and he had marched then in the funeral
procession of Dr. Martin Luther King. This was the
day of the funeral which took place on the campus
about a block from my father's home, and I recall him
remarking that this crowd, a large crowd of people,
had been peaceful, had been orderly, and he expressed
his hope that similar crowds in Chicago could behave
in the same manner.

\* \* \*

The Court: Oh, I am a little weary of your saying everything is different for the Government.

Mr. Kunstler: You tell me, your Honor, in—

The Court: It isn't at all.

Mr. Kunstler: You tell me, your Honor, how this is different. I will be glad to listen to the reason.

The Court: I will rule as I see fit under the law, sir, and I
am not going to be a speech maker for you.

Mr. Kunstler: But all I am saying is Tom Newman's
speech was permitted in. He is not a defendant. Mr. Bond's
speech is excluded. It is the same type of speech, the same
type of relationship.

\* \* \*

*Direct examination of Defense Witness Charles Kis-
singer by Mr. Kunstler*

Q. Mr. Kissinger, would you please state your full name.

A. Charles Clark Kissinger, Jr.

Q. What is your occupation?

A. I am unskilled factory worker now.

Q. Where are you working?

A. I would rather not answer that question, since I understand a previous witness has been fired from his job.

\* \* \*

Mr. Kunstler: Do you strike the observation of Mr. Foran
dealing with comic book defense and words to that effect?

The Court: I would describe it differently but I will let
that stand.

*Direct examination of Defense Witness George Misner,*

*Associate Professor of Criminology at Berkeley, by Mr. Weinglass*

Mr. Schultz: Your Honor, if the Court please—your Honor, please would the Marshal instruct the defendants not to laugh and make comments at objections and rulings?

The Court: I have already directed the Marshal to do that, and Mr. Marshal, I again direct you to do, and watch it carefully.

Mr. Kunstler: Your Honor, there is no evidence that there were any comments or laughter.

The Court: Oh, but there is. I have seen and heard it myself.

Mr. Kunstler: Every time Mr. Schultz says there is, your Honor goes along with it.

**January 14, 1970**

Mr. Kunstler: I would just like to add for the record, your Honor, we did exhibit 287, which is the original NBC film, to the attorneys for the Government during the lunch hour. We did this to save time and not use up any time of the jury while we were doing this.

The Court: How about mine?

Mr. Kunstler: Your, too. Everybody's. I didn't want to exclude anybody.

. . .

The Court: When you come to save time, please include me, will you?

Mr. Kunstler: I will, your Honor. I also have thirty cases waiting for trial, too, so all of us, everybody is included. All our time is saved.

The Court: I must inform you, I'm sure you don't know, that I come first. . . .

* * *

The Court: Mr. Marshal, I am not here to be laughed at by these defendants, particularly Mr. Rubin.

The Marshal: Mr. Dellinger, also, will you refrain from laughing?

Mr. Dellinger: That is a lie. And it wasn't Mr. Rubin. We laugh enough and you can catch us when we do but you just happened to get that one wrong.

* * *

Mr. Kunstler: You don't mind if they laugh at me or if they laugh at someone else.

The Court: I will ask you to sit down.

Mr. Kunstler: I don't think your Honor's ultra-sensitivity should make a difference in rulings in this Court.

The Court:   It isn't ultra-sensitivity. It is a proper under-standing of the conduct of a trial in the Federal District Court.

\* \* \*

Mr. Dellinger:   If you can make an honest mistake, that's all right, but to lie about it afterwards and say you saw me talking when you didn't, that is different.

The Court:   Will you ask that man to sit down.

Mr. Dellinger:   You will go down in infamy in history for your obvious lies in this courtroom of which that is only the most recent one.

. . .

Mr. Dellinger:   You will be ashamed of that for the rest of your life, if anything can shame you.

\* \* \*

Mr. Dellinger:   I want to make the record clear. Mr. Rubin did not laugh and you are standing there saying you heard it. That is why I called you a liar. He did not laugh. I was sitting next to him.

The Court:   Mr. Marshal—

Mr. Dellinger:   And you made it up. It is about time this got out into the open so everybody could know what you are doing here. It is one thing to be prejudiced, it is another to be a liar.

. . .

The Court:   I have never sat in fifty years through a trial where a party to a lawsuit called the judge a liar.

Mr. Dellinger:   Maybe they were afraid to go to jail rather than tell the truth, but I would rather go to jail for how ever long you send me than to let you get way with that kind of thing and people not realize what you are doing.

\* \* \*

The Court:   Will you let the record show—I don't know, I get twisted between the defendants—the one in the middle.

Mr. Weiner:   Weiner.

A Defendant:   Davis.

Mr. Weiner:   Weiner.

The Court:   Mr. Weiner applauded after that speech.

. . .

The Court:  . . . Now, Mr. Weineruss—Weinglass.

Mr. Weinglass:   Weinglass, your Honor.

The Court:   Whatever your name is. Continue with the examination of this witness. Mr. Weinglass. Somebody held up the name. [on a placard—ed.]

Mr. Kunstler:   We have the name here, your Honor.

The Court: Yes.

Mr. Hoffman: Here it is. Shall we put it on him?

\* \* \*

*Direct examination of Defense Witness James Simon Kunen, author of "The Strawberry Statement" and a student at Columbia University, by Mr. Kunstler*

O. Would you state to the jury what Mr. Rubin said while you were listening at this demonstration?

A. Yes. Well, he began by saying that Humbert Humphrey was an ass hole, and he meant that very specifically—or he went on to elaborate that he meant that very specifically, not the buttocks or the anal sphincter, but the hole, that he was nothing, you know, and the reason he was nothing was because he had long since sold his soul to the great corporation which is the United States of America and said that Mr. Humphrey had done this because for anyone to arrive at any position of political power in this country, he has to kiss asses all the way up and he said that since the country was like a giant corporation and was run from the top down, that the elections which were to follow that November were meaningless and that the people would not fall for them. . . .

\* \* \*

*Cross-examination of Mr. Kunen by Government Attorney Schultz*

Q. And he made an obscene statement, did he not?

A. He said—

Mr. Kunstler: Your Honor, I don't know what the word obscene means.

Mr. Schultz: I think the witness knows—

The Court: Oh, Mr. Kunstler.

Mr. Kunstler: Napalm on children seems to me obscene and the word "obscene" has many meanings and I would like Mr. Schultz to identify—

The Court: Oh, I can't believe that—

Mr. Kunstler: —what he is talking about.

The Court: I can't believe that statement, you don't know what the word "obscene" means.

Mr. Kunstler: The massacre of 300 women and children at Song My by American soldiers is obscene.

The Court: I am perfectly willing to let the record show that you have said you do not know what the word "obscene" means.

\* \* \*

[*Colloquy concerning testimony of another witness*]

184

Mr. Weinglass: Your Honor, the witness misunderstood a date. It's clear and obvious. Why isn't she just permitted to explain that? It's so simple.

. . .

Mr. Foran: This crybaby stuff he goes through, your Honor, every time he asks a wrong question, is just—

Mr. Kunstler: Crybaby? Did you ever hear Mr. Foran when he sinks into his seat—"So are we going through this again"—in his dying quail voice that I have pointed out on past occasions?

Mr. Foran: He has been remarkably contained, your Honor, in case—

The Court: Try to go to a diction coach before tomorrow's session, Mr. Foran, so that you don't have a dying quail's voice.

## January 15, 1970

*[Recross-examination of Defense Witness Walter Schneir, a writer, by Mr. Foran]*

Q. Mr. Witness, you just said that—you gave the substance of what you said you heard Mr. Hayden say at the bandshell, is that correct, on cross-examination—or on redirect examination of Mr. Kunstler?

A. Yes. I was just hesitating—my name is Schneir.

Q. What did I call you?

A. Mr. Witness.

The Court: We get used to that in the courts. We call distinguished men "Mr. Witness." We call distinguished lawyers "Counsel." We call the judge who has a name "The Court" or "Judge."

Don't be offended by that. Being a witness in the United States District Court is a privilege.

\* \* \*

*Cross-examination of Defense Witness The Reverend Richard Fernandez by Mr. Schultz*

The Witness: Can we repeat the question, your Honor?

The Court: Certainly. I have already asked the official reporter to read it, please.

The Witness: More games than a church.

The Court: What did you say about the church?

The Witness: Nothing.

\* \* \*

Mr. Weinglass: The question was did he indicate—

The Court: Keep it down. Don't shout. Our hearing is good. At least mine is.

Mr. Weinglass: It is sometimes difficult to get the Court's attention when I am attempting to address the Court.

The Court: Difficult to get my attention?

Mr. Weinglass: Occasionally.

. . .

The Court: I just don't—I resent the fact that you say that it is difficult to get my attention.

Mr. Weinglass: Mr. Schultz was speaking at the same time.

The Court: I can't imagine anybody having been more attentive during this trial . . .

\* \* \*

The Court: . . . What did you say about comparing a courtroom with a church, Mr. Witness? I am interested in that.

The Witness: I said you play more games in the courtroom than we do in a church.

The Court: I play games? Well, do you play games in a church?

The Witness: Some people do.

The Court: They do. I didn't think clergymen did that of my faith.

The Witness: Nor judges, I guess.

. . .

The Court: . . . Reverend—I will call you Reverend.

The Witness: Thank you very much, Judge.

The Court: Even though you think games are played in a courtroom.

. . .

Mr. Kunstler: If your Honor has been in any church discussions, your Honor will know exactly what the witness means.

The Court: Many, many, many church discussions.

Mr. Kunstler: Then your Honor ought to know what the witness means. All institutions—

The Court: Paraphrasing a statement that is frequently made in other areas, some of my best friends are clergymen of all faiths.

Mr. Kunstler: Well, if it is used in the same category as I have heard it used about black people, your Honor, it is not the best compliment.

\* \* \*

[*Direct testimony of Defense Witness Arlo Guthrie, a folksinger, by Mr. Kunstler*]

A. Anyway, I finally came to see the very last person in the induction center who had asked me if I had ever been arrested. I told him yes, I was. He said, "What for?" I

186

said. "Littering," and he said, "Did you ever go to court?" and I said, yes, and I was unacceptable to the draft because I had been a litterbug in Stockbridge, Massachusetts.

The end of the song is the chorus which goes: "You can get anything you want—"

The Court:   Oh, no, no. No. I am sorry.

Mr. Kunstler:   Your Honor, that's what he sang for the defendants.

The Court:   I don't want the theater owner where this picture shown to sue me.

Mr. Kunstler:   We'll represent you, your Honor.

The Court:   No singing. No singing. No singing, sir.

. . .

The Court:   I have had everything else. I think I will forego that pleasure.

\* \* \*

*[Direct testimony of Defense Witness Cora Weiss, a National Co-Chairman of the Mobilization Committee, by Mr. Kunstler]*

Mr. Kunstler:   Mrs. Weiss suggested it is Dr. King's birthday today which I had forgotten and since she and I were both in the Gandhi Society with Dr. King, she suggested perhaps a moment of silence for Dr. King.

Mr. Schultz:   Your Honor, I don't think it would be appropriate at this time.

The Court:   I don't think it is appropriate of the witness to make any—voluntary statements. I strike that request from the record. I wouldn't even have you stand a minute for my birthday. I don't know whether anybody would stand or not.

Mr. Kunstler:   Your Honor, I am not sure how the comparison is to be taken.

\* \* \*

Mr. Kunstler:   Your Honor, just before you leave, there is one matter.

An envelope was received by Mr. Hoffman from Portsmouth, New Hampshire, dated January 13, 1970, containing some plant life.

The Court:   Some what?

Mr. Kunstler:   Plant life of some sort.

Mr. Schultz:   It looks like plant life we have seen in some of our criminal trials.

Mr. Kunstler:   It has an odor, your Honor, that leads me to believe that it might be marijuana or some substance like that. I don't know why it was sent other than to implicate

187

someone here, but we didn't want to leave it in the waste basket here without an explanation.

I have the envelope here and I have whatever is left of it. I don't know whether—

The Court: I think a lawyer who is resourceful as you are in other matters can make a disposition of that item. I will trust you to see that that very important item is safe.

**January 16, 1970**

*Direct examination of Defense Witness Arthur I. Waskow, historian and researcher, by Mr. Weinglass*

The Court: Are you a clergyman, sir?

The Witness: No, sir.

The Court: You will have to remove your hat.

Mr. Schultz: Your Honor, we don't object. I know that he—

The Court: I object.

. . .

The Witness: Your Honor, I am observant and religious, too; I cannot remove my hat.

The Court: I will not permit him to remain on the witness stand.

Mr. Kunstler: Oh, your Honor—

The Court: I will not permit him—I've had that before. You and I have argued that.

Mr. Kunstler: I know, but we have argued only about spectators, your Honor. This is a witness.

[The Court subsequently reversed its decision at the Government's request—ed.]

\* \* \*

The Court: . . . [Y]ou participated in an argument during the direct examination in support of Mr. Weinruss' position.

. . .

*Direct examination of Defense Witness Richard Goodwin, former White House aide, by Mr. Kunstler*

The Court: When you get to be as old as I am and have tried as many thousands of cases as I have, you will be able to rule properly—rapidly, too. And I don't rule too rapidly.

Mr. Kunstler: Your Honor, we have the same birthday, you and I. The difference between us is not that great.

The Court: You must have put an FBI man on me.

Mr. Kunstler: July 7—

The Court: How did you find out?

Mr. Kunstler: No, I compared our Who's Who in Who's Who in America, and I saw we had the same birthday.

The Court: Very brief, wasn't it?

Mr. Kunstler:   No, yours was, I think, three lines shorter than mine.

The Court:   I hope you get a better obituary.

Mr. Kunstler:   Well, I know—all I know, your Honor, is I won't be able to read it, unfortunately.

\* \* \*

[*During cross-examination of Mr. Goodwin by Mr. Foran*]

Q. Did Hayden tell you at that time at that place, Mr. Goodwin, or ever, that the political confrontation in Chicago was going to be the first step of the revolution? Did he tell you that in that specific statement? Did he say that to you?

A. No. He never talked in such grandiose terms.

\* \* \*

[*During cross-examination of Defense Witness Jeffrey H. Lynford*]

The Court:   Let me see that book.

I have asked a lawyer to show me a book, and you keep on talking.

Mr. Weinglass:   Well, your Honor, I wasn't finished with my argument.

The Court:   When I was a lawyer your age, I had some feeling about respect for a judge.

Mr. Hoffman:   Times are changing.

## January 19, 1970

*Direct examination of Defense Witness John Sack, a writer for Esquire Magazine, by Mr. Weinglass. [Concerning an observation regarding dialogue between demonstrators and Chicago police]*

The Witness:   The kids would also come by and give the police the V for victory sign and one or two of the policemen would reply with a W for Wallace sign . . .

Mr. Foran:   I object to this. I never heard that before in my life.

. . .

Mr. Weinglass:   Who told you the three fingers stood for Wallace?

Mr. Foran:   I object to that, your Honor.

The Witness:   The police.

\* \* \*

Q. Do you recall what he [Abbie Hoffman—ed.] said the twenty-minute period of time that you were there?

A. Yes. He told—he was telling the people not to call the

189

policemen pigs. He said that the Yippie candidate for President was a pig, and they wanted a pig in the White House, so it was no insult to the policemen to call them pigs. . . .

\*     \*     \*

[*Direct testimony of Defense Witness Robert G. Levin, a college professor, by Mr. Kunstler. Mr. Levin has with him a motorcycle helmet, previously labeled Defendants' Exhibit 15, for identification*]

Q. Mr. Levin, my heart goes out to you. Take off the helmet for a moment. You are making me uncomfortable.

A. Terrible acoustics.

The Court: You say your heart goes out to him. You said that twice, and yet you smile.

. . .

The Court: How can your heart go out to a man and you smile at the same time?

Mr. Kunstler: Well, your Honor, I think that is essentially the difference between us.

## January 20, 1970

Mr. Kunstler: I am not going to stand by and have him— a colleague of mine called anything like that.

The Court: Sit down.

Mr. Kunstler: I am not going to sit down unless I am directed—

The Court: I direct you to sit down.

Mr. Kunstler: Am I to be thrown in the chair by the Marshal if I don't sit down?

The Court: I haven't asked the Marshal to throw anybody in the chair. . . .

\*     \*     \*

The Court: I will permit only one defense counsel to participate in the examination of this witness.

Mr. Kunstler: I am not participating in the examination. I am only defending Mr. Weinglass.

Mr. Dellinger: He's my lawyer.

Mr. Kunstler: And I speak for three defendants here.

The Court: He does need defense here.

Mr. Kunstler: You say he does?

The Court: He does need it, but you are not the proper person for him at this time.

Mr. Kunstler: I don't think that remark is a proper remark, your Honor. He needs no defense here. He is an American lawyer here doing what every American lawyer has done since Peter Zenger had his problems with lawyers and judges, and he is doing it here, and I think your remark that he needs a defense is an erroneous remark and should be stricken from the record.

\* \* \*

Mr. Kunstler:   Your Honor, Mr. Weinglass and I speaking for all the defendants would like to at this time move for a mistrial. The initial ground and the motivating ground is the remark which your Honor just made in front of the jury that Mr. Weinglass needs a defense. This standing by itself would in our opinion be enough to warrant a mistrial. It is in our opinion a grossly improper statement leading the jury to believe that there is something so wrong with Mr. Weinglass that it is tantamount to criminality, and that is the reason that he needs a defense.

But, in addition to that, there is the constant repetition and refrain by your Honor in front of this jury of derogatory comments about counsel on the defense side. . . .

The judge is the figure of authority, as I have mentioned, in the courtroom, to the jury, particularly to laymen. The judge occupies a very special place and has a very special responsibility in American jurisprudence. He cannot by any means indicate any personal animus towards counsel on either side or towards the parties on either side. He must remain aloof from that type of conduct. Otherwise a trial in the courts of the United States or elsewhere in the state courts becomes a mockery if the judge ex[hibits] any bias whatsoever. . . .

Admittedly it is a hard fought case, hard fought by both sides, but that does not excuse the type of personal attack that should never occur in a courtroom. If a courtroom is to hope for the ideal of justice, it cannot be a place where personal attacks on counsel occur in front of the jury which is to decide the fate of seven men on trial for an extremely serious crime as far as penalty is concerned.

So I make this motion for a mistrial before your Honor.

\* \* \*

Mr. Weinglass: . . . The defendants are entitled by virtue of the Sixth Amendment of the Constitution to have a defense. Courts have interpreted the Sixth Amendment to mean a vital and effective and, I think in this type of case, a hard defense. Mr. Kunstler and I have endeavored to give them that consistent with the Constitution requirement of what they are entitled to.

Now, by the Court's consistent ruling, indicating that there will be reprisals taken against both Mr. Kunstler and myself, the effect of it has been—

The Court:   Not reprisals. I interrupt you to say that our Court of Appeals has required trial judges to admonish counsel when they're doing or engaging in contumacious acts or using contumacious language.

. . .

Mr. Weinglass:   In being entitled to an effective defense, I think the Constitution recognizes that every criminal trial is an adversary proceeding. There are spokesmen for one side and spokesmen for another. If the spokesmen for one side are permitted in court to characterize the spokesmen for the other side in an unprofessional way and yet when the spokesmen for the other side attempt to answer that characterization they are threatened with contempt citations, your Honor has broken down the adversary process that is necessary for a finding of truth, because you have hobbled one side, and you have permitted the other side license to attack. We cannot—

The Court:   I interrupt you now to tell you to be cautious about your characterization of the conduct of the Court. I am willing to rest—if your clients don't stop laughing aloud, I won't listen to you.

Mr. Marshal, will you ask those defendants who are laughing aloud to please remain quiet. Their lawyer is talking.

Mr. Weinglass:   If your Honor please, this is the one room in which a citizen of the country can come into an organ of government on an equal footing with the Government.

The Court:   That's right, and your clients have come in—

Mr. Weinglass:   And that equal footing has been destroyed in this case because you had permitted the Government certain license in advocacy here that you have not permitted the defense, and that is what's essential to a fair trial.

\*        \*

The Court:   I am willing, Mr. Weinglass, to rest my judgments and orders made in this case on the record which to date consists of 16,000 pages. I have never heard anything like this. I really have never had—I have had to wait at every intermission for your clients to come in. I have waited, I have waited without comment, I've waited, I've waited, I've waited. Now, I object to your generalizations. We have 16,000 pages of testimony. They will be gone over by the Court to determine what action is thought to be appropriate, if any.

Mr. Weinglass:   Is your Honor referring to now an appeal, or is your Honor referring to—

The Court:   I will go over them first. You talk about an appeal. Nobody's been convicted yet.

\*        \*        \*

192

*[Following the Court's denial of the defense's motion for a mistrial]*

The Court: Have a look on the expression on the face of Mr. Hoffmann directed at me.

*(Laughter and applause.)*

The Court: Listen to the applause. You talk about dignity in the courtroom.

Mr. Weinglass: Well, your Honor, if your rulings are being affected by the expression on my clients' faces, that is precisely what our problem is. I say this respectfully. The Court is allowing its ability to judge this case to be influenced by the way my clients appear in the court.

*Direct examination of Defense Witness Country Joe McDonald, a musician, by Mr. Kunstler*

Mr. Schultz: For the record may we have the witness' full name? Country Joe is really not sufficient.

The Court: I assuming that his Christian name is Country. He is under oath. He was asked his name.

Mr. Schultz: It might be the name that he uses and not the name that was originally his.

The Court: Is Country your first name?

The Witness: Yes.

The Court: That is your first name or Christian name, is that right?

The Witness: Some people call me Country, yes.

The Court: What is your real name?

The Witness: Country.

The Court: You say some people call you that. What is your real name, sir?

The Witness: I am afraid I don't understand what real means.

The Court: What is the name—Were you baptized?

The Witness: No, I wasn't.

The Court: What were you called when you went to school as a child?

The Witness: Joe.

The Court: Joe?

The Witness: Yes.

. . .

The Court: And you are familiarly known as Country Joe, is that right?

The Witness: Country Joe McDonald, yes.
Joseph, sometimes.

\* \* \*

The Court: You still call him Country Joe even though his name is McDonald?

193

Mr. Kunstler: I know, your Honor, but he is known throughout the world as Country Joe.

The Court: That is what you say. I have never heard of him.

* * *

[*Testifying regarding a conversation with Defendant Hoffman concerning the Festival of Life*]

The Witness: . . . that is was very important that we try to say something in Chicago which would be positive, natural, human, and loving, in order to let the people of America know that there are people in America who are not tripped out on ways of thinking which result only in oppression and fear, paranoia, and death.

At that point Abbie Hoffman wanted to know what the song was, and then I—then I sang the song. It goes:

"And it's one, two, three, what are we fighting for? Don't ask me, I don't give a damn.

"The next stop is Vietnam.

"And it's—"

The Court: No, no, no, Mr. Witness, No singing.

## January 21, 1970

The Court: What is the Government's position in respect to what has been described by Mr. Weinruss as an offer of proof?

Mr. Foran: The Government objects to it.

The Court: For the reasons I have indicated here before and for other reasons, I sustain the objection to what Mr. Weinruss has characterized as an offer of proof.

* * *

The Court: Miss Reporter, will you remain here? I may want to have you read the last question put by Mr. Weinruss.

Mr. Weinglass: Weinglass.

The Court: I have a good friend named Mr. Weinruss, and I am so used to it. I have occasion to see him not infrequently and that is why I confuse your name with his. I am sorry. Only on occasion. I might say he is a very nice man.

* * *

[*Testimony of Defense Witness Paul Krassner, editor of the* Realist *Magazine, by Mr. Kunstler*]

A. I said that Yippie, coming from the Youth International Party, that these were not just coincidental letters, that the word "Youth" represented the kind of generational struggle that was going on in America now. The word "International" because it's happening all over the world, from Japan to France to Germany to Czechoslovakia to Mexico, and "Party" because if this was our alternative party—was a double—deliberately intended as a double meaning, to take off on the Democratic Party and also a party in our sense of the word which was the way it should be, with ice cream and balloons, and that whole thing, that whole going back to the values of childhood, and that the fact that Robert Kennedy had entered the race at this point, I said that he had—he had said that he hesitated entering because he didn't want to divide the Democratic Party, and I said that human life was more important than the Democratic Party and the Republican Party put together, and then I said that—then I announced that we were going to go to Chicago to try to get permits for our festival.

**January 22, 1970**

Mr. Foran: Your Honor, I note there are a couple of defendants missing.

The Court: Are the defendants not here? You lost your gallery, Mr. Kunstler. Your clients aren't here.

Mr. Kunstler: Well, your Honor, my clients are not my gallery. They are clients.

The Court: Oh, they are not interested?

Mr. Kunstler: They are clients.

The Court: Well, they have walked out on you.

Mr. Kunstler: Well, "gallery" doesn't mean interest or lack of interest.

The Court: Well, they've gone, so I'll wait until they return. They left without permission. I don't know where they are.

A Defendant: They went to get a witness.

\* \* \*

Mr. Kunstler: Your Honor, I would state that—I don't know where I left off, and I'm sure Mr. Foran was not unaware of that when he made the comment.

May I find out where I was?

The Court: You mean not unaware of the fact that you didn't know where you left off?

Mr. Kunstler: No, that he deliberately does his little reminders to the Court that clients are not here in the middle of arguments, and he's done it on so many numerous occasions, knowing that it's hard to pick up your thread of argument.

Mr. Schultz: Your Honor, Mr. Kunstler repeats himself

195

so many times, he can just go in another circle, and we'll find out where he was.

\*      \*

[*At this point, groans were heard from the audience*]

The Court:   Mr. Marshal, I wish you'd take care of that.

Mr. Kunstler:   Your Honor, those groans were highly appropriate. I get no help from you, so a groan of a client once in a while at least keeps my spirits up.

\*      \*      \*

The Court:   The United States Attorney was protecting the rights of the defendants, who have a right under the law to be present at every stage of the proceeding, and they were not here.

The Marshal:   Will you be quiet, Mr. Dellinger.

Mr. Kunstler:   They are most appreciative, your Honor, but they have waived that protection a long time ago, as I recall.

The Court:   I don't know which one you represent. Some days you represent only three, some days you represent all seven. I can't tell.

Mr. Kunstler:   Well, I don't have to consult any of them on this.

The Court:   There were times when you said you represented eight. . . .

\*      \*      \*

*Direct Examination of Defense Witness Judy Collins, a singer, by Mr. Kunstler*

Q. Now, Miss Collins, I call your attention to March 17 of 1968 at approximately noontime on that date. Do you know where you were?

A. I was at the Americana Hotel in New York City attending a press conference to announce the formation of what we have now come to know of as the Yippie Movement.

. . .

Q. Now, what did you do at that press conference?

A. Well, where have all the flowers—

The Court:   Just a minute, young lady.

The Witness:   —where have all the flowers gone?

Deputy Marshal John J. Gracious:   I'm sorry. The Judge would like to speak to you.

The Court:   We don't allow any singing in this Court. I'm sorry.

. . .

Mr. Kunstler:   . . . She sang "Where Have all the Flowers Gone," which is a well known peace song, and she sang it, and the jury is not getting the flavor—

196

The Court: She wasn't even asked to sing.

Mr. Kunstler: That is what she did at the press conference.

The Court: You asked her what she did, and she proceeded to sing.

Mr. Kunstler: That is what she did, your Honor.

The Witness: That's what I do.

* * *

The Court: . . . [T]hat has no place in a United States District Court.

Mr. Kunstler: Your Honor, that song has a place in any district court and any place, and this is what she did at the occasion.

The Court: We are not here to be entertained, sir. We are trying a very important case.

Mr. Kunstler: This song is not an entertainment, your Honor. This is a song of peace, and what happens to young men and young women during war time.

. . .

Mr. Schultz: . . . Now, there is no question that Miss Collins is a fine singer. In my family my six kids and I all agree that she is a fine singer, but that doesn't have a thing to do with this lawsuit nor what my profession is. which is the practice of law in the Federal District Court, your Honor, and I protest Mr. Kunstler constantly failing to advise his witnesses of what proper decorum is, and I object to it on behalf of the Government.

[The objection was sustained—ed.]

*By Mr. Kunstler*

Q. What did you say at the press conference?

A. I said a great deal. I said at the press conference that I want to see a celebration of life, not of destruction. I said that I personally, as a singer, which is, by the way, my profession, as your profession is a lawyer, sir, that my soul and my profession and my life have become part of a movement toward hopefully removing the causes for death, the causes for war, the causes for the prevalence of violence in our society, and in order to make my voice heard, I said that I would indeed come to Chicago and that I would sing. That is what I do, that's my profession. . . .

* * *

The Court: Yes. This witness' observations as just expressed are irrelevant and do not contribute to the resolution of the issues created by the pleadings in this case.

Mr. Kunstler: Your Honor, the lives and deaths of American soldiers I think is highly relevant. It was the whole purpose or one of the main purposes people came to Chicago.

The Court: Life and death are really very wonderful. This is a great place to live in and be alive. I agree with you. But those things are not in issue in this case.

\* \* \*

Mr. Kunstler: Your Honor, the FBI sits at that table, the prosecution table. That's where the FBI is. There's Mr. Stanley.

Mr. Schultz: That's right, and the FBI also sat at the tables of the cases which involved the prosecution of the policemen because—

Mr. Kunstler: That's why they were acquitted.

(*Applause.*)

\* \* \*

The Court: . . . I just have never sat through a trial where defendants applauded in a courtroom.

The Marshal: Will you remain quiet, Mr. Rubin.

The Court: I have never, in over fifty years, observed such conduct. I want the record to show that.

\* \* \*

The Court: Don't break the Government's lectern. I don't allow lawyers to pound on a lectern.

Mr. Kunstler: Well, it wasn't a karate blow, your Honor.

The Court: I don't permit that, sir. I don't like to hear them shout either, and I don't like to have them try to over-talk me. I am trying to rule here, and it seems that when I rule, you don't respect my rulings.

\* \* \*

Mr. Kunstler: The defendants call themselves the Conspiracy.

. . .

Mr. Kunstler: . . . The Conspiracy is the defendants.

The Court: Now you are saying something else again. . . .

Mr. Kunstler: That is "Conspiracy" in quotes, your Honor.

### January 23, 1970
*Direct examination of Defendant Rennie Davis by Mr. Weinglass*

The Court: The exhibit [of a bomb—ed.] is wholly ir-relevant and immaterial. If an exhibit like this were to be permitted, you could fill this room with bullets. Of course life-taking devices have been used in all wars. I am not trying the Vietnamese War here, as the United States Attorney pointed out. There is no such charge in the indictment. . . .

. . .

Mr. Weinglass: Well, that goes to the question, your Honor, of the relevance of the war as an issue in this trial. . . .

Now, Mr. Davis, together with six others, is charged with coming to the city to incite a riot. That's the Government's contention.

Our contention is they came to the city to demonstrate peacefully about two overriding social issues, the war and racism.

Now, if we are not permitted to show why they came here, then it's only one side that gets into evidence.

The reasons for their coming here are critical to their defense. They did not come here for a reason of violence. They did not come here without good reason. There were things occurring in the country, and these things caused them to come here.

[*The Court did not admit the evidence*]

\* \* \*

Marshal Joneson:   Will you be quiet, Mr. Dellinger.

Mr. Dellinger:   After such hypocrisy I don't particularly feel like being quiet. I said before the Judge was the chief prosecutor, and he's proved the point.

The Court:   Will you remain quiet. Will you remain quiet, sir.

Mr. Dellinger:   You let Foran give a foreign policy speech but when he [Kunstler] tries to answer it, you interrupt him and won't let him speak.

There's no pretense of fairness in this Court.

. . .

Marshal Joneson:   Be quiet, sir.

Mr. Dellinger:   —just like you gagged Bobby Seale because you couldn't afford to listen to the truth that he was saying to you. You're accusing me. I'm a pacifist.

Mr. Joneson:   Sit down, please, and be quiet.

Mr. Dellinger:   I am employ[ing] non-violence, and you're accusing me of violence, and you have a man right here, backed up by guns, jails, and force and violence. That is the difference between us.

\* \* \*

Mr. Kunstler:   By Attorney General Mitchell's press conference—

Mr. Schultz:   We complied with the rules of this Court. We have made no statements to this press, to any press, since this case was indicted. Mr. Kunstler, on a regular basis, has been falsifying, falsifying, to the press, violating the rules of a court prohibiting every attorney in this case from making press conferences, and he has been doing it and he stands before this Court and says the Government has.

Mr. Dellinger:   And they had rules like that in Nazi Germany.

\* \* \*

A. I said that I felt that given the reports that had—we had seen in the past, that there was some question about our purposes and intentions in coming to Chicago, I said I did not understand any other explanation for the military sort of sabre rattling that was going on at that time, the constant talks in the past about disruption of the Convention, and I said that we had had a similar kind of situation on April 15, 1967, where we called for a peace demonstration in New York City, and that we had applied for permits through the government of New York and city officials in New York had said that we were going to tear up the UN or disrupt the United Nations, and I said finally the New York City officials did grant a permit, and 400,000 people marched up Fifth Avenue to the United Nations as we had announced, peacefully and orderly.

**January 24, 1970**
[*Continued direct examination of Defendant Rennie Davis by Mr. Weinglass*]

A. . . . Tom said that he thought that we should be very sober to the possibility that the strategy of Convention Week will be to not only deny permits for this demonstration but to round people up all through the week so that by the time the march is about to take place there really is no one left, there is no one left to demonstrate, that everyone is in jail. . . .

\* \* \*

A. . . . Mr. Simon then told me that Soldiers Field was not available during the week of the Democratic Convention for the Mobilization, and he also said that the 11 p.m. curfew in parks would be enforced . . . I told Mr. Simon that many of the people who were coming with us to the Convention were black people and poor people and middle-class students without a lot of money, and that it would be just simply impossible to have them rent motel space and then commute back and forth. . . .

. . . I said, "What is going to happen is that they are going to go into the parks, police are going to then come into those parks and clear those parks, and the kids are going to fight back, and the police are going to use Mace and clubs and gas, and it's going to lead

200

to violence, and that's the kind of situation that more than anything else I want to avoid."

\* \* \*

A. I indicated to Mr. Simon that inasmuch as the Mayor recognized that we were in an emergency situation with nearly 40,000 military personnel poised at the edge of our city and with permits being given out to the military to use parks . . . it seemed wholly reasonable to me that park space could be made available to American citizens. . . .

Then Mr. Simon told me that we were not in any emergency situation; the Mayor had not said we were in an emergency situation. I said then, "What does that mean? It is just so coincidental that there happen to be 40,000 military men ready to come into Chicago?"

\* \* \*

Mr. Kunstler: Your Honor, why can't the jury then have a view of the premises? Nothing is more important than to see what the premises looked like.

The Court: Mr. —

Mr. Kunstler: Kunstler.

The Court: — Kunstler. I ought to know—you're right—by now.

Mr. Kunstler: No, names aren't important, your Honor. Whether you know my name or Mr. Weinglass' is completely unimportant—both "X" and "Y"—but let's look at the Amphitheatre.

The Court: Names are important. They are to me . . .

\* \* \*

*[Concerning a conversation with Mr. Dellinger]*

A. . . . Dave said that if the police indicate that they are going to prevent this march by force, prevent constitutional rights by decree, that we have to at that time say to the world that there are Americans who will not submit to a police state by default; that they are prepared to risk arrest and be taken away to jail rather than to submit to the kind of brutality that we had seen all through the week of the Convention . . .

\* \* \*

Mr. Foran: . . . In this case, your Honor, we have heard these people adopt or attempt to adopt Dr. King, attempt to adopt Senator McCarthy, Robert Kennedy, both of whom were better friends of mine than they ever were of theirs.

Mr. Dellinger: Oh, my God.

201

Mr. Foran:  Mr. [Robert] Kennedy appointed Richard Schultz, your Honor.

Mr. Kunstler:  Oh, your Honor—

Mr. Dellinger:  Rev. Abernathy was the Co-Chairman of the Mobilization and I worked intimately with Martin Luther King and Ralph Abernathy.

. . .

Mr. Kunstler:  Your Honor, I represented Dr. King for five years, and I never heard the word "Foran" cross his lips.

The Court:  I am not interested in your representation of—

Mr. Kunstler:  You used that comment with Mies van der Rohe with me . . .

**January 26, 1970**
   *Cross-examination of Defendant Rennie Davis by Mr. Foran*

Q. He [Deputy Mayor Stahl—ed.] told you there was an 11 p.m curfew that did not permit sleeping in the parks, did he say that?

A. But in the context at that time it would be waived as it was waived all the time for the Boy Scouts and the National Guard troops.

Q. Well, you didn't consider the Yippies Boy Scouts, did you?

A. Well, I considered that under the Civil Rights Act that American citizens have equal protection of the law, whether Boy Scouts or people with long hair, Mr. Foran. That is a part of this country.

Q. You think that the Yippies with what they were advertising they were going to do in Lincoln Park are the same as the Boy Scouts? Is that what you are saying?

A. Well, as someone who has been very active in the Boy Scouts during all of his young life, I considered—

Q. Did you ever seen the Boy Scouts advertise public fornication, for heavens sake?

A. The Yippies talked about a Festival of Life and love and—

Q. They also talked about public fornication and about drug use and about nude-ins on the beach? They also talked about that, didn't they?

A. They talked about love, yes, sir.

Q. You and I have a little different feeling about love, I guess, Mr. Davis.

\*   \*   \*

The Court:  Mayor Daley, as far as I am concerned, and so I am told, is a good mayor. I don't think I have ever spoken three sentences to him other than—I don't know whether I spoke to him when he was on the stand here or not. Perhaps I did direct him to answer some questions, I don't know.

\* \* \*

The Court:  I didn't want anybody to get the impression that anybody but President Eisenhower nominated me for this position on the bench and that I was confirmed by the Senate of the United States unanimously. I want the witness to feel easy.

### January 27, 1970
*Continued cross-examination of Defendant Davis by Mr. Foran*

Q. Did you say, "I want to talk about a campaign of building in the United States in 1968 a national liberation front"?
A. Yes. The idea was to build in the—
Q. You didn't say "American"?
A. I said—well, building in the United States a liberation—
Q. —in 1968 a national liberation front?
A. Well, yes, those may be the words, but it is the same idea exactly.
Q. The National Liberation Front in Vietnam is the Viet Cong, isn't it?
A. Well, that's your term. Yes. I am an American, sir, and I think that it is time that we began to talk about liberating Americans.
Q. Like the Viet Cong are liberating the Vietnamese?
A. Well, I think that anywhere in the world where people are working to—
Q. The same way that the Viet Cong are liberating the Vietnamese people?
A. I hardly said that—
Q. I didn't say you said that. I am asking whether that is what you mean; do you mean that you should have a national liberation front in the United States that liberates America the way the National Liberation Front in Vietnam is liberating the Vietnamese people?
A. I hardly think it appropriate that we build an army in the United States.

\* \* \*

Q. And what you want to urge young people to do is to revolt, isn't right?
A. Yes, revolt. That is probably right.
Q. And you have stated, have you not, "That there can be no question by the time that I am through that I have every intention of urging that you revolt, that you join

203

the movement, that you become a part of a growing force for insurrection in the United States." You have said that, haven't you?

A. I was standing right next to Fred Hampton when I said that that, and later he was murdered.

Q. You said that, did you not, sir? You stated that, did you not?

A. Side by side with Fred Hampton who was murdered in this city by policemen.

*　*　*

The Court: This trial is going on. Call your next witness. Three of the defendants have gone out.

Mr. Kunstler: They are bringing him in.

The Court: Oh, it takes three to bring the next witness in?

Mr. Kunstler: No, but he likes company.

The Court: Does he want to hug the witness too, the way they hugged this witness? I have never presided at a trial where there was so much physical affection demonstrated in the courtroom.

Voices: RIGHT ON.

The Court: Perhaps that is part of the love-in, I don't know.

Mr. Kunstler: Maybe this is not a bad place for it to happen, in the United States District Court.

*　*　*

*Direct examination of Defense Witness Norman Mailer, author, by Defense Attorney Kunstler*

Q. Now, Mr. Mailer, can you give us some idea of your experience in the political arena? Have you run for public office?

A. Yes, I ran in the Democratic Primary for Mayor last spring, and I came in fourth in a field of five.

The Court: You didn't say what city, sir.

The Witness: I am sorry, Judge, in New York City.

The Court: I knew I haven't seen your name on our ballot.

The Witness: It is my deep desire, Judge, to run for Mayor in Chicago.

Q. Where did you first meet Abbie Hoffman?

A. I met Mr. Hoffman at the Provincetown Airport after I had refused to see him at my house.

Mr. Schultz: Your Honor, would you instruct the witness please to be responsive to the questions.

I ask that your Honor instruct the witness to be responsive to the questions. He was asked when he met him and where.

204

We don't have to know the story behind it, or what was being done at the time, but simply when and where.

The Court: You are too high-priced a writer to give us all that gratis, Mr. Mailer. Just answer the question.

\* \* \*

Q. Now, Mr. Mailer, in that conversation was there anything else said by Mr. Rubin to you or you to him which did not go into the evaluation of David Dellinger as a person?

A. Mr. Rubin said that his political philosophy and Mr. Dellinger's political philosophy were so different that he hesitated to attempt to explain Mr. Dellinger's philosophy to me because he felt that he was not certain that he could be fair to him since they were at odds. And I asked him to make the attempt in Mr. Dellinger's absence and Mr. Rubin then proceeded to explain to me to the best of his ability what he thought Mr. Dellinger was up to in the march on the Pentagon.

\* \* \*

Q. What was said by Mr. Rubin or by yourself?

A. Mr. Rubin said that he was at present working full time on plans to have a youth festival in Chicago in August of 1968 when the Democratic Convention would take place and it was his idea that the presence of a hundred thousand young people in Chicago at a festival with rock bands would so intimidate and terrify the establishment, particularly the Johnson Vietnam war establishment, that Lyndon Johnson would have to be nominated under armed guard.

And I said, "Wow."

I was overtaken with the audacity of the idea and I said, "It's a beautiful and frightening idea."

And Rubin said, "I think that the beauty of it is that the establishment is going to do it all themselves. We won't do a thing. We are just going to be there and they won't be able to take it. They will smash the city themselves. They will provoke all the violence. . . ."

\* \* \*

Mr. Schultz: . . . We ask that you only relate conversations pursuant to questions.

The Court: That is right.

Mr. Schultz: If you are asked about a telephone call, then you can tell about it, but you can't mix them all up.

The Witness: You are quite right. I have been exposed to the world as a man possessed of a rambling mind.

205

Mr. Schultz:   We are to determine facts here.
The Witness:   Facts are nothing without their nuance, sir.

\* \* \*

*By Mr. Kunstler:*

Q. Can you recall what you said?
A. Yes, I said that Chicago was a city run by a man who had
   been a giant and had ended as a beast. I was referring
   to Mayor Daley. And then I went on and said that the
   country was being run or had been run by a man from
   Texas who begun as a giant and ended as a beast.

\* \* \*

Q. Can you, just so that we can get to the next point, state
   what you did say on Wednesday in Grant Park?
A. I merely said to the people who were there that I thought
   they were possessed of beauty, and that I was not going
   to march with them because I had to write this piece,
   and it was a particularly informal atmosphere in Grant
   Park. One got up and spoke and just said what one felt
   like saying. They were not formal speeches. I just said,
   "I don't feel right about not marching with all of you
   because one never knows whether you do this for the
   best of reasons, or because one is afraid to march. I can't
   take the chance of getting arrested because I have to
   write this piece, and so I just came to say, 'Bless you.
   Do your business, and I'm with you. Thank you.'" And
   they all said, "Write, Baby." That is what they said from
   the crowd.

\* \* \*

The Court:   You may relate what you saw, and not what
you think is clear.
A. I saw the police attack and they charged into the crowd
   wielding their clubs. They cut through them like sheets
   of rain, like a sword cutting down grass, and they would
   cut off a group of people down there on the street and
   then they would charge into them again and cut them
   into smaller pieces, cut them again into four, then into
   eight. They beat them up, left them on the street. Then
   they would come and pick up more people—in other
   words, pick up these people who were beaten up and
   threw them into ambulances. As they did that, they
   would beat them further.

. . .

A. The police kept attacking and attacking. When they had
   driven people in every direction, they then chased them

206

into the park. They chased them into the barricade that had been set up by the police in front of the Conrad Hilton where people who were just standing there watch-the parade were pushed into the police, beaten up. They pushed—as far as I could see, they then pushed people into the wall of the Conrad Hilton. I was not able to see them push people through the plate glass window because that was out of my view.

\* \* \*

*Cross-examination of Mr. Mailer by Government Attorney Schultz*

Q. Now your speech in Grant Park—Just a second. Let me get it.

In your speech didn't you say that "We are at the beginning of a war which would continue for twenty years and the march today would be one battle in that war"?

A. Yes, I said that.

Q. But you couldn't go on the march because you had a deadline?

A. Yes. I was in a moral quandary. I didn't know if I was being scared or being professional and I was naturally quite upset because a man never likes to know that his motive might be simple fear.

\* \* \*

Q. Could you state if Mr. Rubin didn't use the word "intimidate" as you have answered Mr. Schultz, what word did you use? What was his language?

. . .

A. . . . I use the word "intimidate" because possibly since I am a bully by nature, unlike anyone else in this Court, I tend to think in terms of intimidation, but I don't think Mr. Rubin does. He thinks in terms of catalysm, of having people become aroused, to reveal their guilt, their own evil, if you will. . . .

**January 28, 1970**

Mr. Schultz: . . . I wish Davis who was such a gentle boy on the stand for the last couple of days, smiling at the jury and pretending he was just the little boy next door, would stop whispering and talking to me while I am talking.

Mr. Davis: You are a disgrace, sir. I say you are a disgrace. I really say you are a disgrace.

Voices: Yes, yes.

Mr. Schultz:   I think he has a split personality, like a schizophrenic.

Mr. Weiner:   Now he is a psychological student.

\*     \*     \*

[*Argument concerning Government's motion that Ramsey Clark, Attorney General at the time of the events named in the indictments, be barred from testifying as a witness for the defense.*]

Mr. Kunstler:  . . . If your Honor grants their motion [to bar former Attorney General Ramsey Clark from testifying—ed.], you will be the first federal judge in the United States to grant such a motion, and I know of no case within which that has ever occurred with a willing witness. There have been willing witnesses who have taken the stand and had much of their testimony objected to and sustained. That is another thing. That is the way the procedure goes. But I've never heard of a willing witness being prevented from taking the stand or made to testify in the vacuum of a court without a jury.

The Court:   Suppose a fair and reasonable construction of the regulation referred to by Mr. Schultz is that it is illegal for a former employee of the Government to give information as described in that regulation. . . .

If it is illegal, then I ask you, Mr. Kunstler, whether or not the Court may forbid this former employee of the Government, prestigious witness though he might be, from testifying. Then may not the Court forbid him from testifying?

Mr. Kunstler:   Well, I will say this, that if there was—if the regulation was so worded and there was such a regulation of the type which your Honor has visualized, perhaps there might be a legal argument, except that the regulation doesn't exist in that form, and of course I might say that the testimony of Mr. Wilkins and the testimony of Mr. Pomeroy, both of whom testified here without any objection from the Government, then must have been illegal if you interpret it that way . . .

\*     \*     \*

Mr. Kunstler:  . . . Your Honor has read the rules of evidence against us as strictly as it is possible to do. There has not been one given in discretionary areas in favor of the defense. You have read those rules like a straight jacket here, and while I am not going to dispute the legality of it at this time, if they are convicted, that will be for another court to decide.

There is no question that you have read them to the point of extremism as far as the defendants are concerned, every possible exercise of discretion.

The Court:   I will have to see how those last remarks look in print.

208

Mr. Kunstler:   I am telling you it is a legal argument. If you are trying to terrify me from making a legal argument—

The Court:   There is one thing I learned early in this case, Mr. Kunstler. You don't frighten very easily, not at all. I don't terrify you at all.

* * *

Mr. Kunstler:   I don't think your Honor should raise contempt in the middle of my argument, because perhaps you don't like what I am saying.

The Court:   That is your word. You must be thinking about that.

Mr. Kunstler:   I am reading your Honor's mind in this case.

The Court:   I didn't use the word.

Mr. Kunstler:   Your Honor has never used the word "contempt." I agree with that. Your Honor has let filter through the air the unspoken threat that this will be the fate of the lawyers in this case. I know that, and I think that your Honor cannot deny that that is a strong possibility in this case. If your Honor wants to make it after my argument, fine, but I don't think in the middle of my argument when I am presenting a legal point, it should be raised. I don't think it is fair.

* * *

Mr. Schultz:   . . . There is absolutely nothing that the Attorney General can contribute to this case . . . It is absolutely not relevant that he made a call to the Mayor. But they want to get him here to pull the stunt in front of the jury, and we are objecting to it. They are not going to, in our opinion, make this trial the mockery that they are trying to make it. They are not going to stand here and ask that man improper questions as they have done with other witnesses if we can help it, and we are asking your Honor not to let them do that again, not to let them parade people before this jury and create false impressions knowing their conduct is contumacious, but not caring, but willing to practice the civil disobedience that their clients participated in to prove to their clients that they are in the fold, that are in the movement. If that is what Mr. Kunstler has to do, he can do it elsewhere, but not in this courtroom. We can—

Mr. Davis:   Outrageous.

* * *

[*Following a noontime recess*]

The Court:   Now we get to the matter we were discussing this morning.

The defendants propose to call as a witness the former Attorney General of the United States to give testimony in their behalf. This is consistent with the announced intention of the defendants to call a number of persons who have held high public office. The Mayor of Chicago has testified already, and reference has been made to the former President of the United States, President Johnson.

As a matter of fact, I believe a subpoena directed to President Johnson has been filed.

It is the Court's view that during the course of this trial the defendants have attempted to inject irrelevant and extraneous evidence despite repeated Court rulings prohibiting such evidence. The experience with the Mayor's testimony was that he was called with much fanfare but was able to give virtually no evidence that was material to this case.

Because of past experience of that nature, I am concerned that additional witnesses will be called or might be called that are unable to give material testimony with the attendant needless delay of this trial. While the defendants have a right to compulsory process to obtain witnesses in their behalf under the Sixth Amendment, the determination of whether or not to allow a witness to take the stand is a matter within the discretion of the trial judge. Thus, where the defense has attempted to introduce substantial extraneous matter into the case, the Court is justified in requiring the defense to demonstrate by voir dire questions of a witness or the witness, referring to Mr. Clark, the testimony it expects to elicit from him.

I have no way of knowing what testimony at this time—that is, I have no way of knowing what testimony the defendants intend to elicit from the former Attorney General, but I shall permit the defendants to call him out of the presence of the jury and to put to him the questions which they believe —by "they," I mean counsel for the defendants—are material and relevant, and if there are such questions put to the witness, I shall later deal with the matter of permitting the questions to be put to the witness in the presence of the jury.

. . .

Mr. Kunstler: Your Honor, we are going to do this under protest. We believe it is a process to screen a witness prior to his testimony, and we think it is grossly unconstitutional to force us to do this, so we want the record to be quite clear that we examine him out of the presence of the jury under protest.

\*     \*     \*

[*Voir dire examination of William Ramsey Clark, former Attorney General of the United States, by Mr. Kunstler to determine whether the Court will permit him to testify*

210

*as a defense witness. The following takes place out of the presence of the jury*]

Q. Now, Mr. Clark, do you know Wes Pomeroy or Wesley Pomeroy?

A. Yes, I do.

Q. Do you know what position he held in July and August of 1968?

A. Yes. He was Special Assistant for Law Enforcement Coordination to the Attorney General.

Q. Do you know Roger Wilkins?

A. Yes, I do.

Q. Do you know what position he held in July and August of 1968?

A. Yes. He was the Director of the Community Relations Service.

. . .

The Witness: . . . I called Mayor Daley to ask him to meet with Roger Wilkins and Wes Pomeroy. I suggested that he have Supt. Conlisk of the Chicago Police there and describe the purpose of their visit at an interchange of information and ideas.

I described the background and experience of Mr. Wilkins and Mr. Pomeroy, and he said the—Mayor Daley said that he would meet with them and he did meet with them within two or three days.

. . .

Q. Can you give the specific instructions which you gave to them pertinent to this situation, which would be the meeting with Mayor Daley?

A. Well, it was somewhat different for the two.

For Mr. Pomeroy it was to be sure that there was a full and free flow of information among all of the law-enforcement agencies that had any role to perform in the city of Chicago at the time that the Democratic National Convention would be held here. . . .

. . .

Q. What about Mr. Wilkins?

A. Mr. Wilkins had a more general assignment.

As the Director of the Community Relations Service, it was his responsibility to do whatever he could to maintain stable community relations among all the elements that might be involved in the coming convention, so that would involve the major black community here in Chicago, including the community immediately around the Stockyards, and it would involve the leadership of

211

the several groups that had indicated their intention to
come here to protest at the time of the convention.

\* \* \*

Q. All right. Now, after Mr. Wilkins and Mr. Pomeroy met
with the Mayor on July 25, 1968, did one or both
report back to you as to that meeting, the results of that
meeting?
. . .
A. Yes. He said that, you know, roughly, the meeting was not
very satisfactory, that he didn't feel that we were likely
to get the cooperation that we hoped for and that the
attitude from the Mayor's office didn't seem conciliatory.

\* \* \*

Q. . . . [D]o you know what, if any, action was taken with
reference to federal troops?
A. Yes. There were federal troops pre-positioned—is the
phrase we have used—in the Chicago area sometime
during the weekend before the beginning of the Democratic National Convention here in August of '68. I
believe they were pre-positioned—they were flown in
from quite some distance, probably Fort Hood or Fort
Sill. You know, there were some other occasions on
which this happened. I think that's where they came
from, and they came to Glenview and probably Great
Lakes Naval Training Station.

. . .
Q. Now, in your opinion, General Clark, was this pre-posi-
tioning of federal troops necessary in the Chicago area?
Mr. Schultz:  Objection.
The Court:  Sustain the objection.
*By Mr. Kunstler:*
Q. General Clark, in your opinion, were the amount of police
and National Guard and Sheriff's deputies available to
the Mayor of Chicago sufficient for the purposes needed
with reference to expected demonstrational activities
around the Democratic National Convention?
Mr. Schultz:  Objection.
The Court:  I sustain the objection.

\* \* \*

Q. Now, General Clark, I call your attention to August 30,
1968, and ask you if you can recall a telephone call to
Thomas Foran, the United States Attorney for the
Northern District of Illinois?
A. Yes, my notes show and I recall from having read them

212

and having refreshed my memory, that I talked with Tom Foran on that day. Whether he called me or I called him, I am not sure.

Q. Could you state what you said to him and what he said to you?

A. Well, I can state the things that I can recall. I told him that we wanted to investigate the occurrences during that week concerning the National Convention. . . .

. . .

A. I asked him to check on a report that Car 100 of the Chicago Police Department and whoever might have used the car with that license were involved in an order to sweep the streets late on that Wednesday evening near the Conrad Hilton Hotel. That's about all.

\* \* \*

Mr. Kunstler:  . . . This witness is here; he has come a long way to be here, and he is prepared to give some relevant conversations if only the fact they existed, so that this jury can understand that there was an attempt to have a federal presence here in Chicago—

The Court:  You are repeating your arguments.

Mr. Kunstler:  I don't think I mentioned federal presence, but if I am repeating, I am sorry. I don't think your Honor should exclude this testimony from the defendants in this case.

\* \*

The Court:  Let me say this gentlemen: This morning when this matter was presented to me and the meeting at Attorney General Clark's home on Sunday was discussed, and knowing in a general way, at least, what the responsibilities of the Attorney General of the United States are, I had the strong feeling that this witness could not testify to anything material or relevant. I had that strong feeling. I said I'd take it during the noon hour, and I did reflect on it, and carefully, and concluded that I should give the defendants, as I did, the opportunity to ask the witness the questions that they proposed to ask him if he were permitted to testify before the jury, and it is my conclusion, without extending my remarks any further, that I have given the defendants every opportunity here to demonstrate that this witness could make a relevant or material contribution. They have failed to so demonstrate.

I therefore sustain the objection of the government to having the defense call this witness, Attorney General Clark, before the jury, and. I also order both counsel for the Government and the defense not to refer to this hearing or the subject matter thereof before the jury after the jury is brought in.

* * *

[*Testimony of Defense Witness, Chicago Detective Frank Riggio*]

Q. . . . [W]as it necessary to carry a night stick to conduct a surveillance on that day? Was a night stick necessary for a surveillance?

A. It was evidently necessary at that time because I had it in my hand. If it wasn't necessary, I wouldn't have carried it.

## Jaunary 29, 1970

*The following are excerpts from a news film shown at the trial*

Mr. Davis: We have said again and again that we are not coming to the city of Chicago to confront police, National Guard, or people in the United States Army. Our fight is not with these men. Our fight is with the policies that have created a situation where the Democratic Party feels it is necessary to create a police state during the time that the world is regarding this democratic process in action. We oppose this police state, this militarization. We oppose the policies that have now been carried out here in Chicago just as we oppose the aggression and militarization in Vietnam.

* * *

Mr. Dellinger: Certainly we cannot abdicate at a point like this. I believe Senator McCarthy and Albert Weinstein were grossly wrong when they said, in effect, "If you come to Chicago you may actually be confronted with the violence of the police and therefore you must stay away." I think that is the time when democratic-loving people and peace-loving people have to stand up and be counted. They have to come here and they have to face this challenge. We think that at the last minute the Mayor will probably come to his senses and try to avert that kind of bloodshed. If he does not, the onus will be on him.

. . .

Interviewer: Let me ask one of the ladies of the group a question. Nancy, give us the female point of view.

Nancy Kurshon: Oh, I mean, you are asking what the female point of view is. You know, that is a symbol of the poor values of the American society because I don't see why the female point of view should be any different

214

from the male point of view because it is a personal point of view.

*  *  *

Interviewer: This may be your last appearance on Chicago television for a while. What's your final good-bye to our city?
(*Laughter.*)
Voices: Reach out. This is a city where you rub shoulders with rifles, and clubs and Mace. Hog butcher of the world. Hog butcher of the world. That is what Mayor Daley says.

*  *  *

*Direct examination of Defense Witness Bobby Seale, Chairman of the Black Panther Party, by Mr. Kunstler [Mr. Seale is walking to the witness stand. The jury is out of the room.]*
Voices: Hey, Bobby. Right on, right on.
The Marshal: Sit down, please.
The Court: You are Mr. Bobby Seale.
Mr. Seale: Yes.
(*There was laughter in the courtroom.*)
Voice: He doesn't know that yet?

. . .

The Court: . . . Do you wish to testify?
Mr. Seale: Yes.
The Court: All right.
Now, Mr. Garry, out of the presence of the jury, I am glad to see you after all of the many months, but I hope your standing at the lectern doesn't mean that you are going to interrogate this witness.
Mr. Garry: That is what it means, your Honor.

. . .

The Court: . . . I am not going to permit a lawyer even though your appearance is of record to do this. I haven't heard from you in all of these months. But I will permit either one of the lawyers whose names were signed to the petition to examine this witness.

. . .

Mr. Schultz: The jury, your Honor, should also know that both Mr. Garry and Mr. Kunstler are of record for Mr. Seale. Mr. Kunstler's statement that Mr. Kunstler is not his attorney is not so.
Mr. Kunstler: Your Honor, I am not going to go through that weary subject again. I have made my point before the jury forty times.
The Court: You made the statement, but the Government

215

has a right to reply. It doesn't make it weary because you brought it up.

\* \* \*

By Mr. Kunstler:

Q. Would you state what is the Black Panther Party for Self Defense?

A. The Black Panther Party—

Mr. Schultz: Objection.

The Court: I sustain the objection.

. . .

Mr. Schultz: We are not litigating the Black Panther Party.

The Court: I will let my ruling stand.

Mr. Kunstler: We are litigating the Black Panther Party, your Honor, in this case.

The Court: I will let my ruling stand, sir.

\* \* \*

[*Cross-examination of Defense Witness Bobby Seale by Mr. Schultz*]

A. . . . Revolutionary tactics are broad. I could send three or four people out with a community control, the police petition; easily at the same time the community can be occupied by policemen shooting, brutalizing, killing, and what I would tell black people then was don't get up in large numbers because all you're going to do is get a lot of them shot. Go in small groups, threes and fours. You can dissemble the pig police force, as we put it and say it, by circulating the petitions to get enough registered voters to place it on the ballot to vote it out. That's what we mean by being a political party and that's what a political party does, it produces revolutionary tactics on a broad level. . . .

\* \* \*

Q. When you told the people in Lincoln Park, "Pick up a gun, pull the spike from the wall, because if you pull it out and you shoot well, all I'm gonna do is pat you on the back and say, 'Keep on shooting.'" That was part of your revolutionary tactics, too, was it not, sir?

A. Yes, sir, and if you look generally—

Mr. Schultz: Please, that is all.

The Court: You have answered the question.

The Witness: I strike that answer on the grounds that that particular question is wrong because it ain't clear.

The Court: I have some news for you, sir.

\* \*

[*Following applause in the courtroom.*]

The Court: . . . [W]ill the marshals exclude from the

courtroom anyone who applauded. We don't applaud here. This isn't a theater. . . .

\* \* \*

[*Redirect examination by Mr. Kunstler*]

Q. What was the name of your party at that time?

A. The Black Panther Party. Prior to that, it was the Black Panther Party for Self Defense, but after about seven months, so many people were mixing up our organization and trying to call it a paramilitary group which it wasn't, so the central committee of the Black Panther Party took the suggestion of our Minister of Defense, Huey Newton, that we drop the "Self Defense," so people could see we actually have a 10-point basic political program which deals with employment, housing, decent education, fair treatment in the courts, a jury of members of our peers on the jury, and things like this here, and our major political objective was so people could see this and we dropped the "Self Defense," because we wanted a United Nations Plebiscite to be held in the black community to deal with the political aspirations and desires and needs of political, economic and social injustice that we were subjected to.

\* \* \*

*Direct examination of Defense Witness John Conyers, a Congressman from Michigan, by Mr. Weinglass*

Mr. Weinglass: I represent to the Court that Congressman Conyers is being called primarily by the defense as an expert witness and his qualifications in the House of Representatives is essential to qualify him as an expert.

Mr. Foran: An expert on what subject?

Mr. Weinglass: He shall testify as an expert on the political and economic oppression and repression of black people within the United States as it existed in August of 1968.

Mr. Foran: I object to that.

The Court: I will sustain the objection to the question. . . .
. . .

Mr. Weinglass: Your Honor, the problem always has been that the Forans have always been permitted to speak about it but not the Congressmen Conyers.

The Court: You have said that all too often here, sir, and you have repeated it time and again. I have labored four months, probably four and a half, I haven't checked lately. I have given you a respectful hearing on every disputed question and I get remarks such as you just made in return and I disapprove of them. . . .

\* \* \*

Mr. Kunstler:   Your Honor, if the bitterness and frustration of a man like Bobby Seale and what he feels about life in the United States can [sic—ed.] be fully explored and you cannot show that black men are murdered in their beds in this city—

Mr. Foran:   Your Honor, the theater is beginning again. May we have the jury excused, your Honor, since the Government is unable to respond, since the Government is bound to proper conduct in a courtroom?

*   *   *

Mr. Foran:   Your Honor, you will note, of course, that Mr. Hayden shouted out in the courtroom about the Attorney General not testifying before the jury after a direct and clear direction from the Court after the Attorney General had testified extensively on voir dire that it should not be mentioned before the jury. Mr. Hayden jumped to his feet and shouted that out while the jury was filing out of the room.

Mr. Weinglass:   That statement is as accurate as other statements made by Mr. Foran. This time it was done right in the presence of the Court. Your Honor must—your Honor does not have to be reminded if there is a shout in the courtroom and I think the fact that Mr. Foran had to state it is proof of the fact that it didn't occur. The Court has never failed to note for the record when there was a disturbance in the courtroom.

. . .

Mr. Schultz:   Your Honor, would [you] inquire of Mr. Weinglass whether or not he heard Mr. Hayden make the statement?

The Court:   No. I will let the record determine that.

Mr. Hayden:   Your Honor, I did make the statement. I did not intend to, as the Government said. It came about because I lost my temper after listening to what Mr. Foran said. I am sorry that I did it. I did not intend it.

The Court:   You got the answer.

Mr. Hayden:   I did not understand—

Mr. Weinglass:   He did not jump to his feet. He did not shout.

The Court:   That rather convicts you, doesn't it, by your own client?

## January 30, 1970

[*Direct examination of Pete Seeger, a folksinger, by Mr. Kunstler*]

Q.   Mr. Seeger, recently you conducted your singing on board a vessel, did you not?

Mr. Foran:    Objection, your Honor.

Mr. Schultz:    Objection.

The Court:    I sustain the objection.

Mr. Kunstler:    Who is going to do it?

Mr. Schultz:    We haven't decided yet.

Mr. Foran:    Flip a coin.

Mr. Schultz:    I'm taller, your Honor. I object.

The Court:    I sustain the objection.

Mr. Foran:    He's only an inch, Judge. I'm smarter.

*    *    *

*[Direct examination of Martinsen by Mr. Weinglass]*

The Court:    The last statement of the witness, "Unfortunately the truth did not come out," those words may be stricken from the record and the jury is directed to disregard them.

You are asked, sir, to give the conversation you had with these other men.

The Witness:    Yes, your Honor, but I am very deeply committed to the truth.

The Court:    But I am committed to trying this case in a proper manner under the law and I can't permit you to engage in any personal philosophy here.

The Witness:    Yes. Please forgive me for being committed to the truth.

The Court:    I will forgive you if you don't do it again.

*    *    *

*Direct Examination of Defense Witness Staughton Lynd, professor of American History, by Mr. Weinglass*

Mr. Weinglass:    If the Court please, the defense offers Professor Lynd as an expert in the area of American Revolution and I am about to ask him several questions relating to that subject matter and the facts of this case, but in the light of the other objections and the other rulings of the Court, I feel perhaps my motion in this regard should be had outside the presence of the jury.

Mr. Foran:    I would think that is quite likely, your Honor. As to the American Revolution, there is no charge in this indictment about that.

Mr. Weinglass:    The witness will testify about the right of Americans to petition for redress for grievances, a right which was fought for and won in the American Revolution and was not threatened until—

Mr. Foran:    Your Honor . . .

. . .

*[Without the jury present, Professor Lynd was questioned and testified as follows]*

Q. Would you state your opinion.

A. I have the opinion that the right which is enumerated in the First Amendment, adopted shortly after the ratification of the United States Constitution, the right to petition for redress of grievances, had a much broader meaning to the men who made the American Revolution and who wrote the United States Constitution than we ordinarily assume. . . .

And what they were doing in this petitionary process prior to the American Revolution was not asking for the passage of a particular law, but crying out against what the Declaration of Independence called a long train of abuses evincing the design of the attempt to create an absolute despotism. . . .

This is what the petitioning meant to them, and the reason that I think this concept of petitioning is relevant to the situation before this Court is that it seems to me that the First Amendment was involved in what happened in Chicago in 1968 in a far broader sense than in its particular senses of the right to march, the right to use a public park, the right to free speech, and the right of free press. It seems to me that the jury might wish to consider the entire process of the demonstration, that which made people come to Chicago, as a kind of petitioning process in which people who felt that their elected government was no longer responsive to them, felt themselves to be in the same position as the colonists before the American Revolution and came to Chicago to make one last direct appeal to the men of power who were assembled in the Democratic Convention . . .

I don't see how we can say that the American people has a right to revolution as a last resort against total oppression and say that they lack a right of resistance short of revolution to a partially oppressive situation. . . .

. . . This is a form of intermediate resistance full of precedent from the American Revolution, very much in the American tradition, and it seems to me at least quite appropriate in the circumstances of 1968.

Mr. Weinglass: If the Court please, that completes the offer of proof.

The Court: What is the position of the Government in respect to what has been described here by Mr. Weinglass as an offer of proof?

Mr. Foran: The Government objects.

The Court: I sustain the objection. . . .

*  *  *

*Direct examination of Defense Witness Donald Peterson, the Chairman of the Wisconsin delegation to the 1968 Democratic Convention, by Mr. Weinglass*

Mr. Weinglass: . . . I represent this to the Court: if the Court's position is—if the Court's ruling is that anything that occurred on the floor of the Convention is irrelevant to this case, I have no further questions, but if the Court does not make that ruling, I will again attempt to elicit from this witness what occurred on the floor of the Convention.

I am just asking the Court what the basis of the ruling is.

The Court:   I am not obligated to answer that question.

Mr. Weinglass:   Well, then, we will have to go on. Now I don't want to waste this time.

Mr. Schultz:   Then let Mr. Weinglass, without asking a leading question, ask the witness what happened on the floor of the Convention at about a certain time without suggesting—

Mr. Weinglass:   I thought I did that.

Mr. Schultz:   No, Mr. Weinglass.

If he asks that question—

Mr. Weinglass:   Okay. I won't argue that.

Mr. Schultz:   I will object to that question. But if he asks it nonleading, then we can resolve Mr. Weinglass' dilemma.

*By Mr. Weinglass:*

Q. Mr. Peterson, what happened on the floor of the Convention at approximately ten o'clock?

Mr. Schultz:   Objection.

*(Laughter.)*

The Court:   I sustain the objection.

Mr. Weinglass:   It is incredible.

Mr. Schultz:   Now Mr. Weinglass has the ruling of the court in this area.

*By Mr. Weinglass:*

Q. What happened on the floor of the Convention at approximately ten-thirty?

Mr. Schultz:   Objection, your Honor.

The Court:   I sustain the objection.

*By Mr. Weinglass:*

Q. What happened on the floor at any time that night after nine p.m.?

Mr. Schultz:   Objection.

The Court:   I sustain the objection.

*By Mr. Weinglass:*

Q. What did you do on the floor of the Convention?

Mr. Schultz:   Same objection, your Honor, relevancy.

The Court:   I sustain the objection.

Mr. Schultz:   Now Mr. Weinglass has the Court's ruling

221

that what happened at the Convention on Wednesday night is not material to the case.

Mr. Weinglass: Is Mr. Schultz correct in his interpretation of the Court's ruling? If he is, I will desist.

The Court: My rulings are correct. You interpret my rulings, sir.

\* \* \*

*(Witness excused)*

The Court: That didn't hurt a bit, did it?

The Witness: I think it did, your Honor.

*(Applause)*

\* \* \*

Mr. Schultz: Your Honor, conduct like this has never gone on in the courtroom before and what makes it worse is that Mr. Weinglass and Mr. Kunstler countenance it. They countenance it. They smile, they enjoy it.

The Court [sic—ed.]: Oh, Mr. Schultz—

Mr. Schultz: It is just incredible.

The Court: I am aware of that. I am aware of that.

Mr. Kunstler: Your Honor, I sat there and heard you exclude testimony that the defense thinks is quite relevant to this case which the jury can evaluate and judge for themselves. They have not heard one quarter of the available testimony that we presented in this case. They have been in and out today as our witnesses were brought and they never even heard them.

The Court: Call your next witness.

Mr. Schultz: Your Honor, we could call irrelevant witnesses, too, and claim the same thing.

Mr. Kunstler: My God, what did they come here for but the Democratic National Convention and every word about the Convention is excluded.

\* \* \*

*[Colloquy between the Court and counsel]*

Mr. Foran: Your Honor, I would ask that the defendants at counsel table try to look a little less like we are sitting in a living room in front of the fire. We have had a young lady kneeling with her arms in his lap. This is a federal courthouse, your Honor.

The Marshal: Mr. Weiner, sit up.

The Court: Mr. Foran, they are laughing at you back there when you say that. I have tried four and a half months unsuccessfully, I might add, to maintain a modicum of dignity in this courtroom. I have never in all the years undergone what I have undergone in this trial. I have repeatedly requested various people to conform. The marshals have requested the defendants, for example, not to read the newspapers. They didn't even listen to their own expert witnesses, so-called, but insisted on reading newspapers while the testimony was being given.

We have to have the defendants here when they are tried under the Constitution, and it is difficult to control that sort of thing during the trial. I will do my best. I have done my best up to now. . . .

\*     \*     \*

*Direct examination of Defense Witness, the Reverend Jesse Jackson, Director of Operation Breadbasket, the economic arm of the Southern Christian Leadership Conference, by Mr. Kunstler*

A.   I guess what I really wanted to say—I hope I have not been out of order, Judge.

The Court:   I didn't hear what you said.

The Witness:   I said I hope I have not been out of order. I don't quite understand court procedure.

The Court:   Well, I don't think I'd make a perfect minister, either. So we're even.

The Witness:   Okay, Judge. We're going to get along.

\*     \*     \*

*[The Reverend Jesse Jackson, telling of a discussion with Defendant Davis]*

A.   . . . I told him I hoped he got the legal permit, but even if he didn't, that it would be consistent with Dr. King's teaching that we then get a moral permit, which, rather than getting permission from the city, if we couldn't get it that way, we'd have to get a commission from our consciences and just have an extralegal demonstration, that probably blacks shouldn't participate, that if blacks got whipped, nobody would pay any attention, it would just be history. But if whites got whipped, it would make good news—that is, it would make the newspapers—we expected the blacks to get killed, so Rennie told me he didn't understand what I was saying. I told him that I thought long-haired whites was the new style nigger, and if he didn't think they would get whipped, to try it, and we continued the conversation, and then he called me back, I guess, trying to get clarity on what a new style nigger was, and I felt that the country was in some bind as to being able to absorb people with different kinds of values.

\*     \*     \*

The Court:   I wanted to say to counsel for the defendants and the defendants, if they will listen, that it has been brought to my attention that there was a speech given in Milwaukee discussing this case by one of the defendants—not that that was the first time a speech was given about this case by one of the defendants during this trial. I want to say that if such a speech as was given is brought to my attention again, I will give serious consideration to the termination of bail of the person who makes the speech. I think he would be a bad risk to continue on bail. . . .

* * *

Mr. Dellinger: I made the speech.

The Court: What did you say?

Mr. Dellinger: I made the speech. Was there anything in the speech that suggested I won't show up for trial the next day or simply that I criticized your conduct of the trial?

The Court: I didn't ask you to rise, sir, and I am certainly not going to be interrogated.

Mr. Dellinger: Why are you threatening me with revocation of bail for exercising my freedom of speech? What has that got to do with it? I am here, aren't I?

A Voice: RIGHT ON.

Mr. Hoffman: We all give the same speech.

* * *

Mr. Weinglass: Another spectator was physically carried by the marshals from the courtroom.

The Court: Yes. From what I have observed here, I think that that sort of thing should have been done before.

Mr. Weinglass, I repeat, I have never seen or heard anything in the many, many years such as occurred during this trial.

* * *

The Court: . . . I haven't heard either lawyer for the defendants try to quiet their clients during this trial when they spoke out, not once in four and half months, not once.

Mr. Weinglass: If your Honor please, the question of bail revocation as a right to speak, though, I think the Court should clarify it.

The Court: I will determine what to do if and when speeches of a certain kind and character are brought to my attention. Free speech is not involved here.

**February 2, 1970**

Mr. Kunstler: I want to comment on this your Honor, because I think what you have just said is about the most outrageous statement I have ever heard from a bench, and I am going to say my piece right now, and you can hold me in contempt right now if you wish to.

You have violated every principle of fair play when you excluded Ramsey Clark from that witness stand. The New York

Times, among others, has called it the ultimate outrage in American justice.

Voices: RIGHT ON.

Mr. Kunstler: I am outraged to be in this Court before you. Now because I made a statement on Friday that I had only a cameraman, and I discovered on Saturday that Ralph Abernathy, who is the chairman of the Mobilization, is in town, and can be here, and because you took the whole day from us on Thursday by listening to this ridiculous argument about whether Ramsey Clark could take that stand in front of the jury, I am trembling because I am so outraged. I haven't been about to get this out before, and I am saying it now, and then I want you to put me in jail if you want to. You can do anything you want with me, if you want to, because I feel disgraced to be here, to say to us on the technicality of my representation that we can't put Ralph Abernathy on the stand. He is the co-chairman of the MOBE. He has relevant testimony. I know that doesn't mean much in this Court when the Attorney General of the United States walked out of here with his lips so tight he could hardly breathe, and if you could see the expression on his face, you would know, and his wife informed me he never felt such anger at the United States Government as at not being able to testify on that stand.

Voices: RIGHT ON.

* * *

Mr. Kunstler: . . . I have sat here for four and a half months and watched the objections denied and sustained by your Honor, and I know that this is not a fair trial. I know it in my heart. If I have to lose my license to practice law and if I have to go to jail, I can't think of a better cause to go to jail for and to lose my license for—

A Voice: RIGHT ON.

Mr. Kunstler: —than to tell your Honor that you are doing a disservice to the law in saying that we can't have Ralph Abernathy in the stand. You are saying truth will not out because of the technicality of a lawyer's representation. If that is what their liberty depends upon, your Honor, saying I represented to you that I had a cameraman, and that was our only witness, a cameraman, whom we can't get, incidentally, then I think there is nothing really more for me to say.

The Court: There is not much more you could say, Mr. Kunstler.

* *

Mr. Kunstler: I am going to turn back to my seat with the realization that everything I have learned throughout my

225

life has come to naught, that there is no meaning in this Court, and there is no law in this Court—

Voices: RIGHT ON.

Mr. Kunstler: —and these men are going to jail by virtue of a legal lynching—

Voices: RIGHT ON.

Mr. Kunstler: —and that your Honor is wholly responsible for that, and if this is what your career is going to end on, if this is what your pride is going to be built on, I can only say to your Honor, "Good luck to you."

(*There were shouts of "Right On" and there was applause in the courtroom.*)

\* \* \*

The Court: Out with those applauders.

Mr. Davis: I applauded, too, your Honor. Throw me out.

The Court: Unfortunately, you have to remain, Mr. Davis, but we note that you applauded. . . .

\* \* \*

Mr. Kunstler: We have a right to state our objection to resting before the jury.

The Court: Don't do it.

Mr. Kunstler: I am going to have to put my liberty in your hands on that score.

Mr. Schultz: Mr. Kunstler is simply inviting it.

Mr. Kunstler: Oh, of course I am inviting it because what your Honor is doing is a disgrace in this Court.

The Court: He did more than invite.

\* \* \*

Mr. Kunstler: . . . [A]s far as the embracing of Dr. Abernathy goes, I have known and represented Dr. Abernathy for 10 years from Albany, Georgia, through Birmingham, Danville, Virginia, and Selma, Alabama, and St. Augustine, Florida, and dozens of other places, and I have not seen him for some time, not since Martin Luther King's funeral, and I don't really think that my putting my arms around him is going to prejudice anybody in favor of or against anybody. . . .

\* \*

The Court: . . . I have seen witnesses kiss and kissing as they got off the witness stand right down there in the well of the courtroom in the presence of the jury. If that is what you call touching, so be it.

Mr. Kunstler: I was using "touching" in the physical sense, your Honor.

The Court: I have never seen that in a courtroom.

Mr. Kunstler:   But you have never seen us before, your Honor, and the movement —

The Court:   That's right.

Mr. Kunstler:   —and the movement has a physically touching quality to it which is sort of irrepressible sometimes.

The Court:   There are certain kinds of conduct one engages in in a courtroom and in other places.

Mr. Kunstler:   Well, there is, your Honor, because there are different life styles in this courtroom.

\* \* \*

Mr. Kunstler:   Your Honor, how can a lawyer remain silent when he has a witness with crucial testimony who is not available?

The Court:   If that is the way you want to do it, I can't control you. There is nothing I can do to control a lawyer's conduct. I can't put words into your mouth. I can't keep you from kissing a witness a few feet from the witness stand. I can't prevent that after it is done. Those are things that I can't prevent.

Mr. Kunstler:   Your Honor, a greeting by an embrace or a handshake—

The Court:   I have, as you suggested here, a recourse, but I am not eager to send men to prison, especially lawyers. You have invited being sentenced to jail, as you put it. I am not here to get any sadistic pleasure out of that.

\* \* \*

Mr. Kunstler:   I just want to say one very brief thing, your Honor, as to what has happened in this courtroom. I think in the last analysis, it will have to be history that judges whether you were right or we were right. The New York Times has indicated one position from an historical point of view.

The Court:   Oh, I never—

Mr. Kunstler:   I am not citing them as the ultimate authority, your Honor.

The Court:   —I never try cases in the newspapers.

Mr. Kunstler:   That is not my point. It is just the first voice of history.

\* \* \*

The Court:   Oh, I have gone back into the record. You don't know how carefully. I sometimes read things in this record, and I find it hard to believe that they are things on the record.

**February 3, 1970**

Mr. Kunstler:   Your Honor, when court closed yesterday

227

the status of Reverend Abernathy was still in doubt. I spoke with Mr. Abernathy where I found him last night in Clarksdale, Mississippi, and he asked me to make the following statement to your Honor about his appearance here and I will give it as he gave it to me.

"I left Chicago yesterday after being informed that the Court had ruled that I could not testify in this case. I left heavy of heart because I had interrupted my overloaded schedule and traveled through sleet and snow to tell what I knew this jury only to be refused the right to do so because I was sixteen minutes late in getting to the courthouse.

". . . I cannot close this statement without saying that I have just returned from abroad as an ambassador of good will for my country. When I was asked questions about my country's system of justice and equality, I groped for words to explain that both existed. When foreigners said, 'You have no democracy, no justice in America,' I attempted to prove that we did. After my experience yesterday in this Court I can no longer defend my country against such attacks." . . .

\* \* \*

[*At this point in the trial the defense rested its case and the Government proceeded to call additional witnesses in an attempt to rebut the evidence of the defense.*]
*Cross-examination of James Murray, a Chicago newspaper reporter called as a witness in rebuttal by the Government*

Mr. Kunstler: . . . [T]his is improper rebuttal testimony. You cannot rebut on Tuesday what a witness said about Wednesday night, and if you can explain to me how that can be done—

The Court: I am not here to explain anything to you, sir.

Mr. Kunstler: Then would you please rule on my objection.

The Court: Crowd out of your mind that I am going to explain anything to you.

\* \* \*

The Court: . . . [T]here is a man, the Defendant Hoffman, just laughing just as warmly as he can at me.

Mr. Kunstler: Your Honor, I object to your remark.

The Court: What do you say?

Mr. Kunstler: I object to your remark. You miss no opportunity in front of the jury to deride the defense table.

The Court: I overrule your objection, sir, and I think it is up to you as counsel for these men to tell them to behave.

Mr. Kunstler: These men are reacting to provocation

228

from the bench and that has been constant and consistent.

The Court: I am reacting to bad manners.

\* \* \*

Mr. Kunstler: Your Honor, I am right in this. You know I am right.

The Court: Don't say what I know.

Mr. Kunstler: Read the transcript, your Honor.

The Court: I know a lot you don't think I do.

Mr. Kunstler: This man under oath said he saw Viet Cong flags.

Mr. Foran: Your Honor, this man was asked—

The Court: Get back there.

Mr. Kunstler: I am not going to leap over, your Honor.

The Court: I don't like you shouting at me so closely.

Mr. Kunstler: I am trying to get above Mr. Foran's interrupting voice.

The Court: That will be all, sir.

\* \* \*

*(Witness excused)*

The Court: Call your next witness.

Defense Table: Thanks a lot. Thanks a lot.

Mr. Schultz: Your Honor—

Mr. Foran: Look at that—

Mr. Schultz: These men who say they have such compassion and love for human beings are trying to humiliate a man, a poor man, a man who is frightened enough to be in this courtroom, who has—

The Court: I have personally noted that the Defendant Rubin stood up as the witness was walking out with dignity and tendered his hand.

Mr. Rubin: I wanted to shake his hand.

Mr. Kunstler: Your Honor, we wanted to thank him. We thought that testimony was helpful.

Mr. Froines: I beg your pardon. That man wants to put us away for 10 years by lying and we think this proves it . . .

**February 4, 1970**

*Cross-examination by Mr. Kunstler of Richard Phillips, a Chicago newspaper reporter called as a witness in rebuttal by the Government*

Mr. Kunstler: Your Honor, before I ask the next question, is it possible to get a little more heat in the courtroom?

The Court: I am not the janitor. I told you that before. I have a lot of responsibilities; among them is not tending to the furnace.

229

Mr. Kunstler: I realize, but the governor of the trial has to keep us alive.

The Court: I would like awfully much to satisfy everybody. I have a robe but I can't let you borrow it.

Mr. Kunstler: Your Honor, I am not asking you to stoke the furnace; I am merely asking you to find someone to—

\* \* \*

Q. What about Mr. Hoffman?

A. Which one is Mr. Hoffman?

Q. You are the first one who hasn't identified him. This is Mr. Hoffman over here.

*(There was laughter in the courtroom.)*

The Court: Let the record show that Mr. Hoffman stood up, lifted his shirt up, and bared his body in the presence of the jury—

Mr. Kunstler: Your Honor, that is Mr. Hoffman's way.

The Court: —dancing around.

*(There was laughter in the courtroom.)*

Mr. Kunstler: Your Honor, that is Mr. Hoffman's way.

The Court: It is a bad way in a courtroom.

Mr. Kunstler: I remember President Johnson bared his body to the nation.

The Court: Well, that may be.

Mr. Kunstler: Over national television.

The Court: Maybe that is why he isn't President any more.

\* \* \*

*Direct examination by Mr. Schultz of James Riordan, a Deputy Chief of Police of Chicago, called as a rebuttal witness by the Government*

The Court: I say that there seems to have grown up a feeling amongst the lawyers here for the defendants that every manner of abuse can be heaped on a judge of the United States District Court and treat it as a joke. This morning I was asked by Mr. Kunstler whether I wasn't taking things too seriously. I certainly do take them seriously. . . .

\* \* \*

Q. Did you see where he went?

A. He left with the head of the group that were carrying the flags.

Mr. Dellinger: Oh, bullshit.

The Court: Did you get that, Miss Reporter?

\* \* \*

Mr. Kunstler: Sometimes the human spirit can stand so much, and I think Mr. Dellinger reached the end of his.

The Court: I have never heard in more than a half century

of the bar a man using profanity in this court or in a court-room.

Mr. Hoffman: I've never been in an obscene court, either.

The Court: I never have as a spectator or as a judge. I never did.

Mr. Kunstler: You never sat here as a defendant and heard liars on the stand . . .

*　*　*

Mr. Schultz: Your Honor, we had to sit with our lips tight, listening to those defendants, to those two defendants, Mr. Hayden and Mr. Hoffman, perjure themselves.
. . .

Mr. Dellinger: You're a snake. We have to try to put you in jail for ten years for telling lies about us, Dick Schultz.

Marshal Joneson: Be quiet, Mr. Dellinger.

Mr. Dellinger: When it's all over, the Judge will go to Florida, but if he has his way, we'll go to jail. That is what we're fighting for, not just for us, but for all the rest of the people in the country who are being oppressed.

A Spectator: Damn right. Assert ourselves.

Voices: RIGHT ON.

*　*　*

The Court: . . . May I say that I think I have demon-strated great patience during this trial in trying to insure a fair trial both for the Government and for the defendants. Some people have the notion that there is only one party to a case and that is the defense. There are two parties. The title of this case is "United States of America vs. Dellinger and others." . . .

I do not, if I can help it, intend to permit such tactics to make a mockery out of this trial. . . .

*　*　*

The Court: Now, I have up here a transcript of what was said and done this afternoon. I do not intend to use the ob-scenities engaged in or used or applied by Mr. Dellinger. I don't use that kind of language myself. And I don't even like to use it in court here to quote a defendant. I shall turn over this transcript which has been prepared by the official reporter for me to the United States Attorney, and I hereby, Mr. Clerk, terminate the bail of the defendant David Dellinger and re-mand him to the custody of the United States Marshal for the Northern District of Illinois for the remainder of this trial.

*　*　*

Mr. Kunstler: I would like to say my piece. He is my client, and I think this is an utterly—

*(There was disorder in the courtroom.)*

I would like to—

You brought this on, your Honor. This is your fault. This is what happened in Chicago. You made the power move. You exerted the power, and I would like to argue the point.

The Court: You won't argue that point.

Mr. Kunstler: I will argue, your Honor, that your Honor's action is completely and utterly vindictive, that there is no authority that says because a defendant blurts out a word in court—

The Court: This isn't the first word, and I won't argue this.

Mr. Davis: This Court is bullshit.

The Court: There he is saying the same words again.

Mr. Davis: No, I say it.

\* \* \*

Mr. Davis: Mr. Rubin's wife they are now taking—

Mr. Rubin: Keep your hands off her. You see them taking away my wife?

Mr. Davis: Why don't you gag the press, too, and the attorneys, gag them?

\* \* \*

Mr. Kunstler: Your Honor, is there no decency left here? Can't we just argue the point?

The Court: Oh, wait a minute. I have another contempt matter here, or, rather, it is a contempt matter as distinguished from the last, and you will have to go away from that lectern. You can't stand there and insult the United States District Court.

Mr. Kunstler: I am not insulting you. I am asking for argument. Everything you characterize as such an insult—

The Court: Yes, you are.

Mr. Kunstler: Everything in this case is an insult.

The Court: You just insulted me again and you have done it often.

Mr. Kunstler: Every argument is not an insult.

The Court: This case is recessed. . . .

\* \* \*

The Court: Clear the courtroom.

Mr. Davis: You can jail a revolutionary, but you can't jail the revolution.

Mr. Hoffman: You are a disgrace to the Jews. You would have served Hitler better. Dig it.

The Marshal: That was Mr. Hoffman, your Honor.

The Court: I saw him and I heard him.

Mr. Rubin: You are a fascist, Hoffman—

Mr. Hoffman: I heard you haven't let anybody free in four years. That's right, stop me.

The Marshal: That was Mr. Rubin the last time, your Honor.

Clear the court.

The Court: Clear the courtroom, Mr. Marshal.

Mr. Davis: Get as many people as you can. Just like the Convention all over again.

The Marshal: Clear the court.

The Court: Clear the court.

A Female Voice: You little prick.


**February 5, 1970**

Mr. Weinglass: What the Court has indicated by the elaboration of its comments yesterday, this morning I think it is very clearly that the Court intends to punish David Dellinger for what he said. Now I have no quarrel with that, that your Honor has a contempt power, and at the end of this proceeding your Honor can punish—

The Court: I have more power than that.

Mr. Weinglass: No—

The Court: I don't like the use of the word "power."

Mr. Weinglass: You have the—

The Court: I never use the word 'power" if I can avoid it.

Mr. Weinglass: You have the power to punish but—

The Court: I have the authority to maintain order in this courtroom.

Mr. Weinglass: But—

The Court: I haven't succeeded very well at all times.

\*   \*   \*

Mr. Rubin: That is called justice? That is called justice?

The Court: Will you ask your—is he your client? Is Mr. Rubin one of your clients?

Mr. Weinglass: Your Honor, I am—

The Court: Will you ask him to remain silent?

Mr. Weinglass: I am an officer of this Court, but I am not a United States Marshal.

The Court: At times you have not acted as one.

\*   \*   \*

Mr. Weinglass: Your Honor will not permit me to continue a legal argument?

The Court: You heard what I said. I deny the motion.

Mr. Davis: May we defend ourselves if our lawyers can't?

Mr. Kunstler: I think the Marshal is going to have this

time me put in my seat. I am not going to sit down unless I am forced to sit down.

* * *

Mr. Hoffman:   Your idea of justice is the only obscenity in the room. You schtunk. Vo den? Shanda fur de goyem? Huh.

Obviously it was a provocation. That's why it has gone on here today because you threatened him with cutting off his freedom of speech in the speech he gave in Milwaukee.

The Court:   Mr. Marshal, will you ask the Defendant Hoffman to—

Mr. Hoffman:   This ain't the Standard Club.

The Marshal:   Mr. Hoffman—

Mr. Hoffman:   Oh, tell him to stick it up his bowling ball. How is your war stock doing, Julie?

You don't have any power. They didn't have any power in the Third Reich either.

The Court:   Will you ask him to sit down, Mr. Marshal?

The Marshal:   Mr. Hoffman, I am asking you again to shut up.

Mr. Rubin:   Gestapo.

* * *

Mr. Rubin:   You are the laughing stock of the world, Julius Hoffman; the laughing stock of the world.

Mr. Hoffman:   Mies van der Rohe was a Kraut, too.

Mr. Rubin:   Every kid in the world hates you, knows what you represent.

Marshal Dobowski:   Be quiet, Mr. Rubin.

Mr. Rubin:   You are synonymous with the name Adolf Hitler. Julius Hoffman equals Adolf Hitler today.

. . .

Mr. Hoffman:   You know you cannot win the fucking case. The only way you can is to put us away is for contempt. We have contempt for this Court, and for you, Schultz, and for this whole rotten system. That's the only justice. That is why they want this because they can't prove this fucking case.

The Court:   I order the defendants and their counsel not to make reference to this motion made.

Mr. Rubin:   And the reason is because it is a hung jury, and you know it. You want to get us in jail anyway. That is the reason because you know you are losing the jury trial, but you have got to get us in jail, because the people will decide that we are not guilty, so you are going to railroad us into jail.

* * *

[*During examination of another witness*]

Mr. Hoffman:   You put him [Dellinger—ed.] in jail be-

234

cause you lost faith in the jury system. I hear you haven't lost a case before a jury in 24 tries. Only the Krebiozen people got away. We're going to get away, too. That's why you're throwing us in jail this way.

Contempt is a tyranny of the court, and you are a tyrant. That's why we don't respect it. It's a tyrant.

. . .

Mr. Hoffman: The judges in Nazi Germany ordered sterilization. Why don't you do that, Judge Hoffman?

\* \* \*

The Court: Mr. Marshal, will you have Mr. Hoffman remain quiet, please? Order him to remain quiet.

Mr. Hoffman: Order us? Order us? You got to cut our tongues out to order us, Julie.

You railroaded Seale so he wouldn't get a jury trial either. Four years for contempt without a jury trial.

The Marshal: Mr. Hoffman. Will you shut up.

Mr. Hoffman: No, I won't shut up. I ain't an automaton like you. I don't want to be a tyrant and I don't care for a tyrannical system.

Best friend blacks ever had. Huh. How many blacks are in Drake Towers? How many are in the Standard Club. How many own stock in Brunswick Corporation?

\* \* \*

The Court: Mr. Marshal, please have that man refrain from using those epithets.

Mr. Rubin: It is just descriptive. Just describing what I see.

The Marshal: For the sixth time, shut up.

Mr. Hoffman: Epithet.


**February 6, 1970**

The Court: May the record show defendants Hoffman and Rubin came in at 1:28 with their—

Mr. Rubin: The Marshal just came and asked us to come in. We came as soon as we were asked.

The Court: And also attired in what might be called collegiate robes.

Mr. Rubin: Judges' robes, sir.

A Defendant: Death robes.

The Court: Some might even consider them judicial robes.

Mr. Rubin: Judicial robes.

The Court: Your idea, Mr. Kunstler? Another one of your brilliant ideas?

Mr. Kunstler: Your Honor, I can't take credit for this one.

The Court: That amazes me.

**February 7, 1970**

The Court: The time has come and will come when the United States Court will be respected by everybody in this case.

Mr. Kunstler: I know, but your Honor, is it more important that you get the modicum of respect here or the truth get before the jury?

The Court: Modicum of respect? I haven't even had a modicum.

\* \* \*

The Court: I won't sit here and grant courtesies to people who misbehave as they do.

Mr. Kunstler: Your Honor, we are not asking for a courtesy.

The Court: Bring in the jury.

Mr. Kunstler: We are asking to show a film. The Government has agreed to the film.

Mr. Davis: Is it not possible to put on our defense?

\* \* \*

Mr. Weinglass: If the Court please, this matter involves the incarceration of Mr. Dellinger, bail was revoked, and Mr. Dellinger was returned to the custody of the Marshal. . . .

My motion is to request the Court to ask the marshals to keep Mr. Dellinger in this building until 4:30 so that it would be possible for him to meet with his family briefly, I think maybe 20 minutes.

. . .

The Court: I don't think there is anything in the record here that warrants any special treatment from the Court.

Mr. Weinglass: Not even the man seeing his family?

The Court: Think of those things beforehand. You lawyers, give your clients some good advice about conduct, not law, just good ordinary conduct.

\* \*

Mr. Weinglass: Your Honor contends this man is not being punished for what he said.

The Court: Oh, no.

Mr. Weinglass: That has been the official position of this Court.

The Court: Oh, no. He is being punished, if you can call it punishment.

Mr. Weinglass: You cannot use bail revocation for punishment. You can only use it for the orderly process of the administration of justice.

The Court: The United States Court of Appeals unanimously in a panel consisting of three judges has affirmed this Court's action.

Mr. Weinglass: On the representation of this Court that it was not punishment, but rather, it was to insure the orderly process of the trial. Now the Court is indicating clearly on the record that it was punishment. That is what we object to.

The Court: I deny your motion. Let the record show, Mr. Clerk, I deny the motion. . . .

\* \* \*

The Court: Mr. Marshal, the Court will be in recess until Monday morning.

Marshal Dobowski: Everyone please rise.

Mr. Dellinger: You now have my respect, Judge, I am sure you know.

Mr. Davis: Have a good weekend, Judge.

Marshal Dobowski: Everyone please rise.

The Court: You have got all of that, have you?

The Reporter: Yes, your Honor.

A Defendant: One more, Julie, and you'll be a saint.

**February 9, 1970**

The Court: That is the first time I have ever been charged with overwhelming. I have been charged with a lot of stuff here in the last few days, even in a language that probably you are not familiar with, although you are—

Mr. Kunstler: I am glad your Honor is laughing and that no one is being put down for that.

The Court: What did you say?

Mr. Kunstler: I am glad your Honor is laughing because you know I have always advocated that there is room in the courtroom for a little laughter.

The Court: I am laughing now. I don't promise to laugh the rest of this trial. . . .

. . .

The Court: And I guess I am laughing because of what I was about to say. I am not even certain that you understood the references that were made here by one of the defendants in one of the most ancient languages. I don't think it was a dead language, but the language out of which the language came was a dead language.

Mr. Kunstler: The defense would have no objection, your Honor, if you used that language for your charge.

The Court: Referring to who?

. . .

Mr. Kunstler: You mean Mr. Hoffman's Hebraic expressions?

The Court: Yes. Well, if you can call them Hebraic.

Mr. Kunstler: We would even consent to that, your Honor.

237

The Court:   I would think the authorities would call that Yiddish, wouldn't they? I don't know whether you understand that or not.

Mr. Kunstler:   I understand the intonation of it, your Honor, and then Mr. Hoffman explained it to me later.

The Court:   Oh, he translated it?

Mr. Kunstler:   He translated some of it, some of the more esoteric—

The Court:   I had the benefit of a not too accurate translation in one of the newspapers.

Mr. Kunstler:   Schtunk I had heard before. The other expression I had to have translated for me.

# IV

# Summation

Transcript pages 20431–21356

[After twenty weeks of presenting their exhibits and witnesses, the attorneys for the defense and government were given the opportunity to summarize their cases.

[As in all criminal cases, the prosecution maintains the burden of proving guilt beyond a reasonable doubt throughout the trial. It is thus afforded the right to make the first statement, and to later respond to the summation of the defense. This order is reflected in the following chapter.

[The process of summation is difficult, at best. Each side must condense literally thousands of pages of testimony into a few hours of court time. The burden of the editors has been equally weighty. We have excerpted a few of the major arguments in order to capture the essence of the proceedings.

[As always, we remind the reader that the dialogue that follows is the verbatim language of the participants in the trial. —ed.]

February 10, 1970
   *Summation. Argument on behalf of the Government by Mr. Schultz*
Mr. Schultz:   Ladies and Gentlemen of the Jury, Gentlemen of the Defense:
We finally have reached the stage in the proceedings after five months, five months, twenty weeks, twenty weeks of trial time where you are finally getting ready now to receive the case for your deliberations. . . .
The Government rested its case over two months ago and it is hard to remember what all that evidence was, especially when the defendants put in their evidence during the last two months and they never met the Government's case. So there was really nothing to refresh you as to what the issues were, what the charges were, what you were listening for, listening to, because in the last two months you have hardly heard any evi-

dence that relates to the case, to the charges in this indict ment. . . .

Now the defendants repeatedly state they didn't war violence, they were here for peace, but we have proven throug their own statements, we have prove through their own action that that is not so, that they came here for violence and for rio

\* \*

Mr. Schultz: Now the first question that you must as yourselves is why would anybody want to incite a riot? Wh would anybody want to incite a situation where people ar beating each other, where policemen are beating demonstrator where demonstrators are beating policemen? Why should the want that? Why should they want demonstrators to destro property or police to destroy property pursuant to a riot? Why Why would they want this?

Well, in answering this question we can look at the defend ants' own statements as to why they would want a riot.

Davis wanted the President to use troops to secure [the nomination. . . . He wanted to use the violence to precipitate to precipitate the National Liberation Front in the Unite States where people would group together in anger against th Government and that would be precipitated by a riot. . . .

\* \* \*

Mr. Schultz: Hayden wanted to create what he referre to after the Convention, the very day after the Convention, a the first step towards the revolution. . . .

Hayden wanted in Chicago, as he and Davis wrote after th Convention, wanted to show that since the United States in stitutions cannot be changed from within, people will take t the streets. And you show that by violence and riots in th streets. . . .

Dellinger said that he wanted to bring the U. S. militar machinery to a halt. He referred to the people in Chicago a freedom fighters, and on Thursday, after the violence, that hor rible violence, he compared the Americans who were fightin in the streets, compared their actions to the actions of th revolutionaries in Cuba and read a telegram from Cuba. Tha was the purpose, to precipitate, to solidify, to turn against. . .
. . .

Mr. Schultz: Rubin—Rubin told Norman Mailer, accord ing to Mr. Mailer, their witness, in December of '67 that th presence of one hundred thousand people at the Festival o Life would so terrify the establishment that the Conventio would be held under armed guard and the resulting violenc by the establishment itself, the resulting violence will be suc that the establishment will smash the city, and then he said h

240

was going to devote full time to getting a hundred thousand people here to do just that, to smash the city. . . .

Hoffman stated, right after the Convention, in the book that he wrote, five days after, that he wanted to smash this system by any means at his disposal. He intended, as he stated in an interview which was published, which we established on his cross-examination, "He wanted to wreck this fucking society." That's what he said. . . .

They got what they wanted. So while the defendants profess that they came here for non-violence, their own statements belie that, their own statements contradict that.

\* \*

Mr. Schultz: They brought people to the city to incite a riot, where the authorities, the Government, the city and the federal authorities, would have to enforce its civil laws by using force. When people don't obey, you start arresting them, they start fighting, and you have violence. But to grab that person to make the arrest, to spark the riot, that is what they wanted, to disobey the laws and force arrests and then a riot, and by having the riot and by having sufficient violence, right during the Democratic National Convention, they could make the Government look like it's oppressing its citizens because the citizens were opposed to the policies of the government. . . .
. . .

Mr. Schultz: Furthermore, they couldn't publicly state they were coming here for violence because people wouldn't come. Just as Mr. Rosen said—Mr. Rosen was the witness who was at the resistance meeting on March 14, 1968, where Hayden spoke. Rosen said that Hayden said, "We can't announce we're going to have violence in Chicago. We can't have violence because people won't come." And that is exactly right. People wouldn't come here. They'd end up with five hundred people. So for those two reasons they had to say their purposes were peaceful. One, if they said that they were violent, when they were violent, people would blame them, and two, if they said the purposes were violent, people wouldn't come.

So they told people, many people, and many groups, that they had planned non-violent, peaceful activities. They told this to the McCarthy supporters. They told it to Julian Bond. They told it to Dick Gregory. They told it to Jesse Jackson. They attempted to enlist the support of these people, to bring these people both to Chicago and also to have these people think that they were non-violent. . . .

\* \* \*

Mr. Schultz: Now what I would like to do is go separately looking at the proof relating to each of the defendants and take you through the proof of Rubin and Hoffman and Davis, Dellinger, Froines and Weiner individually as it was presented, referring both to the proof in the Government's case and the defense, so that you can analyze the proof, so that you can see it all capsulated into one. . . .

Rubin. Let's take him first. He is charged in Count I, the conspiracy count, but let's specifically discuss Count VI. He is charged with traveling from New York to Chicago with the intent to incite a riot and when he got here he, in fact, incited a riot. He screamed and yelled for people to kill everybody. We will get into it.

During Convention Week Rubin was clearly the most active of all the defendants on the streets. He repeatedly urged the crowds to attack the police, fight the police in defense of the park, disrupt the city and the Convention. . . .
. . .

Mr. Schultz: . . . [H]e said to about two hundred people that the park belongs to the people. The park belongs to the people. Rubin's from New York. Hoffman's from New York. They are all from out of town. The park belongs to the people; that's their park, and they should not let the pigs push them from the park. Arm themselves, he said. Fight the pigs, break into small groups, wait for instructions from the marshals. Wednesday's the big thing, that they're going to stop the Convention. That's Rubin. . . .

[There followed approximately 40 pages of Government summation concerning the activities of Jerry Rubin during Convention Week, 1968—ed.]

Mr. Schultz: So we proved with regard to Rubin that he came to this city to incite to violence. On Sunday and Monday, on Tuesday and on Wednesday, he was awfully busy inciting. He led groups against the ten policemen against the field house. He screamed at the crowd to arm themselves and to fight the pigs. He incited by his screaming and his actions, he incited by his screaming and his actions, he incited the people to fight the police in the park.

We have proved that Rubin came here with the intent to incite the violence and that he, in fact, incited it, and that on Count VI of the indictment where he is charged with that he is guilty. . . .

\* \* \*

Mr. Schultz: There is Davis next. Let's look at Davis. Davis is much more complicated, much more sophisticated, but with the exact same objects. . . .
. . .

Mr. Schultz: Let's look at how Davis organized the violence and planned the violence, and then during the Convention, incited, personally invited the violence.

First, his statements and organizations of the violence prior to the Convention. . . .

Now, Davis was quick to tell you that everything he planned and discussed was peaceful, and yet practically every time he spoke, most of them were conversations and speeches that he gave to his own people, but practically every time he spoke, except on national television or publicly, where the whole world could hear, he talked about mill-ins, disruptions, disabling jeeps, using Mace, getting the Guard out, there would be war in the streets. But he says it was all peaceful planning. . . .

> [*There followed approximately 30 pages of Government summation concerning the activities of Rennie Davis during Convention Week, 1968—ed.*]

Mr. Schultz: . . . [J]ust on what we have been through on Tuesday night, all of the meetings he participated at, where he planned violence and then the violence that he both incited and attempted to incite—all of that evidence, excluding Wednesday, which we will get into in a minute, proves beyond all doubt that Davis came to Chicago from Cleveland, Ohio, about July 20 with the intent to incite and organize and encourage and promote a riot in this city, and when he got here he did things to plan it and incite and and he did, in fact, plan it and incite it during the Convention. . . .

\* \* \*

Mr. Schultz: Let's look at Abbie Hoffman. He is charged in Count V with traveling from New York to Chicago with the intent to incite a riot, as the other defendants are charged in Count I.

When he arrived here, he planned and organized and incited a riot.

As we have done with the other defendants, let's look at his statements of intent, his plans, what he did and how he incited.

Like Rubin, Hoffman got people here with his Festival of Life. He said his reason for coming here was to have a music festival and he and Rubin talked to all of these musicians that I discussed including Arlo Guthrie, Ed Sanders, Judy Collins, Country Joe McDonald, Peter Seeger—he talked to them and said, "Come on to Chicago and sing. Sing and perform. It's going to be delightful."

And they succeeded in bringing these musicians to Chicago, they would have succeeded in bringing hundreds of thousands of youths to Chicago to hear the music, and just like Rubin said, if they get 100,000 people here, the Establishment will smash the city, and he is going to devote full time to it.

Well, Hoffman with Rubin used the Festival of Life for that purpose, to get the people here and then create the confrontation where violence would be precipitated and the Establishment, as they call it, would be weakened or destroyed.

The very day Hoffman arrived in Chicago on August 7, and he arrived with Rubin and met with David Stahl—and we will discuss the permits when I get to it, after we discuss the defendants—he told David Stahl that he was prepared to tear up the town and the Convention and he was willing to die in Lincoln Park.

\* \* \*

He [Mr. Hoffman—ed.] testified that part of his so-called Yippie myth was that Yippies would be all over the city diverting troops. He testified that it was part of the Yippie myth that there would be so much paranoia, fear, in Chicago that the delegates would need helicopters to fly to and from the Amphitheatre. A Festival of Life? . . .

Prior to the Convention, Hoffman admitted on cross-examination, that he predicted 6,000 arrests in Chicago, 20 to 30 people killed, and 2,000 to 3,000 beatings based on 50,000 people coming here. Did he tell that to any of the youngsters? Did he tell that to any of the musicians? . . .

[*There followed approximately 50 pages of Government summation concerning the activities of Abbie Hoffman during Convention Week, 1968—ed.*]

Mr. Schultz: Well, I think that's enough about Hoffman. We've proved on the substantive count, as well as the conspiracy count, which I will discuss in a minute that he came here on August 7 from his home in New York, came here with Rubin from New York, to organize and incite and promote and encourage violence. When he got here, he did just that. He organized, promoted, and encouraged violence, and during the Convention he incited violence, he incited people to attack, and he's guilty as he's charged in that count. . . .

\* \* \*

Mr. Schultz: Now, let's look at the activities and the planning of Hayden and Dellinger. Their primary role, their primary role, was the Wednesday bandshell. I am going to take them together for that reason. . . .

. . . He and Hayden wrote that throughout the final day of the Convention, among other things, they would have disruptions to dramatize their demands. They were going to pin the delegates in the Amphitheatre on their funeral march to the

Amphitheatre. They'd have another Pentagon right at the Amphitheatre. . . .

\* \* \*

Mr. Schultz: . . . Both Hayden and Dellinger spoke on July 25. Mr. Dellinger was in California addressing a crowd there. Mr. Hayden was in New York. Mr. Sweeney, a New York businessman, an advertising executive, testified that he was at the Hayden speech in New York. . . . He said that Hayden in his speech said that "The United States is an outlaw nation, it had broken all the rules and therefore peace demonstrators should break all the rules, too." He spoke about demonstrations in Berkeley, Paris and Berlin, and about the demonstrations in Chicago. And he said that the North Vietnamese were shedding blood and that demonstrators when they came to Chicago should be prepared to shed blood, too. He said that in Chicago and throughout the election there would be more arrests than the jails could hold.

Now there is nothing illegal about the speech, but it shows what he was coming here for. The United States had broken the rules: they were going to break the rules.

They are shedding blood in Vietnam, the Viet Cong are, and we, the peace demonstrators, are going to shed blood.

All right. The defendants say that he didn't say that. . . .

\* \* \*

Mr. Schultz: Now Dellinger on the same day was speaking in the evening in San Francisco—in San Diego. Mr. Gilman, the young newsman in his early thirties, testified here near the beginning of this trial. . . . Mr. Gilman heard Dellinger talk about Vietnam and the fighting and the brainwashing of the United States prisoners of war by the American Government after they got them from North Vietnam; after being released by Hanoi, the United States was brainwashing prisoners of war.

Then after Dellinger said that, Mr. Gilman related the end of the speech where Dellinger said to the group, "Burn your draft cards. Resist the draft. Violate the laws. Go to jail. Disrupt the United States Government in any way you can to stop this insane war." The audience cheered wildly. And then he said, "I am going to Chicago to the Democratic National Convention where there may be problems." And the crowd went wild.

Then he said, "I will see you in Chicago," with his fist up. It is not a crime to state that, but it tells you, did he come here for a vigil? Did he come here, as they say, for workshops?

"Violate the law. Go to jail. Disrupt the United States Government in any way you can to stop the war."

245

Peaceful? Vigil? And "I will see you in Chicago." And the crowd goes wild. . . .

* * *

[There followed, over two days, approximately 40 pages of Government summation concerning the activities of Tom Hayden and David Dellinger during Convention Week, 1968—ed.]

**February 11, 1970**

Mr. Schultz: [Continuing] We have proved beyond all doubt that Hayden and Dellinger came to this city for the purposes of organizing, aiding, and inciting, and encouraging a riot, and they did on Wednesday. They did just that at the morning meeting on Wednesday morning alone. They then executed it at the bandshell, and then after the bandshell.

* *

Mr. Schultz: All right. Now let's look briefly at Weiner and Froines.

Weiner and Froines are charged in Count VII not with crossing state lines to incite a riot, but with teaching and demonstrating to others the use and application of a Molotov cocktail, an incendiary device, teaching it to be used at the underground Grant Park garage for the purpose of diverting the troops so the people could go in the city, and, as they said disrupt.

I had planned to go through all of the meetings of Weiner and Froines prior to the date of their activities, but there isn't really time. . . .

. . .

Mr. Schultz: . . . Weiner said they should have some cocktails. . . . [H]e said, "They're easy to make. All you need are gasoline, sand, rags, and bottles." And Weiner said that a good mobile tactic would be to pick a target in the Loop and bomb it. He said that such a diversionary tactic as bombing the wooden fence across from the Federal Building, this Federal Building, the fence across the street here, or the underground Grant Park garage, would draw the police away from the demonstrators so the demonstrators could take their actions in the Loop, they would be free, no one would be there to stop them.

Weiner said that the police and the firemen rushing to the underground Grant Park garage or to the fire at the fence would leave the demonstrators free to do their actions.

. . .

Mr. Schultz: And Froines, who participated in the conversation and who recommended the underground Grant Park

246

garage as the alternative, as the best place, and who said he had four cans of gasoline but didn't know whether he was going to use them or the butyric acid, but who helped in making a determination in how they were going to proceed, aided Weiner and abetted Weiner in that activity, and he, too, is guilty of that charge.

The last thing with regard to Froines is the butyric acid, the stink bombs. They are not charged with stink bombs; they are charged with coming here to disrupt, incite a riot, and disruption with stink bombs helps you conclude whether they came here for the purposes of disruption. . . .

\* \* \*

Mr. Schultz: We have shown that these defendants, all seven of them, had a mutual understanding to accomplish the objects of the conspiracy, that they had a common purpose of bringing disruption and inciting a violence in this city, and that all seven of them together participated in working together and aiding each other to further these plans. Oh, they never explicitly said, "You do that to blow up that," and "I will do that to incite that crowd," that is not how they did it. It was tacit understanding, a working-together in all these meetings and all of these conferences that they had, and that is how they conspired, and agreed, and worked together for the same goal. And that goal was to organize and precipitate a situation in the city where they could have a confrontation with the troops, a confrontation with the police, where violence would occur, and they could start their movement. . . .

Mr. Schultz: . . . We have proven, ladies and gentlemen, we have proven in this case, we have proven beyond all doubt, all conceivable doubt, that these defendants, all seven of them, every one of them, came to Chicago, came to this city to incite people to riot, bringing them here under peaceful guise, getting them here and manipulating so a riot would result from the confrontation. They wanted the riot, to start a Vietnam in the United States. They are guilty of coming here to incite a riot. They came here and they incited a riot.

\* \* \*

*Argument on behalf of the defendants by Mr. Weinglass*
Mrs. Burns, Ladies and Gentlemen of the Jury, Judge Hoffman, Mr. Foran, Mr. Schultz, Mr. Cubbage:
This has been a long and tedious trial for all of us. Words have been exchanged in this courtroom. But I must confess at the outset that it is not easy to follow Dick Schultz whom you have been listening to since yesterday morning. I think Mr. Schultz has exhausted, utilized every shred and piece of

247

evidence that the Government has been able to accumulate against these seven men since they started their investigation apparently on November 20, 1967 . . .

\* \* \*

Mr. Weinglass: Now they [the government—ed.] have to prove their case beyond a reasonable doubt and you have to believe it beyond a reasonable doubt, and if you can believe the starting premise of the Government's case, that these men plotted to put themselves in jail, that these men conspired to have this trial, then you could find them guilty. But I suggest to you that the whole foundation upon which this case is built, the whole structure of it, that whole sense of it, put in terms of common sense, is just not acceptable as a rational proposition.

Abbie Hoffman and Rennie Davis signed their names to applications in one case five months before the Convention. Abbie flies here three times to meet with city officials. Rennie is here constantly meeting with them. Rennie meets with a sub-Cabinet officer of the Justice Department, Roger Wilkins, and finally meets with the prosecutor, Mr. Thomas Foran, and when they can't get what they want, what do they do, these men who want this quiet violence, they file a lawsuit in this building, in the Federal Court, compelling the city who won't negotiate with them to come into court. And Rennie Davis puts his statements on the record before Judge Lynch where it is stenographically transcribed.

And all of this the Government would want you to believe these men did while they intended to have violence and a civil disturbance in the city.

I could rest my case on that fact. I think that fact alone is hard enough to digest. I think that fact alone inserts more than reasonable doubt into this case. . . .

\* \* \*

Mr. Weinglass: Doesn't the Government have the obligation to present before you the whole truth? Why only city officials? Why only policemen, undercover agents, youth officers, and paid informers? In all of this time, couldn't they find in this entire series of events that span more than a week one good, human, decent person to come in here to support the theory that Mr. Schultz has given you in the last day? . . . . . .

Mr. Weinglass: Who is trying to project the truth in this courtroom? My clients wouldn't change a single garment to curry your favor. They won't put on a tie or wear a suit. They won't get a haircut. They want you to judge them as they are.

248

There is no make-believe here. This is the way they are. The outbursts, the laughter—that is the way these men are.

When the Government calls in a police officer who was just a patrolman—do you remember the man who was on the stand last week? I believe his name was Officer Butler.

"Why aren't you wearing your uniform today, Patrolman Butler?"

"The United States Attorney told me not to wear my uniform in this courtroom." . . .

\* \* \*

Mr. Weinglass: I will not deny that some of these men, during sometime in their lives, used strong words, stronger words than I would use, or probably you would use. People with strong convictions who live the way they live do not use the same language we use. Clearly, Bobby Seale does not, but by virtue of the language used, they [the Government—ed.] are attempting to say that they are criminals and that they are violent, and you should consider the fact that men who have had strong convictions for peace and strong convictions for non-violence have spoken in strong words, and these men are no exception. . . .

. . . They were a crowd that wanted to go to the Amphitheatre, that wanted to march. They walked past the Hilton. They were pushed back up to the Hilton. They wanted to march, and they weren't permitted to march. They stayed in the streets, and they chanted. But does that fact mean the police should wade into them and beat them and club them? Is that the way we have come to deal in this country with people who adamently insist on the right to gather together in the streets and to protest?

If the '60's as a decade meant nothing more, the '60's in this country, historically and socially, meant that Americans literally took to the streets, as Tom Hayden said, and Jerry Rubin said, to protest their grievances. They took to the streets. That is what Martin Luther King had done in Selma, Alabama, and that is what has been done ever since.

[This last remark was objected to as immaterial and the objection was sustained.]—ed.

\* \* \*

Mr. Weinglass: Every conceivable avenue of approach, flying in here, meeting with Corporation Counsel Simon, meeting with the Deputy Mayor, appointing local Yippies to negotiate, getting a lawyer, filing a lawsuit, going to the Park District, filing all of their papers properly, everything conceivable was done to get that permit application, and they know it. And they know it. And that's why so little attention was paid to it in the course of Mr. Schultz' summation, because it is the weakest part of their case. . . .

. . .

Mr. Weinglass: What was the city afraid of? Why wouldn't they talk to these men?

We could give a number of reasons, but I think you saw one demonstrated right here in front of you, right before your very eyes. What was employed to keep the Yippies out of Chicago was demonstrated in court when we brought before you two men, Allen Ginsberg, a poet, and Jacques Levy, a doctor in clinical psychology, a former instructor at the Menninger Clinic, and now a director, who testified about what happened at the Festival of Life. And when Allen Ginsberg testified about his meeting with David Stahl and about everything that happened during Convention Week, including the Om-ing and sunrise ritual, was he cross-examined on the truth of what he said or the truth of the events? Did Mr. Foran attack his believability or his credibility? No. What was attacked— Do you remember that cross-examination?—was his poetry, his poetry. "Didn't you write a poem where you had a man in bed with a honeymooning couple?" "Didn't you write a poem where there was some allusion to homosexuality?"

No attempt on the part of the Government to deal with the truth of what the man said or what he stands for, but just a complete misunderstanding of him as a person and an attack on his poetry. . . .

### February 12, 1970

[*Conclusion of Mr. Weinglass' argument*]

Mr. Weinglass: I merely want to indicate to indicate to you in finishing that this case is more than just the defense of seven men. It involves the more basic issue of whether or not those who stand up to dare can do so without grave personal risk and I think it will be judged in that light, and I think while you deliberate on this case, that history will hold its breath until you determine whether or not this wrong that we have been living with will be righted by a verdict of acquittal for the seven men who are on trial here.

Thank you.

\* \* \*

*Argument on behalf of the defendants by Mr. Kunstler*

Mr. Kunstler: . . . I might reiterate some of what Mr. Weinglass said, that these seven men are important to us as human beings, as clients, but they are not really sitting in the dock here. We are all in the dock because what happens to them happens to all of us. What happens to them is the ultimate answer to all of us.

\* \* \*

Mr. Kunstler: I might just indicate to you that the so-called outside agitator, which is the term that is used by the prosecution frequently, the outside agitator brought the Freedom Riders throughout the South that led to integrated interstate travel in 1961.

The outside agitator leading the voter registration drives led to the Civil Rights Act of 1966.

The outside agitator led to the Civil Rights Act of 1964 that there shall be no discrimination in public accommodations.

The outside agitator led to the Civil Rights Act of 1968 that there shall not be discrimination in housing.

The outside agitators in St. Augustine, Selma, Jackson, Mississippi, Birmingham, these places that have become so familiar in the last decade, have led to all of the reforms, and there is a reason for it, and the reason is that it takes the man who doesn't make his livelihood in the community, and who isn't afraid of losing his job, or having his house burned, to come in and give courage to people who live in communities which are repressed.

. . .

Mr. Kunstler: I don't want you to leave for your deliberations without knowing that agitator has an honest, good connotation whether it be Jesus leaving Nazareth, or Debs leaving Terre Haute, or Susan Anthony, or Dr. King, or George Washington, or Mohandas Gandhi, or Harriet Tubman—they are all outside agitators, all in the interest of social change.

\* \*

Mr. Kunstler: Just some fifty years ago, I think almost exactly, in a criminal court building here in Chicago . . . Clarence Darrow said this:

When a new truth comes upon the earth, or a great idea necessary for mankind is born, where does it come from? Not from the police force, or the prosecuting attorneys, or the judges, or the lawyers or the doctors. Not there. It comes from the despised and the outcasts, and it comes perhaps from jails and prisons. It comes from men who have dared to be rebels and think their thoughts, and their faith has been the faith of rebels.

This generation gives them graves, while another builds their monuments . . . And if this jury should make it harder for any man to be a rebel, you would be doing the most you could for the damnation of the human race. It is easier to believe something because somebody tells you it is true. It is

251

easy to run with the hounds and bay to death those who may be better than yourself. It was easy for the people of New England to join in the mad rush and hang old women for witchcraft. It was easy for the people who lived in the days of the inquisition to light the fires around men who dared to think, but it is those same rebels whose burning bodies have been the flame that has lighted the human race to something better than the world has known.

\* \* \*

The Court: Unless you get down to the evidence, I will direct you to discontinue this lecture on history. We are not dealing with history.

Mr. Kunstler: This is not a lecture, your Honor.

The Court: This is a lecture. It is not a summation of the evidence which is the function of a final argument in the trial of a jury case.

Final argument is intended to help the jury understand the evidence better than they might without a final argument.

Mr. Kunstler: But to understand the overriding issues as well, your Honor—

The Court: I will not permit any more of those historical references and I direct you to discontinue them, sir.

Mr. Kunstler: I do so under protest, your Honor.

## February 13, 1970
[*Continuation of Mr. Kunstler's argument*]

Mr. Kunstler: . . . Now we come to one question that Mr. Schultz raised clearly with you. He said that the defendants here were dupers and manipulators, that they brought people to Chicago for their own purposes. They were going to manipulate everyone. They were unconcerned, self-seeking manipulators, that they used these proper things, like racism, the war aganist racism, the fight against the war in Vietnam, youth culture, and poverty, they used all these things.

He is trying to tell you that they were just friends and cynics, and that their lives have been all of this type of activity, and they came to Chicago with the dirtiest possible kind of intention, to bring people here with rock bands and speeches, and then turn them loose in a mass frenzy so they would be butchered in the streets.

I think you have to look at these people, and you have to reach a determination as to just who was being duped in Chicago. Was it the people who came to Chicago, including all these men, who were being duped and misled by the city of Chicago and its mayor, or were these the manipulators that Mr. Schultz would have you believe?

252

I have mentioned Lee Weiner to you. I have mentioned his educational background. Remember, Al Baugher was on the stand, and he said he knew Lee three years ago when he worked for the city of Chicago in the Division of Correctional Services doing social work with families with children, and then he also knew that he had worked in a black community organization on the Near North Side.

. . . This is duper number one.

Duper number two is John Froines. I have mentioned him, and won't repeat it again.

Duper number three is Tom Hayden, a man who was introduced to Dick Goodwin by no less a figure than Senator [Robert—ed.] Kennedy, and was asked by Senator Kennedy whether Tom would work for him on his campaign, who has entree to Ambassador Harriman, with whom he negotiated for the release of American prisoners of war in North Vietnam . . . who worked in the Newark ghettos among black and poor, and whom Julian Bond had known in 1961 when Tom was beaten up by police in McComb, Mississippi during the Student Non-Violent Coordinating Committee program there.

Abbie Hoffman—you remember Abbie Hoffman on the stand who told you a lot about himself, that he was a psychologist in a State Hospital in Massachusetts, that he was a campaign manager for two Senate Peace Candidates in Massachusetts back in the early '60's, that he was in the South from 1964 to '65, first for the Freedom School in McComb, and then with the Southern Christian Leadership Conference of Martin Luther King in Americus, Georgia, on the voter registration program.

Then he organized the Poor People's Corporation in Mississippi to give an outlet to the work product of both black people in Mississippi and poor people whatever color everywhere. . . .

You have heard about Dave Dellinger, that he was a lifelong pacifist, that he attended the War Crimes Tribunal in November of '67, long before Chicago, long before Chicago was really even thought of, that he walked with Julian Bond behind Martin Luther King's coffin in Atlanta, Georgia.

Jerry Rubin ran—and he has so many witnesses tell us from the stand, he met so many people there—one of the first major demonstrations against the war in Vietnam in Berkeley in 1965. The first teach-in was in May of '65, the first large—25,000 people attended—teach-in in the United States. And then a march in October of 15,000 against the war in Vietnam. . . .

He had the first Be-In, the first Festival of Life, in 1966 in

California. Fifty thousand attended; no violence; no disorder.
. . .

Mr. Kunstler: Rennie Davis—you heard him—Oberlin, Bachelor of Arts, attended the University of Illinois, the University of Michigan, attempting to get an M.A. Came here to Chicago to join Community Youth, Jobs Or Income Now, National Coordinator for the Mobilization, went to Hanoi as Mr. Foran questioned him on cross to bring back American prisoners of war . . .

\* \* \*

Mr. Kunstler: We have young people who are depressed and dismayed at what they see about them, who cannot accept the ideals and the dreams and the drives of their parents and their grandparents and who are worried and disturbed and are suffering from a malaise of not understanding where they are going, their country is going, the world is going. These are rough problems, terrible problems, and as has been said by everybody in this country, they are so enormous that they stagger the imagination. But they don't go away by destroying their critics. They don't vanish by sending men to jail. They never did and they never will. To use the problems by attempting to destroy those who protest against them is probably the most indecent thing that we can do. You can crucify a Jesus, you can poison a Socrates, you can hang John Brown or Nathan Hale, you can kill a Che Guevara, you can jail a Eugene Debs or a Bobby Seale. You can assassinate John Kennedy or a Martin Luther King, but the problems remain. These are no solutions to the problems. The solutions are essentially made by continuing and perpetuating with every breath you have the right of men to think, the right of men to speak boldly and unafraid, the right to be masters of their souls, the right to live free and to die free. These things are what cause the eventual solution of maybe not all of the problems, but these things alone will do it. The hangman's rope never solved a single problem except that of one man.

I think if this case does nothing else, perhaps it will bring into focus that again we are in that moment of history when a courtroom becomes the proving ground of whether we do live free or whether we do die free. You are in that position now. . . .

\* \* \*

*Argument on behalf of the Government by Mr. Foran*

Mr. Foran: . . . The defendants in this case—first of all, they kind of argued in a very strange way that there was no violence planned by these defendants at the Democratic National Convention. . . .

To argue it, since they have no evidence that violence wasn't planned, the way they argue it in that they say Bock, Frapolly, and Oklepek and Pierson lied. They lied about all of the meetings that they attended, and everything that they heard, and that Pierson lied about Rubin in his discussions with Rubin. They state that they lied categorically, and this, you know, is what they said, "Because Bock, Frapolly, Pierson, and Oklepek were undercover agents for the police or newspapers, and, therefore, they cannot be honest men."

Now how dare anybody argue that kind of a gross statement? Some of the bravest and the best men of all the world, certainly in law enforcement, have made their contributions while they were undercover. That statement is a libel and a slander on every FBI agent, every federal narcotics agent, every single solitary policeman who goes out alone and unprotected into some dangerous area of society to try to find out information that is helpful to his government. It is a slander on every military intelligence man, every Navy intelligence man who does the same thing. How can anybody make that kind of a terribly gross statement?

* * *

Mr. Foran: I mean, what has happened to us. Are we going to get conned like that: The bad people are policemen. The bad people are FBI agents. The bad people are people who give their lives to Government. The bad people are a kid who goes in the Navy. That you're only a good guy if you like the homosexual poetry of Allen Ginsberg. Or you are only a good guy if you think Paul Krassner is funny. Or you are only a good guy if you think that somebody like that Sanders with the goofy outfit is a decent man. We can't let people use our kids like that. We can't let them do it because what they want to do, what they want to do, right there, they want to stand on the rubble of a destroyed system of government, the new leaders in arrogance and uncertainty. That is all. . . .

* * *

Mr. Foran: You know this case is really an awesome responsibility. In just a minute it is going to pass into your hands.

The vision and ideals that our forefathers had just can't be corrupted by the haters and the violent anarchists. "The future is with the people who will be truthful, pure and loving."

You know who said that? Gandhi. Dr. King.

"Truthful, pure, loving."

Not liars and obscene haters like those men are.

Can you imagine? You know, the way they name-dropped —Can you imagine—and it is almost blasphemous to say it.

255

They have named St. Matthew and they named Jesus and they named Abraham Lincoln. They named Martin Luther King. They named—they even—can you imagine any of those men or the Reverend Jesse Jackson—or can you imagine those men supporting these men if they—

A Spectator: Yes, I can. I can imagine it because it is true.

The Court: Remove those people, Mr. Marshal.

Mr. Dellinger: That's my daughter.

A Spectator: I won't listen to any more of these disgusting lies.

Mr. Dellinger: That's my other daughter. Thank you. Right on. Right on.

Don't hit my daughter that way. I saw you. That man hit her on the head for saying the truth is here.

The Court: The marshals will maintain order.

Mr. Dellinger: Yes, but they don't have to hit 13-year-old girls who know that I was close to Martin Luther King.

The Court: Mr. Marshal, have that man sit down.

Mr. Foran: You see? You see how it works?

"Don't hit her."

Mr. Dellinger: He did hit her.

A Spectator: They hit him. He did hit her.

Mr. Foran: Oh, bunk.

\* \* \*

Mr. Foran: These seven men have been proven guilty beyond any doubt. They didn't attack the planning they were charged with. They didn't say it didn't happen. They are guilty beyond any doubt at all of the charges contained in the indictments against them. They have been proven guilty beyond all doubt of each count in those indictments that charge them with these crimes. . . .

# V

# Charge to the Jury

Transcript pages 21357–21444

The Court:
   I Am About to Discharge My Obligation
   Under the Law to Instruct the Jury With
   Respect to the Law in the Case.

[In criminal cases where both judge and jury sit, the role of each is clearly defined. It is within the judge's province to rule on all matters of a legal nature while the jury decides the factual matters. Before the jury retires to deliberate upon these facts, the judge instructs them about the legal framework in which guilt or innocence must be determined. These instructions are called his charge. On February 14, Judge Julius Hoffman carried out his responsibility.

[Once again, we remind the reader that the dialogue that follows is the verbatim language of the participants in the trial—ed.]

**February 14, 1970**
   *Judge Hoffman's charge to the jury*
   The Court: . . . Members of the jury, when a person embarks on a criminal venture of indefinite outlines with other persons, he may be held responsible for the actions taken by his co-conspirators which tend to further the common objectives as he understood them. The Government need not show knowledge of all those acts or of any particular phase of the scheme. It is necessary, however, that the Government prove from all the evidence and beyond a reasonable doubt that each defendant charged with the conspiracy was aware of the common purpose, that each accepted the purpose, made them his own and that each phase of the conspiracy charged in this indictment was within the scope of those criminal purposes.

   To prove that a defendant knowingly and voluntarily joined the conspiracy, the Government must show more than knowledge, asquiescence, carelessness, indifference or lack of concern. There must be informed and interested cooperation and participation. The mere fact that a defendant knew the other defendants during the period of time here in question, and that they came in contact with each other is not sufficient to support a charge of conspiracy. Proof of mere meetings is not sufficient to prove that any kind of agreement existed between any defendant. Several men may be engaged in doing various acts, even of the same general character, and in similar fields of activity, by which they may come in contact with each other without becoming conspirators.

The prosecution must prove that each of the defendants wilfully entered the alleged conspiracy, participated in the formation or knowing its existence and purpose intentionally joined the conspiracy and knowingly aided in the furtherance of such conspiracy. . . .

* *

The Court: The law distinguishes between mere advocacy of violence or lawlessness without more and advocacy of the use of force or of illegality where such advocacy is directed to inciting, promoting, or encouraging lawless actions. Thus, statements of abstract doctrine or principle or of ideas and beliefs are protected by the First Amendment to the Constitution, even though such statements condone, support or are sympathetic to violence or violations of the law, and even though unlawful actions may occur because of such statements, although unintended by the speaker. But the Constitution does not protect speech which is reasonably and knowingly calculated and directed to inciting actions which violate the law. The essential distinction is that those to whom advocacy is addressed must be urged to do something now or in the immediate future rather than merely to believe in something, and the words must advocate concrete action, not merely principles divorced from action.

Thus a conviction can rest only on advocacy which constitutes a call to imminent unlawful action. . . .

* *

The Court: In determining the guilt or innocence of the defendants or any of them, you must determine whether the words spoken after arriving in Chicago, Illinois, as charged in the indictment, were (1) such as to organize, incite, promote or encourage a riot; (2) were spoken or caused to be spoken to an assemblage of three or more persons having individually or collectively the ability of immediate execution of an act of violence which would result in danger or injury to any other person or his property; and, (3) were spoken or caused to be spoken with this specific intent that one or more persons who were part of that assemblage would cause injury or damage to any other person or his property as an immediate result of such words.

In addition it is a constitutional exercise of the rights of free speech and assembly to march or hold a rally, without a permit where applications for permits were made in good faith at a reasonable time prior to the date of march or rally and the permits were denied arbitrarily or discriminatorily.

\* \* \*

The Court: All of the defendants on trial have pleaded not guilty. The law does not require any defendant to prove his innocence. The burden of proof is upon the Government, and this means that the Government must prove the offense charged against the accused, and must establish each and every material element of such offense beyond a reasonable doubt. . . .

\* \*

The Court: To constitute a crime there must be the joint operation of two essentials: an act forbidden by law and an intent to do the act. Before a defendant may be found guilty of a crime, the Government must establish beyond a reasonable doubt that under the statutes defined in these instructions the defendant was forbidden to do the act charged in the indictment, and that he intentially committed the act. . . .

. . . A defendant's specific intent to further the unlawful purposes of the alleged conspiracy may be proved [in] one of three ways only: by the individual defendant's prior or subsequent statements, by the individual defendant's subsequent commission of the very illegal act contemplated by the agreement; or, by the individual defendant's subsequent legal act if that act is clearly undertaken for the purpose of rendering effective the later illegal activity or activity which is advocated.

\* \*

The Court: . . . I have not intended at any time during this trial, and do not now intend, to express any opinion on any matter of fact. If by chance I have expressed or do express any opinion on any matter of fact, it is your duty to disregard that opinion. . . .

In addition, in reaching your verdict you must not in any way be influenced by any possible antagonism you may have toward the defendants or any of them, their dress, hair styles, speech, reputation, courtroom demeanor or quality, personal philosophy or life style. . . .

# VI

# Contempt Proceedings

Transcript pages 21445–21818

[One of the most controversial aspects of the Chicago trial concerned the contempt proceedings. After the jury had retired for its deliberation, Judge Hoffman imposed jail sentences on all seven defendants and the two defense lawyers, citing specific examples of their behavior throughout the trial.

[In the transcript pages listed above, the Court sets forth each incident of contempt. It would have been a relatively simple matter for the editors to merely reproduce those pages. Instead, we felt that only by seeing the actions of the defendants and lawyers in the chronological context in which they occurred could a fair evaluation be given. The reader therefore will already have read of the events for which jail sentences were imposed. Judge Hoffman did not indicate at those times that the actions were contemptuous. We have therefore included an appendix at the end of the book where dates on which the alleged contemptuous events took place can be found.

[We remind the reader that the dialogue that follows is the verbatim language of the participants in the trial—ed.]

The Court: . . . Contempt by definition is any act calculated to hinder or disrupt the Court in the administration of justice and to lessen the Court's authority. Certainly no one would doubt that it is fundamental to not only our federal system but any state court legal system that the courts conduct their business in an untrammeled and undisrupted way. Therefore, misbehavior, misconduct which tends directly to prevent the discharge of judicial function is not and must not be overlooked. . . .

Our legal system provides adequate and orderly means to challenge and test those rulings. Orderly procedures must be followed because the only alternative is anarchy, and we had during this trial such conduct.

The calculated use of contumacious conduct and the direct encouragement of disruptive outcries from spectators to express dissatisfaction or to intimidate the Court and the jurors are reprehensible and must be punished if our system of justice is to survive. . . .

\* \*

The Court: From the outset of the trial the Court admonished and warned the defendants and their counsel to refrain from such conduct, particularly when committed in the presence of the jury. They chose deliberately to disregard such admonition, right down through yesterday afternoon's hearing and have openly challenged and flaunted their contempt for both this Court and for the system of law it represents.

Particularly reprehensible was the conduct of counsel, who not only disregarded a duty to advise and direct their clients to observe the rules of this Court but participated with their clients in making a mockery of orderly procedure. . . .

\* \*

The Court: Once any party to a law suit has embarked upon a strategy of disruption such as that displayed in this case, rather than proceeding within the bounds of proper procedure, only cumulative sanctions can act as a restraint. Otherwise a first offense would offer immunity for further violations.

\* \*

The Court: This was a case marred by continual disruptive outbursts in direct defiance of judicial authority by the defendants and Defense Counsel. I will specify here the instances of conduct of record which I consider to have been contemptuous, but I also make the entire record of the case of United States of America v. David T. Dellinger, et al., 69 CR 180, a part of this proceeding.

Much of the contemptuous conduct in this case does not show, of record. The constant murmurs and snickering emanating from the defense table were not captured on the printed page. No record, no matter how skilfully transcribed, can adequately portray the venom, sarcasm, and tone of voice employed by a speaker. No record, no matter how skilfully transcribed, can adequately reflect the applause, the guffaws, and other subtle tactics employed by these contemnors in an attempt to break up this trial. I have not focused on these cheap theatrics, histrionics, and affectations. I note them for the record lest my silence be construed as approval. But for the sake of the citations of contempt in this case, I limit myself to that conduct which is clearly and adequately portrayed in the record.

This was a long trail. The behavior of the defendants and Defense Counsel was prepared with direct and defiant contempt for the Court and the federal judicial system as a whole. Here is a record of exceptional circumstances which were disruptive of the proceedings. . . .

\* \* \*

Mr. Kunstler: . . . We place little credence in the notion that the independence of the judiciary hangs on the power to try contempt summarily and are not persuaded that the additional time and expense possibly involved in submitting serious contempts to juries will seriously handicap the effective functioning of the courts. We do not deny that serious punishment must sometimes be imposed for contempt but we reject the contention that such punishment must be imposed without a right to jury trial.

. . .

Mr. Kunstler: The defendants do not consent to your Honor sitting on their contempts and therefore I think your Honor is totally without jurisdiction to do what you are doing today and to sentence people from summary contempt after the trial is over.

\* \* \*

The Court: . . . I will first consider the conduct of the Defendant David Dellinger. . . .

. . .

Defendant Dellinger: You want us to be like good Germans supporting the evils of our decade and then when we refused to be good Germans and came to Chicago and demonstrated, despite the threats and intimidations of the establishment, now you want us to be like good Jews, going quietly and politely to the concentration camps while you and this Court suppress freedom and the truth. And the fact is that I am not prepared to do that. You want us to stay in our place like black people were supposed to stay in their place—

The Court: Mr. Marshal, I will ask you to have Mr. Dellinger sit down.

Defendant Dellinger: —like poor people were supposed to stay in their place, like people without formal education are supposed to stay in their place, like women are supposed to stay in their place—

The Court: I will ask you to sit down.

Defendant Dellinger: Like children are supposed to stay in their place, like lawyers—for whom I thank—I thank you —are supposed to stay in their places.

262

It is a travesty on justice and if you had any sense at all you would know that that record that you read condemns you and not us.

The Court:    All right.

Defendant Dellinger:    And it will be one of thousands and thousands of rallying points for a new generation of Americans who will not put up with tyranny, will not put up with a facade of democracy without the reality.

\* \* \*

Mr. Dellinger:    . . . People no longer will be quiet. People are going to speak up. I am an old man and I am just speaking feebly and not too well, but I reflect the spirit that will echo—

The Court:    Take him out—

Defendant Dellinger:    —throughout the world—

*(Applause.)*

Defendant Dellinger:    —comes from my children who came yesterday—

*(Complete disorder in the courtroom.)*

. . .

Mr. Kunstler:    My life has come to nothing, I am not anything any more. You destroyed me and everybody else. Put me in jail now, for God's sakes, and get me out of this place. Come to mine now. Come to mine now, Judge, please. Please. I beg you. Come to mine. Do me, too. I don't want to be out.

\* \* \*

[Defendant Dellinger was sentenced to 29 months and 16 days on 32 counts of contempt.]

Defendant Davis:    You have just jailed one of the most beautiful and one of the most courageous men in the United States.

The Court:    All right. Now we will talk about you, Mr. Davis. . . .

\* \* \*

The Court:    Mr. Davis, do you care to be heard?

Mr. Davis:    Yes. . . .

I am sorry I do not have the complete transcript with me so that I could report on each of the 23 counts in detail.

This morning you said that the only alternative to what I have done here in the courtroom is anarchy, and perhaps you are right. You have said as well that as a matter of law, there is no defense for what we have done, and I believe that there is a defense for what we have done.

. . .

Mr. Davis:    . . . Judge, you represent all that is old, ugly,

263

bigoted and repressive in this country, and I will tell you that the spirit at this defense table is going to devour your sickness in the next generation.

*　　*　　*

[Defendant Davis was sentenced to 25 months and 14 days on 23 counts of contempt.]

*　　*　　*

The Court: . . . It is the spirit of rebellion against the orders of the Court. I know you don't like courts, but you are going to have to like them or deal with them and you had better decide to just respect them. If you don't want to, that is, [of] course, your privilege, but you are going to have to somewhere along the line take the consequences. That is all. . . .

There was scarcely a day that I came out here that I wasn't the subject of at least of some sarcasm and it went all the way from sarcasm to awful invective. I just don't stand for that kind of treatment and I don't get it from anybody. I have tried some of the most highly and widely publicized criminal cases in the United States. I have never had, but never have I been treated in any of those cases as I have been treated here. And all I was asking for was respect, the same kind of respect that I would extend to any litigant or any lawyer who comes in here.

*　　*　　*

The Court: To be characterized as a racist was an absolute absurdity. There is nothing here that shows me a racist. Is there now? Now is there anything that shows me a racist? You think I disciplined Mr. Seale because of his color? It's what he said and what he did. And a white man would have been disciplined in the same way.

*　　*　　*

Mr. Hayden: . . . [F]or a lot of people who feel the way I do, we are in the movie "Z," I mean there is not going to be a higher court.

The Court: You are going to shout them down right here at the trial level, is that right?

Mr. Hayden: I am not raising my voice. But I find this is the only place I may have or I may in the next two years be allowed to speak to these people, to them and to the press. But the point that I wanted to make about punishment is that the problem that I think people have who want to punish us —Mr. Foran who calls us evil, people who want to punish us, is that what must cause a great problem for the understanding of people like that is why the punishment does not seem to have effect. Even as the elder Dellinger is taken off for two years, a younger Dellinger fights back.

\* \* \*

Mr. Hayden: . . . So, your Honor, before your eyes you see the most vital ingredient of your system collapsing because the system does not hold together.

The Court: Oh, don't be so pessimistic. Our system isn't collapsing. Fellows as smart as you could do awfully well under this system. I am not trying to convert you, mind you.

Defendant Hoffman: We don't want a place in the regiment, Julie.

\* \* \*

The Court: . . . [Y]ou are going to have to abide by the system, the rules of the system, the federal system, when you get into trouble. . . .

\* \* \*

Mr. Hayden: I think the difficulty is trying to try people for political crimes or crimes of consciousness or ideological crimes. That is what brings politics and consciousness into the courtroom. . . .

\* \*

[Defendant Hayden was sentenced to 14 months and 14 days on 11 counts of contempt.]

\* \* \*

The Court: . . . I will hear from Mr. Hoffman if he wants to be heard.
. . .

Defendant Hoffman: You have always referred to—they were my remarks—you said that we did not pay tribute to the highest court in the land, but to us the Federal Court is not the highest court in the land.

The Court: I didn't hear myself say that.

Defendant Hoffman: Oh, yes, you did. You always call it the highest court in the land. Sure.

The Court: The Supreme Court is.
. . .

Defendant Hoffman: We don't consider it the highest. We consider the people the highest court in the land.

\* \* \*

Defendant Hoffman: But when the decorum is oppression, the only dignity that free men have is the right to speak out. Furthermore, you said we so not honor your authority, but we recognize that authority as illegitimate in the same way that the authority that decided the political decisions in that heavy

265

week in August of 1968 was illegitimate and did not represent the will and the desire of the people.

So we cannot respect an authority that we regard as illegitimate. We can only offer resistance to such illegitimate authority. . . .

\* \*

Defendant Hoffman: Furthermore, you have asked us to respect the law but this is a law—I sat there on the witness stand and Mr. Schultz said, "What were you wondering?" as he quoted from my book and speeches. "What were you wondering that night when you stood before a building?"

And I said, "Wonder? Wonder? I have never been on trial for wondering. Is that like a dream?"

He said, "Yes, that's like a dream."

And I have never been on trial for my dreams before. How can I respect the highest court in the land or a Federal Government that puts people on trial for their dreams. I can show it no respect.

\* \* \*

[Defendant Hoffman was sentenced to 8 months on 24 counts of contempt.]

**February 15, 1970**
The Clerk: Everybody is here, your Honor.
The Court: I come now to deal with the conduct of Jerry Rubin during this trial.

. . .

Mr. Rubin: I want to discuss the contempts and the motivation behind them, which would affect your punishment and I want to start with the references that I have made on a number of occasions to Gestapo, fascism and Hitler, and I want to explain what motivated me to say that.

Everything that happened in Nazi Germany was legal. It happened in courtrooms, just like this. It was done by judges, judges who wore robes and judges who quoted the law and judges who said, "This is the law, respect it."

We saw Nazi Germany [as—ed.] immoral, and I think that this is the closest thing that I personally experienced to what happened in Nazi Germany, and it was the closest thing in my experience to say to you, to communicate to you, that just quoting the law is no answer, because the law in the courtroom gagged and chained Bobby Seale and I refuse to stand up and say, "Heil Hitler" when a black man was gagged and chained and I think that any human being sitting in that courtroom refused to stand up and that's why I refused to stand up because I came to this trial. I wanted to be indicted.

266

I issued a statement I was indicted upon the Academy Award protest. I was ready for a trial with lawyers, a full defense. The moment you walked in, I don't know what day it was, for the arraignment, we got from you instantly the message we were going to jail, and I think it's interesting that while the jury is out, before it reaches a verdict, the 10 of us are going to jail. Who has respect for the law?

* * *

Mr. Rubin: By punishing us, you are going to have ten million in two weeks. Deterrent? Putting us in jail is just going to produce more trials like this. You have done more to destroy the judicial system. That's what punishment is going to be; that's what punishment is going to be. Revenge never got you anywhere. By having to punish us, you have shown the world that this judicial system has lost the respect of the youth, and the youth will free us. We're going to jail with smiles on our faces because we know that in jail, there are millions of kids, young kids out there who identify with us, and are going to fight to free us, and that's the revolution. And your jailing us is a vindictive, revengeful act. . . .

* *

Mr. Rubin: Obscenity, I am accused of obscenity. What is obscenity? To me, the war in Vietnam is an obscenity. Racism is an obscenity.

The Court: I will tell you, sir—

Mr. Rubin: My gosh, for you, obscenity is words connected to the body, to the body. That is obscenity. A sexual act becomes an obscenity in your mind, and we get punished for that.

* * *

Mr. Rubin: . . . There were 25,000 people in the Stadium in Los Angeles last night, and there are going to be meetings across the country and demonstrations across the country. And you have destroyed the judicial system. You have done more harm to this country than any other single person alive today.

You should be ashamed of yourself.

The Court: You may sit down.

Mr. Rubin: I am happy to.

* * *

[Defendant Rubin was sentenced to 25 months, and 23 days on 15 counts of contempt.]

* * *

The Court: We now come to the consideration of the conduct of Defendant Lee Weiner. . . .

. . .

Specification 5. On December 1st, while the witness Rochford was on the stand, the Defendant Weiner made the following comment in a voice loud enough to be heard by the Court and others present, including the jurors:

Mr. Weiner: . . . I think the judicial system is a fairly reasonable one—twelve jurors, the evidence—that is kind of good; that is kind of good.

The Court: The judicial system is what?

Mr. Weiner: I think the judicial system as an idea, an abstract idea, is a fairly reasonable one, and so I have a great deal of sympathy, and I guess, pity for Lennie and Bill who have worked so hard to gain some expertise in a system which should, if it functioned adequately, provide some opportunity for some kind of abstract notion of justice to come at least close to, but I think here, you, not necessarily because you are anything necessarily evil, but simply because you are what you are, who you are—you are older than us—

\*   \*   \*

The Court: —I am supposed to be especially tolerant because years ago when I was a much younger man, I was a member of the faculty of the school that you—I don't know whether you still are; at least it has been suggested here during this trial that you are or were a teacher there.

Mr. Weiner: I even understand that there is a plaque naming an auditorium after you at the Law School. At latest report, by the way—

The Court: You are nice to tell the assembled spectators here—

Mr. Weiner: I tell them actually for an evil reason.

The Court: —that there is a Hoffman Hall on Northwestern University's campus.

Mr. Weiner: I am telling them actually because I am suggesting it is evil.

The Court: Perhaps those who think ill of me because of some of the things that have been said might have a little compassion.

Mr. Weiner: I am pleased to report to you that the plaque has been ripped off the wall.

The Court: The plaque?

Mr. Weiner: The plaque has been ripped off the wall in the auditorium. Apparently while the Board of Trustees feel affection for you, the student body does not.

The Court: Did they take the sign off the door?

Mr. Weiner: They have done their best. They have done their best.

The Court: I haven't been there.

Mr. Weiner: I wouldn't suggest immediately appearing at the Law School after you get through with this trial. You might be mobbed, not necessarily as a tourist of our law building.

\* \* \*

[Defendant Weiner was sentenced to 2 months and 18 days on 7 counts of contempt.]

\* \* \*

The Court: . . . I will next consider the conduct of the lawyers in this case—oh, I beg your pardon. We have—I almost forgot to take care of Mr. Froines. Mr. Kunstler has finished. Mr. Froines, I give you the same opportunity I accorded all of the others to speak in mitigation of punishment here, but without saying offensive things to the Court.

Mr. Froines: It's part of being a media unknown that even the Judge finally forgets you're here.

\* \* \*

Mr. Froines: In the Oregon Constitution there is an article which I think describes some of which we do and that is entitled "Natural Rights Inherent in the People." It says that we declare all men, when they form as a social compact, are equal in right, that all power is inherent in the people, and all free governments are founded on their authority and instituted for their peace, safety and happiness and they have at all times a right to alter, reform or abolish the government in a manner as they may think proper. And I think that's what we did . . .

\* \* \*

[Defendant Froines was sentenced to 5 months and 15 days on 10 counts of contempt.]

\* \* \*

The Court: This matter now involves the conduct of Mr. William Kunstler, counsel for some of the defendants here, who has participated in this trial from the very beginning.

I have said here frequently that the Court has never had the occasion to hold a lawyer in contempt, and only on one occasion did the Court hold someone who is not a lawyer in contempt. . . .

I recognize the obligation of a lawyer to defend a client with vigor, and secure for his client the full benefits under the law. Nevertheless, if he crosses the bounds of legal propriety, the Court must deal appropriately with that conduct.

\* \* \*

Mr. Kunstler: . . . I just have a few words, your Honor. Your Honor, I have been a lawyer since December of 1948, when I was first admitted to the bar in the state of New York. Since that time, I have practiced before, among other courts, the Supreme Court of the United States, the United State Court of Appeals for the First, Second, Third, Fourth, Fifth, Sixth, Seventh, Tenth, District of Columbia Circuits, Federal District Courts throughout a great deal of the United States, and the United States Court of Military Appeals. . . .

Until today I have never once been disciplined by any Judge, federal or state, although a large part of my practice, at least for the last decade, has taken place in hostile southern courts where I was representing black and white clients in highly controversial civil rights cases.

Yesterday, for the first time in my career, I completely lost my composure in a courtroom, as I watched the older daughter of David Dellinger being rushed out of the room because she clapped her hands to acknowledge what amounted to her father's farewell statement to her.

I felt then such a deep sense of utter futility that I could not help crying, something I had not done publicly since childhood.

I am sorry if I disturbed the decorum of the courtroom, but I am not ashamed of my conduct in this Court, for which am about to be punished.

I have tried with all my heart faithfully to represent my clients in the face of what I consider—and still consider—repressive and unjust conduct toward them. If I have to pay with my liberty for such representation, then that is the price of my beliefs and my sensibilities.

I can only hope that my fate does not deter other lawyers throughout the country, who, in the difficult days that lie ahead, will be asked to defend clients against a steadily increasing governmental encroachment upon their most fundamental liberties. If they are so deterred, then my punishment will have effects of such terrifying consequences that I dread to contemplate the future domestic and foreign course of this country. However, I have the utmost faith that my beloved brethren at the bar, young and old alike, will not allow themselves to be frightened out of defending the poor, the persecuted, the radicals and the militant, the black people, the pacifists, and the political pariahs of this, our common land.

But to those lawyers who may, in learning of what may happen to me, waver, I can only say this, stand firm, remain true to those ideals of the law which even if openly violated here and in other places, are true and glorious goals, and above all, never desert those principles of equality, justice and freedom without which life has little if any meaning.

I may not be the greatest lawyer in the world, your Honor, but I think that I am at this moment, along with my colleague, Leonard Weinglass, the most privileged. We are being punished for what we believe in.

Your Honor, I am ready, sir, to be sentenced, and I would appreciate it if I could be permitted to remain standing at this lectern where I have spent the greater part of the past five months, while you do so.

Thank you.

*(Applause.)*

\*   \*

The Court: The marshals will remove those who have applauded from the courtroom. Remove them from the courtroom. This circus has to end sometime. . . .

\*   \*

The Court: . . . I approach what I perceive to be my responsibility here just as unhappily as you indicated you are. I, too, have been at the bar for a long time, many years longer than you. I have practiced in the various state and federal courts throughout the land, not all, of course, but many.

I have to repeat what I have said in substance, that I have never heard a lawyer say to a judge in substance the things that you have said to me during this trial. I know you are going to say—if I permitted you to reply—you would say that I deserved them . . .

We decided questions here according to the law, as we perceive the law to be. As I indicated this morning, to one of the defendants, if a lawyer or a party perceives that a ruling is erroneous, you certainly, as a lawyer, know there are courts where you can proceed to have error corrected. We don't correct error doing it the way you have done.

\*   \*

The Court: Now, I know you, from some of the things you said here, ties in your own personal beliefs with those of your clients, and you live your clients' cases as though they are your own. Nobody disputes that anyone under the Constitution of the United States charged with a crime has a right to counsel of his choice, and if he hasn't the money to employ a lawyer, just about every state and the Government, itself, provide counsel at no cost to them. Certainly, that is the constitutional right of any citizen, or anybody who comes in here charged with a crime. But a man with a crime has a right only to a defense properly made, and that does not include what has gone on, the sort of thing that has gone on in this courtroom.

We hear a lot of discussion by men in high political places

271

about crime in this country. I am going to make a rather unorthodox statement. First of all, there is a lot of crime, I know because I have a lot of criminal cases to try, and I have tried many criminal cases. I am one of those who believes that crime, if it is on the increase, and I don't have the statistic before me, in any jurisdiction, state or federal, it is due in large part to the fact that waiting in the wings are lawyers who are willing to go beyond, to go beyond professional responsibility, professional rights, and professional duty in their defense of a defendant, and the fact that a defendant or some defendants know that such a lawyer is waiting in the wings I think, has a rather stimulating effect on the increase in crime.

\* \* \*

Mr. Kunstler: Your Honor, I am glad your Honor spoke because I suddenly feel nothing but compassion for you. Everything else has dropped away.

\* \* \*

[Defense Attorney Kunstler was sentenced to 4 years, and 13 days on 24 counts of contempt.]

The Court: . . . Now we come to the matter of Leonard Weinglass. I will wait until those who wish to leave the court room do so. . . .

. . .

Mr. Weinglass: . . . This has been a long, difficult, highly contested proceeding in which all of us at one time or another have lost their sense of professional control and judgment. I only have to cite to the court Mr. Schultz' reference to the bathroom in front of the jury, for which he later apologized. There were unlawful references to the fact that two of the defendants took the stand and perjured themselves for which he apologized; Mr. Foran's statement that Tom Hayden and Rennie Davis were guilty of a crime for which they had neither been charged nor were before a grand jury, for which he later apologized.

But I have no quarrel with either Mr. Foran or Mr. Schultz. They were attorneys involved in a very difficult adversary proceeding and they are entitled to errors of judgment, to loss of control, which they committed in the course of this four and a half months.

For the same understandable defects, Mr. Kunstler and myself will have to serve time in jail. . . .

\* \* \*

The Court: . . . This trial, whatever the result comes to be, could have been conducted fairly and with dignity and without rancor or ill will. I can recall few instances—oh, I suppose every judge has a run in with lawyers on occasions

272

but there have been few instances that I can recall where I have had acrimonious or anything that approached an acrimonious discussion with a lawyer in respect to his conduct. And I have tried cases in this courtroom and in the old court house across the street where the defendants were widely publicized men in the field of crime and we went through trials involving one or two or three months with no rancor [or] ill feeling. Sometimes there was a conviction, sometimes not. But when a lawyer—but when the lawyers in the main were told what they had to do, they did it. They did it. That is no matter of arrogance on the part of the judge; it is the way a trial should be conducted, and you heard me use the words of Justice Frankfurter in my charge to the jury, "The judge is the governor of the trial." . . .

But there is rapidly growing up a tradition or a belief in this country that the only person on trial is the defendant—that the only party to the trial is the defendant. . . .

\* \* \*

The Court: I will hear you now only on the matter—I took time to digress because of your observations about—

Mr. Weinglass: If I could just answer that digression for a moment: With respect to our different understandings of respect, I was hopeful when I came here that after 20 weeks the Court would know my name and I didn't receive that which I thought was the minimum—

\* \*

The Court: Well, I am going to tell you about that. . . .
. .

The Court: I have got a very close friend named Weinruss and I know nobody by the name of Weinrob— and somehow or other the name of Weinruss stuck in my mind and it is your first appearance here. You have seen lawyers pass before this bar all during your four to five months here whom I know intimately and I scarcely ever forget a lawyer's name even when he hasn't been in for 20 years.

\* \*

Mr. Weinglass: My natural instincts are and have always been to avoid, if possible, a protracted fight. I am not as strong a man as Bill Kunstler by far, and I think I am more vulnerable to what I perceive to be intimidation—whether it is or not. And I have had to fight that instinct here in court, not only because I felt that the rights of other men were involved but because of the inspiration I drew from Bill Kunstler as well as the other persons who have worked with me.

\* \*

273

The Court: Did you ever feel like tapping one of those defendants, one or more of them, on the hand when they were assailing me with vile epithets to say, "Hey, hey, be quiet?"

Mr. Weinglass: Does your Honor seriously believe that what was in conflict here in this courtroom could have dissipated by an admonishment from Bill Kunstler or myself?

. . .

The Court: I judge your whole attitude toward the Court by your omission to do that. But I am obligated under the law to particularize these items of contempt which I have.

Mr. Weinglass: I only need point out to the Court one thing in answer to that. Those men are upstairs now, they are serving long prison terms, the Court made it known to them throughout this trial that they would, and your Honor failed in your attempt to silence what they felt was their right to speak out when they just couldn't stand it any more, to sit and be silent.

\* \* \*

[Defense Attorney Weinglass was sentenced to 20 months and 9 days on 14 counts of contempt.]

# VII

# Verdict and Sentencing

Transcript pages 21819–22302

The Court:
> I understand, gentlemen, that the jury has
> brought in a verdict. Is the jury here? Have
> you brought the jury here?

The Marshal:
> Your Honor, the jury has reached a verdict.

[Thus, after four days of deliberations, the twelve jurors
ended speculation that they would be unable to reach the
unanimous decision necessary for a determination of innocence
or guilt. Each of the seven defendants had been individually
charged in counts 2–8 of crossing state lines with intent to
incite to riot and, collectively, in count 1, of conspiring with
each other, to do the same.

[We remind the reader that the dialogue that follows is the
verbatim language of the participants in the trial—ed.]

**February 18, 1970**

Mr. Schultz: Your Honor, before the jury is brought in,
may I make a statement? May I address the Court, please?

The Court: You certainly may.

Mr. Schultz: Your Honor, I just have a couple of matters
I would like to present to your Honor before the jury is brought
in. The first is that considering what has gone on in this courtroom before, considering the fact that we have had a number
of fist fights in the courtroom and miniature riots right here
in this courtroom and the last especially culminating last week
even during the final arguments with the staff members, relative to the defendants, who have been thrown out repeatedly—
some, in fact, are under charge before the United States Com-
missioner—and further because, your Honor, on Saturday
and on Sunday your Honor issued certain contempt citations

in this case, we would ask your Honor to have the court cleared of all spectators except the press, leaving the press, your staff, the marshals, the defendants, and the attorneys, with orders to the people who remain direct orders to the people who remain not to make any statement in this courtroom in the presence of the jury relating to the contempt citations.

\* \* \*

The Court: You may reply, Mr. Kunstler.

Mr. Kunstler: Your Honor, we would want to voice the strongest possible objection to the first point, the first application by the government, that is, that the court be cleared during the rendering of the verdict. First of all we completely dispute his phrase "miniature riots" and the implication that what occurred here in the courtroom was caused by the defendants. It is our contention—and I think the facts bear it out—that if there was violence in this courtroom, it was provoked in the courtroom by either the Government or the United States Marshals involved and that the violence that was provoked was far in excess of any required.

There was the same overreaction here that we thought we had proved in Chicago in the streets in late August of 1968. . . .

. . . I don't think that you ought to add to what we consider a totally unfair trial the last crowning indignity that you could possibly do as far as these defendants were concerned and that is to let them stand here alone surrounded only by the press, by the prosecution, and with their own attorneys, but really alone in the most lonely way a man can be alone, divorced from his family and friends and supporters at a moment in his life when he is about to hear the verdict of a jury in a criminal case and one involving serious criminal penalties.

\* \* \*

The Court: I will decide to enter this order: The following may remain: of course the defendants and those who have sat at the Government's table throughout this trial—the three lawyers and representatives of the Government. The defendants. The ladies and gentlemen of the press, all media. I direct that no newspapers be exhibited in the presence of the jury. I would say counsel of record, of course, for the defendants may be here.

. . .

Now all of the parties here other than those I have mentioned are directed to leave the courtroom.

A Voice: . . . (T)hey will dance on your grave, Julie, and the graves of the pig empire.

\* \* \*

The Court: Good morning, ladies and gentlemen of the jury.

I am informed by the United States Marshal that you have reached a verdict or come to some verdicts.

Is that true? Is there a forewoman or foreman?

The Foreman: A foreman.

The Court: You are the foreman?

The Foreman: Yes, sir.

The Court: Has the jury reached a verdict or some verdicts?

The Foreman: Yes, your Honor.

The Court: Would you hand the verdicts to the marshal, please, and, Mr. Marshal, will you hand them to the clerk?

I direct the clerk to read the verdicts.

The Clerk: "We, the jury, find the Defendant David T. Dellinger guilty as charged in Count No. 2 of the indictment and not guilty as charged in Count No. 1." . . .

". . . the Defendant Rennard D. Davis guilty as charged in Count No. 3 of the indictment and not guilty as charged in Count No. 1." . . .

". . . the Defendant Thomas E. Hayden guilty as charged in Count No. 4 of the indictment and not guilty as charged in Count No. 1 of the indictment." . . .

". . . the Defendant Abbott H. Hoffman guilty as charged in Count No. 5 of the indictment and not guilty as charged in Count No. 1 of the indictment." . . .

". . . the Defendant Jerry C. Rubin guilty as charged in Count No. 6 of the indictment and not guilty as charged in Count No. 1 of the indictment." . . .

". . . the Defendant Lee Weiner not guilty as charged in the indictment." . . .

".. . the Defendant John R. Froines not guilty as charged in the indictment."

Signed by Edward F. Kratzke, Foreman, and eleven other jurors.

\* \* \*

Mr. Kunstler: . . . [W]e feel that pending appeal of what is going to be an extremely complicated appeal and a long appeal involving the constitutionality of the law and many other aspects, I think that we could at least at the twilight of this case agree together there are many complicated issues of law and fact involved in this case and it would certainly not be called by any person a frivolous appeal under any circumstances, and therefore I would urge that your Honor continue the bond that is presently in effect, even though they have been convicted on one count of the two, and it was thought sufficient to only have a $10,000 bond for that, for the two counts originally, that your Honor continue the bond on appeal, pending appeal of this cause, of the $10,000 bond previously established by this Court for the five men I have mentioned.

. . .

The Court: . . . I have heard the evidence here. I have watched all of the defendants whom you asked me to release on bail with respect to the counts on which they have been found guilty. From the evidence and from their conduct in this trial, I find they are dangerous men to be at large and I deny your motion for bail as to Dellinger, Davis, Hayden, Hoffman and Rubin respectively.

[The Court then adjourned for two days to determine the sentences to be imposed—ed.]

### February 20, 1970

The Court: . . . I now proceed with the imposition of sentence. I will hear you for your clients, Mr. Kunstler.

. . .

Mr. Kunstler: Well, your Honor, I say this. One, the defendents had no way of knowing they are going to be sentenced today. Their families are not even present, which would seem to me in common decency would be permitted.

The Court: The reasons—

Mr. Kunstler: Unless those words are contemptuous, too.

The Court: The reason they were kept out is my life was threatened by one of the members of the family. I was told they would dance on my grave in one of the hearings here within the last week.

Mr. Kunstler: Your Honor, are you serious?

\* \* \*

The Court: . . . Mr. Dellinger, you have the right to speak in your own behalf.

. . .

Giving you the right to speak means you must be respectful, I said in substance, and I say it again. I don't want you to be anything other than respectful.

Mr. Dellinger: What does that mean? Only say things that you agree with, or does it mean I can discuss—

The Court: Go ahead. I give you the right to speak, sir, in your own behalf.

. . .

Mr. Dellinger: . . . First, I think that every judge should be required to serve time in prison, to spend time in prison before sentencing other people there so that he might become

278

aware of the degrading and anti-human conditions that persist not only in Cook County jail but in the prisons generally of this country. . . .

. . .

Like Mr. Kunstler I feel more compassion for you, sir, than I do any hostility. I feel that you are a man who has had too much power over the lives of too many people for too many years. You have sentenced them to those degrading conditions that I am talking about without being aware fully of what you are doing, and undoubtedly feeling correct and righteous, as often happens when people do the most abominable things.

\* \* \*

Mr. Dellinger: . . . I want to say that sending us to prison, any punishment the Government can impose upon us, will not solve the problems that have gotten us into "trouble" with the Government and the law in the first place; will not solve the problem of this country's rampant racism, will not solve the problem of the economic injustice, it will not solve the problem of the foreign policy and the attacks upon the under-developed people of the world. . . .

The Government has misread the times in which we live just like there was a time when it was possible to keep black people in slavery, and then it became impossible. So, this country is growing out of the time when it is possible to keep young people, women, black people, Mexican-Americans, anti-war people, people who believe in truth and justice and really believe in democracy, when it is going to be possible to keep them quiet or suppress them.

\* \* \*

Mr. Dellinger: Our movement is not very strong today. It is not united, it is not well organized. It is very confused and makes a lot of mistakes, but there is the beginning of an awakening in this country which has been going on for at least the last fifteen years, and it is an awakening that will not be denied. Tactics will change, people will err, people will die in the streets and die in prison, but I do not believe that this movement can be denied because however falsely applied the American ideal was from the beginning when it excluded black people, and Indians and people without property, nonetheless there was a dream of justice and equality and freedom, and brotherhood, and I think that that dream is much closer to fulfillment today than it has been at any time in the history of this country.

I only wish that we were all not just more eloquent, I wish we were smarter, more dedicated, more united. I wish we could work together. I wish we could reach out to the Forans, and the Schultzes and the Hoffmans, and convince them of the necessity of this revolution.

* * *

The Court: Mr. Davis, would you like to speak in your own behalf? You have that right.

Mr. Davis: . . . I do not think that it is a time to appeal to you or to appeal to the system that is about to put me away.

I suppose if I were to make any appeals, it really should be to Agent Stanley or to J. Edgar Hoover, because the sentence that I am about to receive comes not from you in my judgment but from the FBI. This trial has been controlled by the police and the FBI and undercover agents from the beginning, from the witnesses that have been paraded with their lies to that witness stand day after day after day right up to the last sentence that is going to be delivered, comes from the FBI, and I don't think the FBI is interested in speeches. I don't think the FBI is interested in words. I think that what moves a government that increasingly is controlled by a police mentality is action. It is not a time for words; it is a time that demands action. And since I did not get a jury of my peers, I look to the jury that is in the streets. My jury will be in the streets tomorrow all across this country and the verdict from my jury will keep coming in over the next long five years that you are about to give me in prison.

* *

I guess if I have any hope at all it is that I am allowed out of prison by 1976 because in 1976 the American people are not going to recount their history, they are going to relive their history, and when I come out of prison it will be to move next door to Tom Foran. I am going to be the boy next door to Tom Foran and the boy next door, the boy that could have been a judge, could have been a prosecutor, could have been a college professor, is going to move next door to organize his kids into the revolution. We are going to turn the sons and daughters of the ruling class in this country into Viet Cong.

* *

The Court: Mr. Hayden, you have a right to speak in your own behalf.

Mr. Hayden: . . . Our intention in coming to Chicago was not to incite a riot. Our intention in coming to Chicago was to see to it that certain things, that is, the right of every human being, the right to assemble, the right to protest, can be carried out even where the Government chooses to suspend those rights. It was because we chose to exercise those rights in Chicago in the jaws of a police state that we are here to-day. . . .

280

We have known all along what the intent of the Government has been. We knew that before we set foot on the streets of Chicago. We knew that before the famous events of August 28, 1968. If those events didn't happen, the Government would have had to invent them, as I think it did for much of its evidence in this case, because they were bound to put us away. They had to put us away in some way that would preserve the image of the system.

\* \* \*

Mr. Hayden: . . . We would hardly be notorious characters if they had left us alone in the streets of Chicago last year. It would have been a few thousand people. It would have been testimony to our failure as organizers. But instead we became the architects, the master minds and the geniuses of a conspiracy to overthrow the government. We were invented. We were chosen by the government to serve as scapegoats for all that they wanted to prevent happening in the 1970's. We were chosen because we had a history in the 1960's of doing things that had to be stopped. . . . So the Government has had every reason to eliminate us because the Government operates from the theory that somebody must be behind these things and because we have been so active and aggressive, it must be us, and by putting us away, that will put an end to the problems.

\* \* \*

Mr. Hayden: . . . I want the press to try to understand how we view the structuring [of] our indictment. First of all pick Weiner and Froines, innocent young men, so if they are found guilty, that will scare every innocent young person who might associate with leaders, who might go to a demonstration, because they are average people, and when people saw them indicted, they said, "Well, that could have been me."

Also it gives you plenty of room to negotiate if the jury doesn't want to feel that it's putting everybody away, the jury can always negotiate out Froines and Weiner—why not, because they'll obviously show up to be much less guilty than the others.

Then give us two counts instead of one so you have a maximum and a minimum. Ten years, that will be nice, but if the jury finds us guilty on one and not guilty on the other, that will look to people like the whole thing came out fairly.

\* \* \*

Mr. Hayden: . . . I think we will not be given bail which is the ultimate example, the ultimate example of the suspension of constitutional rights, the ultimate example of refusing to extend constitutional rights to people who might use them effectively.

281

It is all right to let Mafia people out on bail. It is all right to let murderers out on bail. It is all right to let DeSapio out on bail. They walked right out of the courtroom; it is not going to be all right to let us out on bail because they will say, there is an incendiary situation.

\* \* \*

Mr. Hayden: People have tried through the system, people have tried through all of the avenues to register their feelings. Then they have gone home to watch color TV and have oxtail soup, and to see their four-year-old poodle hoping that nobody blames them. . . .

The tragedy is that people of that older generation do not know yet how to hold out, and probably never will, do not know how to fight to the end. . . . I have no doubt that if we had a jury of our peers, by any definition anybody wants to give to the word peers, if we had a jury of our peers we would have walked out of this place, or we would have had an absolutely hung jury because younger people in the country today know what principles are, and know what bullshit is, and know how to stand up and are not in the least afraid of expressing their convictions in the face of the state, in the face of the troops, in the face of police.

\* \* \*

Mr. Hayden: If you didn't want to make us martyrs, why did you do it? If you wanted to keep it cool, why didn't you give us a permit? You know. You know if you had given us a permit, you know if you had given slightly different instructions, very little would have happened last year in Chicago. Ramsey Clark knows it. He survived many more street confrontations than most people in this room, no matter how much you want to call him an intellectual from Washington. . . .

. . . You don't believe it but we have to do this. We have no choice. We had no choice in Chicago. We had no choice in this trial. The people always do what they have to do. Every person who is born now and every person under thirty now feels an imperative to do the kind of things that we are doing. They may not act on them, they may not act on them immediately, but they feel the same imperatives because they are part of the same generation. They are part of the same body of people that came to life in the 1950's and 1960's and saw things differently from the older people. So they feel an imperative. They are proclaiming that imperative from the streets. Some day they are going to proclaim the imperative from the bench and from the courthouse. It's only a matter of

282

time. It's only a matter of time. You can give us time. You are going to give us time. But it is only a matter of time.

[Following Mr. Hayden's statements, the court recessed for the lunch hour—ed.]

\* \* \*

[*Following the recess*]

The Court:   Mr. Hoffman, the law gives you the right to speak in your own behalf. I will hear you if you have anything to say.

Mr. Abbie Hoffman:   Thank you.

I feel like I have spent 15 years watching John Daly shows about history: You Are There. It is sort of like taking LSD, which I recommend to you, Judge. I know a good dealer in Florida. I could fix you up.

\* \* \*

Mr. Hoffman:   Right from the beginning of the indictment, up until the end of the trial, I always wanted to change my plea. I had just like a great urge to confess; say, "I am guilty," because I felt what the State was calling me was an enemy of the State and I am an enemy of the State, I am an enemy of the America as it is now, with a K. . . .

Mr. Foran says that we are evil men, and I suppose that is sort of a compliment. He says that we are unpatriotic. Unpatriotic? I don't know, that has a kind of jingleistic ring. I suppose I am not patriotic.

But he says we are un-American. I don't feel un-American. I feel very American. I feel very close to the vision of America in that film, the Yippie film you wouldn't allow into evidence, because it didn't go into our intent.

It said it is not that the Yippies hate America. It is that they feel the American dream has been betrayed. That has been my attitude.

\* \*

I know those guys on the wall. I know them better than you, I feel. I know Adams. I mean, I know all the Adams. They grew up 20 miles from my home in Massachusetts. I played with Sam Adams on the Concord Bridge. I was there when Paul Revere rode right up on his motorcycle and said, "The pigs are coming, the pigs are coming. Right into Lexington." I was there. I know the Adams. Sam Adams was an evil man.

Thomas Jefferson. Thomas Jefferson called for revolution every ten years. Thomas Jefferson had an agrarian reform program that made Mao Tse-tung look like a liberal. I know Thomas Jefferson. . . .

Washington? I now respect Bobby Seale's opinion of him

283

as a slaveholder because he was. All men are children of their times, even revolutionaries. We are children of our times and we are not perfect.

Washington grew pot. He called it hemp. It was called hemp then. He was probably a pot head. . . .

Abraham Lincoln? There is another one. In 1861 Abraham Lincoln in his inaugural address said, and I quote, "When the people shall grow weary of their constitutional right to amend the government, they shall exert their revolutionary right to dismember and overthrow that government."

He gave that speech. If Abraham Lincoln had given that speech in Lincoln Park, he would be on trial right here, right here in this courtroom, because that is an inciteful speech. . .

\* \* \*

Mr. Hoffman: It wasn't funny last night sitting in a prison cell, a 5 x 8 room, with no light in the room. . . .

There's no light. It's not a nice place for a Jewish boy to be, with a college education. I'm sure my mother would say that.

Speaking about that, I remember when we were speaking before, you said, "Tom Hayden, you could have had a nice position in the system, you could have had a job in the firm." We have heard that for the past ten years, all of us have heard that. And our only beauty is that we don't want a job. We don't want a job there, in that system. We say to young people, "There is a brilliant future for you in the revolution. Become an enemy of the State. A great future. You will save your soul." . . .

\* \* \*

The Court: The next defendant, Mr. Rubin, so you desire to speak in your own behalf? You have that privilege.

Mr. Rubin: . . . You see, you are not jailing five individuals. You are jailing a historical movement. We are symbols. You can just read the paper and see what is happening. . . .

. . . I am going to jail because I am part of a historical movement and because of my life, the things I am trying to do, because, as Abbie said, we don't want to be—we don't want to have a piece of the pie.

We don't just want to be part of the American way of life. We don't want to live in the suburbs. We don't want to have college degrees.

We don't want to stand before the Judge and say, "Yes, we respect you, Judge, no matter what happens." We don't want that. We are moved by something else. . . .

\* \* \*

Mr. Rubin: . . . There is a family around this table. We have called this the life versus death culture. Anybody walking in the courtroom could see this life versus death culture. People in this courtroom were a family, together like this. The people here were like machines, machines, and so the machines are sentencing the human beings to jail. . . . My gosh, what is happening in this courtroom? What is happening in this country? What is going on? The five of us are to blame for what happened in August of 1968. Incredible. . . .

\* \* \*

Mr. Rubin: A father tells his son, "Respect me or else." That's what America told its youth. America told its youth, "Respect us or else." The kids grow up saying, "I am not going to respect you or else. When you are killing black people, I am not going to respect you." . . .

\* \* \*

Mr. Rubin: We are on trial because we are trying to wake America up. We are on trial because we are trying to wake it up emotionally, because it turned us all into machines, it turned us all into marshals, reporters, judges, prosecutors; it's destroyed our humanity. So the people at this table are trying to wake it up, and the only way we can wake it up is by screaming, yelling, standing on our heads, doing whatever we can do. That's what we tried to do during this trial. That's what our defense was.

Our defense was trying to present our life to this jury. We were doing—we acted in this trial just the way we always act. We didn't do a single thing to try and get a not guilty verdict; to try and get someone's respect. We were ourselves. And you are sentencing us for being ourselves. That's our crime: being ourselves. . . .

\* \*

Judge, I want to give you a copy of this book. I want you to read it on your vacation in Florida, because this is why I am on trial. I inscribed it . . . "Julius, You radicalized more young people than we ever could. You're the country's top Yippie." . . .

. . . [W]e are going to go to jail with smiles on our faces because we are the happiest people in the courtroom because we know what is happening because you are jailing your youth, America. That's what you are doing. You are jailing your youth. And you are jailing it for the crime of dreaming, dreaming of an alternative. You are jailing it for the crime of idealism. Our crime is idealism. That's the only thing. And there is this slogan, you can jail the revolutionary but you can't jail a revolution. . . .

What you are doing out there is creating millions of revolutionaries, millions of revolutionaries. Julius Hoffman, you have done more to destroy the court system in this country than any of us could have done. All we did was go to Chicago and the police system exposed itself as totalitarian. All we did is walk into the courtroom and the court system exposed itself as totalitarian. . . . Maybe now people will be interested in what happens in the courthouse down the street because of what happens here. Maybe now people will be interested.

This is the happiest moment of my life.

The Defendants: RIGHT ON.

* * *

The Court: I call on the Government to reply to the remarks of the defendants and each of them.

Mr. Foran: The Government has no comment on their remarks, your Honor. I think the evidence in the case speaks for itself.

* * *

[*The Court then sentenced Defendants David Dellinger, Rennie Davis, Tom Hayden, Abbie Hoffman and Jerry Rubin to prison for individual terms of five years and fines of $5,000 each, the maximum penalties permitted*]

The Court: —the defendant[s] to stand committed until the fine and costs have been paid, the prison terms to run concurrently with the prison term or prison sentence previously imposed for direct contempt of Court in the presence of the Court.

Not only on the record in this case, covering a period of four months or longer, but from the remarks made by the defendants themselves here today, the Court finds that the defendants are clearly dangerous persons to be at large. Therefore the commitments here will be without bail. . . .

* * *

[*Colloquy between the Court and Mr. Kunstler*]

The Court: I gave you an opportunity to speak at the very beginning. You said counsel did not desire to speak.

Mr. Kunstler: Your Honor, couldn't I say my last words without cutting me off?

The Court: You said you didn't want to speak.

Mr. Kunstler: Your Honor, I just said a moment ago we had a concluding remark. Your Honor has succeeded perhaps in sullying it, and I think that maybe that is the way the case should end, as it began.

* * *

# APPENDIX TO CONTEMPT PROCEEDINGS OF FEBRUARY 14-15

To enable the reader to locate those actions and statements for which the defendants and their attorneys were cited for contempt of court by Judge Hoffman, we include the following examples, cross-referenced to the date on which they occurred. This is a partial, but representative, list.

## DAVID DELLINGER:

| | |
|---|---|
| October 15: | Calling Judge "Mr. Hoffman"—6 months |
| October 28: | Protesting a Court ruling—7 days |
| October 30: | Commenting aloud without permission—7 days |
| November 26: | Cursing in court—4 days |
| December 15: | Protesting removal of Mr. Ball—6 days |
| January 9: | Protesting bathroom facilities—3 days |
| | Laughing—3 days |
| January 12: | Ridiculing Judge's ruling—5 days |
| January 14: | Insulting the Court—6 months |
| January 23: | Arguing with Judge—4 months |
| January 24: | Reacting to a prosecution statement concerning Senator Robert Kennedy—2 days |
| February 4: | Commenting sarcastically—7 days |
| | Using a barnyard epithet—5 months |
| TOTAL: | 32 counts; 29 months, 16 days |

## RENNIE DAVIS:

| | |
|---|---|
| November 26: | Talking back to Judge—14 days |
| December 15: | Laughing—15 days |
| January 9: | Shouting—7 days |
| January 12: | Interrupting the proceedings—1 day |
| February 2: | Applauding—14 days |
| | Objecting to exclusion of Rev. Abernathy—7 days |
| February 4: | Shouting at Mr. Schultz—2 months |
| | Shouting a barnyard epithet—5 months |
| | Asking to defend themselves—14 days |
| TOTAL: | 23 counts; 25 months, 14 days |

## TOM HAYDEN:

| | |
|---|---|
| October 29: | Protesting treatment of Seale—1 month |
| January 9: | Laughing at the Court—1 day |
| TOTAL: | 11 counts; 14 months, 14 days |

## ABBIE HOFFMAN:

| | |
|---|---|
| September 26: | Blowing kiss to jury—1 day |
| October 23: | Showing newspaper in courtroom—7 days |
| November 26: | Renouncing his last name—1 month |
| December 15: | Laughing at the Court—14 days |
| December 30: | Commenting out of turn while on witness stand—14 days |
| January 9: | Laughing at the Court—7 days |
| February 4: | Baring body to jury—4 days |
| | Insulting Judge—5 days |
| February 5: | Insulting Judge in Yiddish—6 days |
| February 6: | Entering courtroom in judicial robes—7 days |
| TOTAL: | 24 counts; 8 months |

## JERRY RUBIN:

| | |
|---|---|
| October 30: | Protesting treatment of Seale and using obscenity—4 months |
| February 3: | Attempting to shake hands with Government witness—2 months |
| February 5: | Berating Judge—6 months |
| TOTAL: | 16 counts; 25 months, 23 days |

## JOHN FROINES:

| | |
|---|---|
| February 3: | Claiming that witness was lying—2 months |
| February 5: | Yelling in court—14 days |
| TOTAL: | 10 counts; 5 months, 15 days |

## LEE WEINER:

| | |
|---|---|
| December 1: | Statement to attorney is overheard by Court—1 month |
| January 14: | Applauding Dellinger's speech—14 days |
| January 28: | Berating Mr. Schultz—1 month |
| TOTAL: | 7 counts; 2 months, 18 days |

## WILLIAM KUNSTLER:

| | |
|---|---|
| October 15: | Participating in Moratorium activities in court-room—14 days |
| October 30: | Berating the Court for its treatment of Seale—3 months |
| | Refusing to cease argument—14 days |
| December 9: | Accusing Court of interfering with defense—14 days |
| January 6: | Disobeying Court order concerning Mayor Daley—6 months |
| January 14: | Continuing argument after Court's order to stop—7 days |
| January 20: | Refusing Court order to sit—14 days |
| January 22: | Refusing to silence defendants—21 days |
| February 2: | Disobeying Court's orders—2 counts, 6 months each |
| February 4: | Admonishing the Court—4 months |
| February 5: | Refusing to sit down when requested—1 month |
| TOTAL: | 24 counts; 48 months, 13 days |

## LEONARD WEINGLASS:

| | |
|---|---|
| September 24: | Continuing argument when told to cease—2 days |
| October 30: | Criticizing Court—14 days |
| TOTAL: | 14 counts; 20 months, 16 days |

## ABOUT THE EDITORS

MARK L. LEVINE is a graduate of Columbia College and the New York University School of Law, and is presently a lawyer with a prominent New York law firm. He took an active part in the 1965 and 1969 mayoralty campaigns and in the McCarthy for President movement.

GEORGE C. MCNAMEE, a member of the New York Stock Exchange, was graduated from Yale University in 1969. On the national staff of the McCarthy for President campaign, Mr. McNamee worked in the California and Indiana primaries.

DANIEL L. GREENBERG received his BA from Brooklyn College in 1966, and a JD from Columbia University School of Law in 1969. Though a member of the New York State Bar Association, he is currently teaching in an experimental elementary school in Harlem.